LEGISLATING INSTABILITY

LEGISLATING INSTABILITY

Adam Smith, Free Banking, *and the* Financial Crisis *of* 1772

TYLER BECK GOODSPEED

Harvard University Press
Cambridge, Massachusetts
London, England
2016

Second printing

Library of Congress Cataloging-in-Publication Data

Goodspeed, Tyler Beck, author.
Legislating instability : Adam Smith, free banking, and the financial crisis of 1772 / Tyler Beck Goodspeed.
pages cm
Includes bibliographical references and index.
ISBN 978-0-674-08888-7 (cloth : alk. paper)
1. Smith, Adam, 1723–1790. 2. Banking law—Scotland—History—18th century. 3. Banks and banking—Scotland—History—18th century. 4. Financial crises—Scotland—History—18th century. I. Title.
HB3722.G665 2016
332.109411'09033—dc23 2015033368

For Madsen

Contents

Figures

LEGISLATING INSTABILITY

1

A Very Melancholy Situation

On 27 June 1772, as the city of Edinburgh reeled from its worst financial crisis since the collapse of the Darien Company in 1700, David Hume posted an anxious letter from the Scottish capital to Adam Smith, in Kirkcaldy, then working on *An Inquiry into the Nature and Causes of the Wealth of Nations.* To his friend, Hume noted that

> We are here in a very melancholy Situation: Continual Bankruptcies, universal Loss of Credit and endless Suspicions. There are but two standing Houses in this Place, Mansfield's and the Couttses . . . Mansfield has pay'd away 40.000 pounds in a few days; but it is apprehended, that neither he nor any of them can hold out till the End of the next Week, if not Alteration happen. The Case is little better in London . . . even the Bank of England is not entirely free from Suspicion. Those of Newcastle, Norwich and Bristol are said to be stopp'd: The Thistle Bank has been reported to be in the same Condition. The Carron company is reeling, which is one of the greatest Calamities of the whole; as they gave Employment to near 10.000 people.

He concluded by inquiring of Smith whether "these Events any-wise affect your Theory? Or will it occasion the Revisal of any Chapters?"[1]

Two weeks earlier, on 10 June, the London banking house of Neale, James, Fordyce, and Down, of Threadneedle Street, had been issued a commission of bankruptcy upon news that one of their partners, Alexander Fordyce, had racked up a staggering £300,000 in trading losses (see Figure 1.1). Fordyce,

FIGURE 1.1. A "Four dice" macaroni gambler. The four dice in the title indicate that this is Alexander Fordyce. In his right hand the man holds a money bag and in his left a Scotch bill for £10,000. Image from Matthew Darly, *Macaronies, Characters, Caricatures & designed by the greatest personages, artists &c graved & published by MDarly, 39 Strand,* vol. 3 (2 July 1772), British Museum. Photo reproduction courtesy of the British Museum via Creative Commons Attribution Non-Commercial Share Alike 4.0 International (CC-BY-NC-SA 4.0) license.

the brilliant but brash youngest son of an Aberdeen hosier who had worked his way up from outdoor clerk to partner in one of London's most prominent banking firms, had for months been shorting some £1,000,000 (approximately £114,200,000 in 2014 prices) of East India Company stock.[2] But with East India share prices flat since late 1771, and facing an additional margin call of 10 percent, Fordyce absconded to France, leaving his partners liable for an estimated £243,000 in debts.[3] Days earlier, in reply to a desperate plea from Fordyce for an emergency line of credit, one London banker, a Quaker, had replied, "Friend Fordyce, I have known many men ruined by two dice, but I will not be ruined by Four-dice."[4] Realizing the extent of their liability, the remaining partners immediately suspended payments in a futile attempt to safeguard creditors from a disorderly liquidation, yet the damage was already done. Runs quickly formed against several of their principal counterparties in Exchange Alley, and by Wednesday following, no fewer than ten London banks had failed, with even the eminent houses of Drummonds and Coutts coming under severe pressure.[5]

The worst, however, was yet to come. It took just forty-three hours for a rider to carry word of the collapse to Edinburgh, where several leading banking firms had been relying heavily on Neale, James, Fordyce, and Down, the largest buyer of Scottish bills in London, to roll over short-term debt. Fordyce himself being a Scotsman, and with two Scottish houses in London having already stopped payment owing to his failure, the fear was that the sudden evaporation of liquidity for Scottish bills, which had lately been flooding the London discount market, would render it nearly impossible for Scotland's banks to obtain vital refinancing as outstanding drafts came due.[6] As one Scottish banker thus put it, Fordyce's downfall "set fire to the mine," blowing up "the whole traffic of circulation" of Scottish bills in which the city had for some years been intensely engaged, with the result that "all those houses in London who had largely accepted bills drawn on them from Scotland . . . finding it no longer possible to discount the remittances that had been made to them for their reimbursement, were instantly compelled to stop payment."[7]

Another contemporary observer, the eminent English historian Horace Walpole, likewise wrote at the time that "it is now thought Fordyce was rather the handle than the cause of this ruin," and that he "only advanced the crash," which "would have happened without his interference, for the Scotch bankers have been pursuing so deep a game by remitting bills and drawing cash from hence."[8] With the news arriving late Friday afternoon, Edinburgh's bankers were largely spared for the weekend, but upon reopening Monday morning, panic set in. By the end of the day, the small private bank of Fordyce, Malcolm & Co. had been forced to stop, followed, on Tuesday, by Arbuthnot and Guthrie.[9] Pressure was particularly intense, however, on Douglas, Heron & Co., the "Ayr Bank," who on Tuesday evening distributed advertisements throughout Edinburgh offering a reward of £100 to anyone who discovered the source "of some ill-grounded reports raised by foolish or malicious persons" respecting the bank's solvency.[10]

In private, however, the banking behemoth, whose balance sheet accounted for an estimated 25 percent of Scottish banknotes in circulation, 25 percent of deposits, and 40 percent of total bank assets, was scrambling to shore up an increasingly desperate internal position. Already the day before, they had approached directors of the Bank of Scotland and Royal Bank of Scotland to insist that, though the extent of their exposure to Neale, James, Fordyce, and Down did not exceed £22,000, they required an immediate six-month loan of £20,000 from *each* bank to resolve what they claimed was a temporary lack of liquidity.[11] The directors of the two chartered banks sensed a bluff, and the Royal Bank promptly responded that although they were "exceedingly sorry for the Bankruptcys that have happened in London," they were "at the same time extremely pleased to be Informed that Messrs Douglas Heron & Company are entirely Covered on their Engagements with the Houses that have failed," and therefore were "of Opinion that it would be Improper for them to Agree to the Proposals" made to them by the bank.[12]

Nevertheless, Douglas, Heron & Co. somehow managed to struggle through till the end of the week. But the following Monday, 22 June—"Black Monday," as it came to be known—their head office at Ayr, where notes could previously be redeemed for specie, did not reopen after the weekend.[13] Two days later, a second entreaty to the chartered banks for an emergency line of credit was refused, with the Bank of Scotland and Royal Bank of Scotland further informing Douglas, Heron & Co. that they could no longer accept the latter's notes in payment.[14] Within twenty-four hours, the largest bank in Scotland finally capitulated, announcing via public advertisement that "the Company of Douglas Heron & Company Bankers in Air, taking into their consideration the present state of the credit of this country, and the uncommon demands that have been made upon them for specie," had resolved to "give over, for some time," the payment of specie for their notes.[15] Total liabilities amounted to nearly one and a quarter million pounds sterling.[16] They assured their creditors, however, that "the country, who have received the most liberal aids from this company, cannot entertain the smallest doubt of the solidity of its foundation," and further pledged that "in order to give full satisfaction to the public, that no person will be a loser who is in possession of their paper," 5 percent interest would be paid on all outstanding Douglas, Heron & Co. notes, until paid, and duly registered a bond to that effect with the Court of Session.[17]

Evidently, the Scottish public was unassuaged. By week's end, just four of Edinburgh's eighteen private banks remained standing. Outside the capital, in addition to Douglas, Heron & Co., the Glasgow Merchant Banking Company and Simson, Baird & Co. both fell, while Dunlop, Houston & Co. (the "Ship Bank"), the oldest bank in Glasgow, was rumored to be on the brink. Of the country's eleven provincial banks, just eight reopened for business on the following Monday morning, of which three—the Ship, Arms, and Thistle Banks, all in Glasgow—were already seeking assistance from Edinburgh.[18] In Perth, the General Bank of Perth would soon wind up. The editors of *The Scots Magazine* were thus by no means dramatizing when they reported that the ongoing crisis was "said to be the greatest that ever happened in Scotland," worse even than the aftermath of the South Sea Bubble or the collapse of the Darien Company.[19] Horace Walpole concurred, writing that "scarce the bubble of the South Sea occasioned greater consternation." As "one rascal," he declared, could thus "shake the mighty credit of such a nation as Great Britain," yet twenty years would be insufficient to "remove the prejudice that men will contract against bankers."[20]

Among those contracting such prejudice was, in fact, none other than Adam Smith, for whom the events of June 1772 did indeed seem to "occasion the revisal" of at least one chapter of the still incomplete *Wealth of Nations,* perhaps not coincidentally, as several of his intimate friends and associates were financial casualties of the Ayr Bank's demise, as well as shareholders in the failed bank itself. In a letter to close friend William Pulteney, Member of Parliament for Cromartyshire, on 3 September 1772—less than three months from Black Monday—Smith admitted that, "tho I have had no concern myself in the Public calamities, some of the friends for whom I interest myself the most have been deeply concerned in them; and my attention has been a good deal occupied about the most proper method of extricating them."[21] Of the bank whose spectacular collapse bankrupted 114 of 226 shareholders and similarly threatened to ruin his pupil and patron, Henry Scott, 3rd Duke of Buccleuch, Smith later wrote that, ultimately, "This bank increased the real distress of the country which it meant to relieve," insisting, moreover, that such calamity served as a stark reminder that "the commerce and industry of the country . . . cannot be altogether so secure, when they are thus, as it were, suspended upon the Daedalian wings of paper money, as when they travel about upon the solid ground of gold and silver."[22]

To be sure, it was not that Smith wished for credit and banking to be rigidly bound by gold and silver manacles; indeed, "The judicious operations of banking" he likened to "a sort of wagon-way through the air," enabling a country to convert its "highways" of gold and silver "into good pastures and cornfields, and thereby to increase very considerably the annual produce of its land and labor." It was rather, he feared, that "over and above the accidents to which they are exposed from the unskilfulness of the conductors of this paper money," the industry and commerce thus suspended "are liable to several others, from which no prudence or skill of those conductors can guard them." Therefore, just as violations of natural liberty are justified where the "exertions of the natural liberty of a few individuals, which might endanger the security of the whole society, are, and ought to be, restrained by the laws of all governments," so too, Smith argued, are "regulations of the banking trade" likewise justified. Such regulation was, he suggested, introducing yet another metaphor, rather like the "obligation of building party walls, in order to prevent the communication of fire."[23]

But the "party walls" Smith advocated to fireproof the banking trade—prohibition of small-denomination banknotes, a maximum legal rate of interest, and prohibition of contingent liability banknotes—could hardly have been expected to deliver effective protection against what Smith called the "accidents" of both the "unskilfulness" of bankers as well as causes against which no amount of "prudence or skill" on their part, but only public regulation, might guard, for the simple reason that all three regulations were already law seven years *before* the crisis of 1772 and the collapse of Douglas, Heron & Co. More curious still is the realization that these restrictions, far from constituting the bequests of enlightened philosophers or prudential public administrators, were in reality the products of intense political lobbying by none other than the very bankers—many of them intimate and lifelong friends of Smith's—whose trade they were intended to regulate. Perhaps oddest of all, however, is that close analysis of the available historical and statistical evidence reveals that, far from attenuating financial sector instability, the banking regulations championed by Smith actually exacerbated the risk of that for which they were purportedly the cure; Smith's financial "party walls," in other words, belong among the contributory causes of the 1772 crisis, not among its mitigators.

That the "Ayr Bank Crisis" in Scotland should be seen, at least in part, as a consequence of bank regulation is itself odd. For, largely unaffected by the Bubble Act and exempt from the Bank of England Act of 1708, which had effectively extended the Bank of England's monopoly on note issuance in England by prohibiting all other banks of more than six partners, Scotland from 1716 to 1845 is widely considered by economic and financial historians to have been one of the closest ever historical approximations to "free banking"—namely, the competitive issuance of convertible currency by non-privileged banks, in the absence of any additional legal or regulatory restriction beyond those applying equally to all commercial enterprises. While scholars of free banking have quibbled over how closely the Scottish financial system during this period fit the true mold of idealized free banking, there is no dispute that from the expiration of the Bank of Scotland's monopoly charter in 1716 to the passage of the Scottish Bank Act of 1845, Scottish banking functioned with no official central bank or lender of last resort, no public (or private) monopoly on currency issuance, no mandated capital or reserve requirements, no legal restrictions on entry, and no limits on bank size analogous to England's six-partner rule. Moreover, there is similarly little dispute that the Scottish economy during these one hundred and thirty years was characterized by *faster* economic growth and *greater* financial stability than occurred contemporaneously in England, or subsequently in Scotland itself. Echoing Adam Smith himself, Kerr and others all conclude, in Kerr's words, that

> In Scotland, banking was permitted to develop as the country advanced in wealth and in intelligence. Nay, it was even enabled to lead the nation on the path of prosperity, and to evolve, from practical experience, a natural and healthy system of banking, which would have been impossible under close state control similar to that followed in other countries.[24]

Meanwhile, White and others argue convincingly that the Scottish "free banking" period was one of substantially greater financial stability and fewer bank failures than experienced concurrently south of the Tweed.[25] Inasmuch as Sechrest contests White's thesis, he does so by citing Checkland on the extent and severity of the Ayr Bank Crisis of 1772.[26]

The central argument of my thesis is thus that the salient financial crisis of the Scottish free banking period, the obtrusive exception to the hypothesis of greater financial stability under free banking in Scotland, was, pace Adam Smith, made more rather than less likely by precisely those regulated or "unfree" elements of Scottish banking which the author of *The Wealth of Nations* promoted. Further, I argue that this conclusion should hardly be cause for surprise once we realize that it was none other than the oldest, largest, and most established banks in Scotland that had lobbied for Smith's legal restrictions on banking; regulations that had the effects of raising barriers to entry, lowering competition in the provision of short-term credit, increasing the efficient scale of banking, and therefore, ultimately, amplifying the level of systemic risk in Scottish credit markets.

Finally, in support of Selgin and White, among others, I find that the relative competitiveness of the Scottish financial system—certainly in contrast to the highly bifurcated English banking sector of the time—along with the unlimited legal liability of shareholders in Scottish private banks, were sources of considerable financial stability, both in 1772 and previously.[27] To be clear, then, it is not my contention that the introduction of legal restrictions into Scottish banking *caused* the 1772 crisis, but rather that they critically undermined the flexibility and resilience previously exhibited by Scottish finance, and thereby elevated the risk that adverse economic or financial shocks might metastasize into broader threats to financial stability.

Readers may, perhaps, wonder why we should even bother to concern ourselves with a comparatively little-known eighteenth-century financial crisis in what was then something of a provincial backwater of the global economy. Aside from the fact that the international shock waves generated by Douglas, Heron & Co.'s ignominious demise reveal that Scottish capital, goods, and labor markets were far more integrated with the global economy than might at first appear, there are, I would argue, four reasons for the episode to detain our attention. These are a philosophical rationale, for the impact of the crisis on contemporary economic thought; a historical rationale, for its magnitude and global political and economic repercussions; a theoretical rationale, for how the Ayr Bank collapse speaks to important topics in the political economy of law and regulation, as well as finance and international macroeconomics; and, finally, a methodological rationale, as the Scottish experience of free banking offers a unique opportunity to more precisely identify and analyze the causal effects of basic financial regulation.

First, then, the financial crisis of 1772 should concern us because it quite evidently concerned Adam Smith (as well, for that matter, as James Steuart and David Hume, who continued to update Smith on the unfolding crisis).[28] It certainly concerned Smith personally; by 1774, his mentor and patron, the Duke of Buccleuch, had been forced to sell his 1,520-acre Adderbury estate, including the extravagant fifty-six-room manor house where Smith had been a frequent guest, to cover his unlimited liability in the Ayr Bank—just one of some £750,000 worth of landed properties that were brought on the market in forced liquidations following the events of June 1772.[29] Ultimately, for each £500 share, the average shareholder of Douglas, Heron & Co. lost nearly £3,000, with the solvent partners facing even steeper bills; the Duke of Buccleuch, holding just two shares, eventually paid out £15,000, while the Duke of Queensberry, with four shares, lost almost £45,000.[30] The families of some shareholders, indeed, were still paying for the bank's folly sixty years after its collapse.[31] In July 1776, moreover, just months after *The Wealth of Nations* went to press, the Duke of Buccleuch joined his fellow partners in Douglas, Heron & Co., many of them also close friends and social acquaintances of Smith's, in commissioning a committee of inquiry into allegations of negligence and gross mismanagement by the bank's managers, resulting in eight legal suits against sixty-one directors and partners for financial redress.[32]

But, more than that, in answer to Hume's question, Checkland, Gherity, and Rockoff have found that the crisis also concerned Smith intellectually.[33] Whereas before 1772 Smith maintained that a legal mandate prohibiting contingently convertible banknotes, possibly allied to a prohibition of small denomination banknotes, would offer sufficient protection against the dangers of overissue, by 1776 he not only doubled down on both counts, even advocating a much higher legal note minimum of £5 to prevent the entrance of what he called "beggarly bankers," but also proposed two additional regulations.[34] Concerned that only "prodigals and projectors" would be willing to borrow at high rates of interest, he expressed support for retaining the existing maximum legal rate of interest, which he thought "ought to be somewhat above," though "not much above the lowest market rate," deeming the then prevailing legal rate of 5 percent to be "perhaps as proper as any."[35] Further, citing the "ruinous" practice of Douglas, Heron & Co. of drawing and redrawing "fictitious" bills of exchange on London correspondent banks to roll over outstanding debts, Smith argued that prudent bankers ought only to discount "a real bill of exchange drawn by a real creditor upon a real debtor," and never "a bill for which there is properly no real creditor but the bank which discounted it; nor any real debtor but the projector who made use of the money," the famous "real bills doctrine."[36] With these "party walls" in place, Smith concluded in the aftermath of 1772, the banking trade may, "With safety to the public," be thereby "rendered in all other respects perfectly free."[37] As Gherity observes, this does indeed constitute a significant "revisal" of Smith's views toward banking regulation from where they stood before 1765.[38]

Second, however, the 1772 financial crisis should concern us because it was not simply a minor, run-of-the-mill regional banking panic, but rather a full-blown global financial crisis. Like Walpole, Dr. Samuel Johnson, the eminent essayist and lexicographer, wrote in August 1772 that "there has not since the year of the South Sea been, I believe, such extensive distress or frightful alarm."[39] Within days, press reports in Holland and France described in detail the unfolding crisis across the Channel, and even the Munich newspapers saw fit to list the names of the failed Scottish banks, documenting in particular the affairs of Douglas, Heron & Co.[40] In Amsterdam, the *Gazette van Gend* relayed an exhaustive account of the Fordyce collapse on 23 June, warning that the firm's heavy engagement in the discount market for Scottish debt threatened other London houses exposed to Scottish paper, as well as their counterparties.[41] While the Dutch bourse had initially shrugged off Fordyce's bankruptcy, news of the deteriorating situation in Scotland triggered a sell-off of West India Company stock, with share prices in the Dutch company sliding 20 percent by the end of the summer.[42]

The French weekly *Gazette de France,* meanwhile, reported on 4 July that the entire city of London was awash "in rumors and tears," noting that suspension of payment by several banking houses had prompted bank-on-bank runs, with "universal bankruptcy" seemingly imminent.[43] The editors further cautioned that the failure of Neale, James, Fordyce, and Down had merely provided the spark; the tinder was the immense quantity of Scottish paper the firm had been discounting, with a nominal face value of as much as £4 million over the preceding five years.[44] The consequent evaporation of liquidity for Scottish bills of exchange, they observed, thus instantly cast doubt on any London houses that had been buying Scottish bank debt, and on those Scottish banks, particularly Douglas, Heron & Co., that had been relying on London to roll over short-term debt. While the *Gazette* acknowledged that "bankruptcies of this kind usually affect the principal commercial firms of Europe," the present crisis was alarming in that it had shaken financial markets not only in Holland but also in France, "which had no connection of trade" with the failed houses.

Three days later, in Amsterdam, the *Gazette van Gend* reported with great concern the extensive credit network of Douglas, Heron & Co., noting that even the empress of Russia was deeply involved with firms financed by the distressed Scottish bank, including one under contract to deliver £500,000 of fabric to Petersburg.[45] In fact, before the crisis had run its course, Tsarina Catherine would eventually intervene "to ward off the impending calamity, and particularly favoured her best customers, the British merchants at Petersburg, by giving them a credit on her own banker for such sums as they should stand in need of."[46] According to one contemporary Dutch source, these sums totaled one million rubles in emergency lines of credit, all advanced by the tsarina's banker, Friederichs.[47] Though Amsterdam's banks survived the summer relatively unscathed, the intensifying credit crunch in England and Scotland increasingly weighed on East India Company shares, in which several Dutch houses had gone long on margin. By December 1772, the Dutch weekly, *De Koopman,* reported that "not a merchant in Amsterdam can raise 50,000 guilders in cash," calling the unfolding crisis worse even than that which had struck the Dutch capital in 1763, at the end of the Seven Years' War.[48] The eminent merchant banking firm of Clifford & Sons, older than the Bank of England, had broken on 27 October 1772, followed not long thereafter by Herman Johan van Seppenwolde, Willem Clifford & Chevalier, Abraham Ter Borch, and André Pels & Sons.[49]

Indeed, as one French journal put it in early 1773, while "traffic is stopped in all branches of commerce" and while "there are few places in Europe which do not suffer from the current successive events," in Amsterdam the effects of the credit freeze were particularly acute. "It is easy to judge," wrote the editors of the *Journal Politique,* "what must be the situation of a country which has no other resource than its trade, nor other wealth than the movement of its money."[50] By January 1773, the situation had become so desperate that the City of Amsterdam established a mutual insurance company, backed by the Bank of Amsterdam, to support its merchant banks.[51] Contemporary Dutch financial commentators were keen to lay much of the blame on "windhandel," or trading/banking in the air, particularly, they alleged, by Amsterdam's Jewish financiers.[52] Within two years, one enterprising Dutch merchant and financial trader, Abraham van Ketwich, seeking to diversify risk at low cost for small investors, invited subscriptions on the Amsterdam bourse for the world's first mutual fund. The closed-end fund was called "Eendracht Maakt Magt," or "Unity Creates Strength," and consisted of one million guilders dispersed among 2,000 shares with a par of 500 guilders each, which Ketwich invested broadly in sovereign and commercial bonds spanning Austria, Denmark, Spain, Sweden, Russia, various German states, and several colonial plantations in Central and South America.[53]

In Hamburg, too, city officials coordinated the formation of a mutual insurance bank in November 1772 "to support those who, in the present circumstances, could run out of cash," while in Stockholm the Bank of Sweden likewise felt compelled to intervene, extending emergency lines of credit to the country's principal banks.[54] As one Hamburg linen merchant put it, "When one link gave way—the charm was instantly dissolved, leaving behind it consternation in the place of confidence, and imaginary affluence changed to a real want and distress; a torrent of ruin from the north."[55] The failure of the Dutch house of Clifford & Sons, especially, brought the crisis to the rest of the continent, with creditors including not only the Bank of England but also Frederick the Great of Prussia and Christian VII, king of Denmark, ultimately recovering just 30 percent of their deposits from the bank's lengthy liquidation, which dragged on at least through 1777.[56]

The effects of the credit crisis in England and Scotland were also felt by European exporters. Figure 1.2 plots total annual imports from the five largest

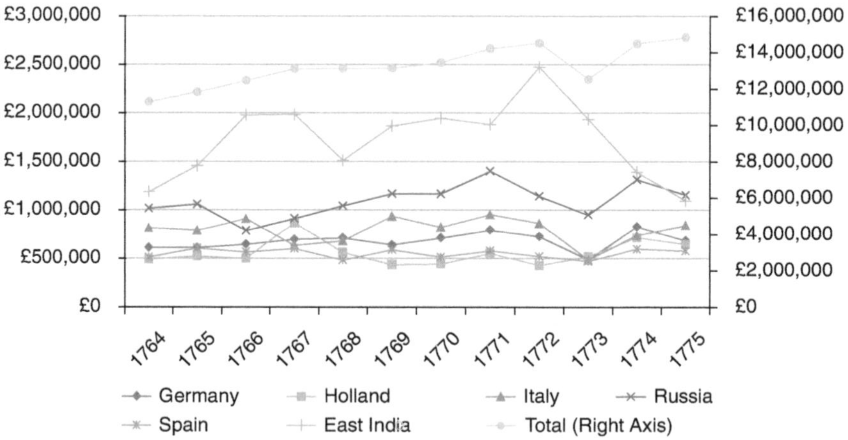

FIGURE 1.2. Total English and Scottish imports, 1764–1775. *Data source:* Macpherson, *Annals of Commerce,* 409–585.

exporters to England and Scotland—the German states, Holland, Italy, Russia, and Spain—as well as imports by the East India Company and total English and Scottish imports. Overall, imports into England and Scotland, having grown at an average annual rate of 3.5 percent since the end of the Seven Years' War, fell 14 percent from 1772 to 1773, with imports from Germany (down 33 percent), Italy (down 44 percent) and Russia (down 17 percent, following an 18 percent decline in 1772) hit particularly hard. For England and Scotland's top five exporters combined, exports plunged 32 percent in 1773, and were still almost 9 percent below their pre-crisis peak as late as 1775.

But as acutely as the crisis was felt throughout the financial and commercial capitals of Europe, it was perhaps Britain's worldwide colonies that were hardest hit by the events of June 1772. For the "ruinous" practice described by Smith of Scottish banks drawing and redrawing bills of exchange on London correspondents had been relied upon not only for financing industrial development and agricultural improvements in Scotland itself, but even more importantly, as Devine, Sheridan, Soltow, and Gipson have demonstrated, for providing a vital source of credit for the transatlantic tobacco and linen trades.[57] Given the relative size of its population and economy, Scotland accounted for a staggeringly disproportionate 42 percent of all imports into Great Britain from the North American colonies in the year before the crisis, and more than 50 percent of tobacco imports.[58] Of 290 outstanding Virginian debts owed to British creditors reported to a British government commission in 1776, 208 were to Scots, with such prominent names as Jefferson, Monroe, Washington, and Lee, along with Browns, Carters, Hancocks, Harrisons, Jacksons, Randolphs, Watts, and Whartons, among those owing £1,000 or more to Scottish lenders.[59] No fewer than fifty-five Virginians owing £500 or more were members of the House of Burgesses from 1769 to 1774.[60] For the North American colonies as a whole, as much as £1.4 million of an estimated £4–5 million owed to British creditors on the eve of the revolution was due to Scottish lenders.[61] The poet Thomas Moore was thus hardly unduly cynical when he later wrote of "Those vaunted demagogues, who nobly rose; From England's debtors to be England's foes; Who could their monarch in their purse forget; And break allegiance but to cancel debt."[62] He simply mistook the creditor to be England alone.

It was smaller-scale planters, though, who were particularly reliant on Glasgow for credit. When William Cunninghame & Co., the largest tobacco merchants in Glasgow, submitted claims for £135,631 of debts lost in Virginia and Maryland due to the American War of Independence, they revealed thousands of separate debtor accounts, the vast majority owing less than £10. Before the war, in testimony to a committee of the House of Commons during the Stamp Act crisis, John Glassford, founding partner in the Glasgow Arms and Thistle Banks, had estimated that Chesapeake borrowers owed no less than £500,000 to Glaswegian lenders—including some £50,000 to his own enterprises—with relatively small loans of under £30 comprising the bulk of that sum.[63] All told, on the eve of the revolution thirty-seven Glasgow firms held some 31,000 debts owing to 112 Virginian stores.[64] The standard method of financing was for agents of Glaswegian firms to advance to colonial planters and farmers imported goods, the cost of which was to be repaid in twelve months in currency, bills, or crop for export. Unpaid balances after twelve months were then charged 5 percent interest per year, typically secured by personal bonds renewed annually.[65] The custom of thus rolling over outstanding debts meant Glaswegian creditors had to wait an average of four years to recoup their investments, with Glassford noting it frequently took five years, and rarely fewer than three.[66]

It was a delicate method of trade finance. Scottish merchants and banks themselves often had to tap London credit markets for short-term funding via sixty-day bills of exchange; which, at 5 percent discount and commission of 0.5 percent per bill, implied a total cost of capital of no less than 8 percent on an annualized basis, with supply highly sensitive to short-run perturbations in London capital markets.[67] As early as 8 July 1772, Alexander McCaul, a Glaswegian tobacco merchant, thus wrote Thomas Jefferson to inform him that recent events had "thrown a damp on Public Credit, and it will be some time before it is perfectly restored."[68] One month later, John Norton, of the London merchant house of John Norton & Sons, wrote his son in Virginia to warn him against accepting Virginian bills of exchange drawn on Scottish creditors, as these were possibly "discharged by drafts on the Heron & Douglas Bank which lately stopt."[69] Even one year on from Black Monday, William Wiatt, a merchant in Fredericksburg, Virginia, reported to his brother in Liverpool that "the late bankruptcies have made prodigious alterations within these 9 months, the factors for the Scotch merchants in Glasgow are forbid to draw, and a great number of their bills come back protested."[70] Benjamin Franklin had in fact even conducted business with the Ayr Bank; in a letter from London to his son-in-law on 7 October 1772, Franklin wrote that amid "the late wreck of credit" he had used his credit with a London bank "to support that of a Friend as far as £5,000," for which he noted with trepidation that he was "secur'd by Bills of the Bank of Douglas, Heron & Co."[71]

Facing an accelerating credit crunch back home, many Scottish lenders began to retrench; on 1 July 1772, William Cunninghame & Co. instructed their agents in Virginia "to force payment of many of our overgrown large debts," and one month later issued orders to sharply limit cash payments for tobacco to no more than 20–25 percent of the purchase price. Already by August 1772, Norton predicted there would be few cash purchases of tobacco in Virginia that autumn, "Owing to the distress many of the Glasgow Merchts have been in for some time past, as also the fall of the Market."[72] As one merchant in Virginia noted in July 1773, "I am much concerned to observe the great difficulties the trade Labours under in Britain by the failure of some great houses, the consequences have extended to this part of the World to a violent degree, and unless our proncipal [*sic*] export, Tobo., can be kept up in value at home, I don't see how we shall be enabled to discharge our debts on your side of the water."[73]

Glaswegian firms and their colonial agents, hitherto willing to roll over debit balances, increasingly began to demand real-estate mortgages or deeds of trust to discharge debts secured by personal bond.[74] Several prominent houses, including R. Bogle & Sons, Perkins, Buchanan & Brown, and John Buchanan & Son—whom Norton called "the father of our Trade"—caught between mounting delinquencies in Virginia and their own debts to London creditors coming due, were bankrupted entirely. Perkins, Buchanan & Brown, who failed for £70,000, were among Jefferson's numerous creditors.[75] Not only did such bankruptcies exacerbate the contraction of fresh credit to colonial borrowers, but the resulting institutional liquidations furthermore intensified demands for the collection of outstanding debts.

At the same time, colonial debtors were also struggling with a sharp drop in demand from Scottish importers, following more than a decade of rapid growth during which they had borrowed heavily to acquire manufactured equipment and luxury goods, purchase slaves, and clear land for cultivation in order to expand production of export commodities. Figure 1.3 plots total Scottish imports from the North American colonies, as well as total Scottish imports of tobacco, the bulk of which originated in the greater Chesapeake Bay area. Having averaged 9 percent growth per year since the end of the Seven Years' War, Scottish imports from the North American colonies dropped 6 percent in 1772, 9 percent in 1773, and 4 percent in 1774. Tobacco imports

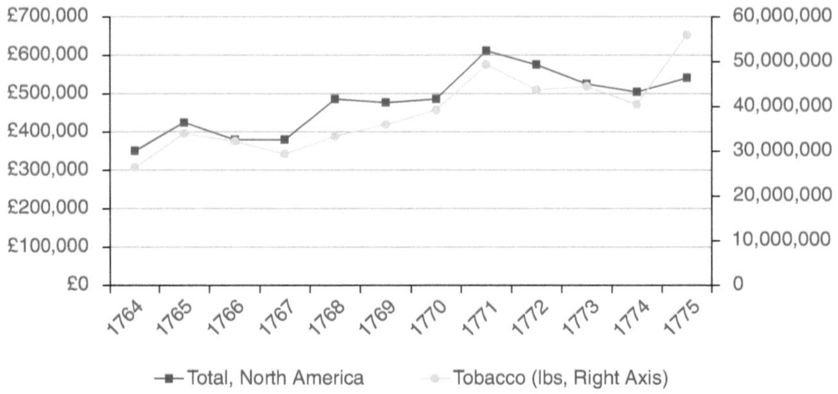

FIGURE 1.3. Scottish tobacco imports and imports from North American colonies, 1764–1775. *Data source:* Macpherson, *Annals of Commerce,* 409–585.

were even harder hit; after averaging 10 percent growth per year since 1764, Scottish imports of tobacco slid 11 percent in 1772, recovered slightly in 1773, before falling a further 9 percent in 1774. The price, which had soared 50 percent from just under 1s. a pound in 1769 to 1s.6d. in 1772, dropped 20 percent to 1s.2d. by 1775.[76] Moreover, as the supply of sterling bills evaporated due to the ballooning trade deficit, the exchange rate swung heavily against American borrowers; Virginian bills fell from 20 percent under par on London in October 1771, to 25 percent under by July 1772, and to 30 percent under by May 1773.[77] American debtors were quite simply getting crushed by the original sin of foreign-denominated debt.

The financial strains generated by the crisis of 1772 thus ignited intense antipathy, long latent, between Virginian and Marylander debtors and their Scottish creditors. As Scottish factors pursued debt claims through the colonial courts, they were often met with intimidation or outright civil disobedience. Ostensibly for political reasons relating to the controversial Boston Port Act, the House of Burgesses was dissolved in May 1774 without having renewed the 1745 Fee Bill, after Richard Henry Lee—himself deeply in debt to Glaswegian lenders—had quietly excluded the bill from a report to the committee responsible for renewing administrative statutes. Expiration meant Virginia courts were thereafter closed for all civil processes, most notably the collection of debts.[78] Maryland shortly followed Virginia's lead; on 25 May 1774, residents of Annapolis adopted a resolution declaring it "the opinion of this meeting that the gentlemen of the law of this Province, bring no suit for the recovery of any debt due from any inhabitant of this Province to any inhabitant of Great Britain, until the said Act [Boston Port Act] be repealed."[79]

Other counties quickly adopted similar resolutions.[80] When one court in Berkshire County, Maryland, attempted to hear civil cases in August 1774, an angry mob overran the courtroom, seized the chief judge, and held him captive until he agreed to an adjournment sine die.[81] One Scottish merchant in Norfolk, James Parker, remarked of the event that "by such methods they meant to avoid the payment of their just debts," having earlier noted that "calling a man a Patriot here is saying he is in bad Circumstances."[82] Within weeks of the Annapolis resolution, William Cunninghame & Co.'s primary agent reported that he was struggling to collect from "some of the worthless kind" who had become "very impudent and daring" since the suspension of civil suits. Another agent similarly lamented that "Patriotism" had apparently come to mean little more than "not to pay anybody."[83] Jefferson himself would never repay his debts to Alexander McCaul, the Glaswegian who had written to apprise him of the credit upheavals of June 1772; shortly before his death in 1827, Jefferson still owed McCaul a hefty £6,580.[84]

As they aggressively sought to rein in credit, Scottish lenders were particularly singled out by colonial debtors. When local communities throughout Virginia and Maryland resolved to hold a day of fasting in solidarity with the city of Boston, James Madison wrote censoriously and with biting sarcasm that "the Europeans especially the Scotch and some interested Merchants among the natives" had discountenanced the observance, "alledging the Injustice and perfidy of refusing to pay our debts to our Generous Creditors at Home." He further noted that it "has been said here by some that the appointed Fast was disregarded by every Scotch Clergyman."[85] Endeavoring to persuade a crowd at the Richmond county court to support a commercial association against the British, Landon Carter appealed directly to prejudice against Scottish traders, recounting in his diary that at the meeting he "took notice of the Part the Gent of the Scotch nation were acting." "They are become a part of us," he told the crowd, "by coming to trade among [us], and . . . seem active in endeavoring to Persuade a submission to this arbitrary taxation." As the Scots had themselves been "bread up under strange feudal tenets," Carter insisted, "they were strangers to Liberty themselves & wanted the rest of mankind to live under the same slavish notions that they had ever done."[86] Two years later, commanding the American rebel forces which burned

Norfolk, Virginia—including the property of several Glaswegian firms—William Woodford would boast that he was indebted to two Scottish merchants for "more than he was worth . . . but never had the least inclination to pay," and looked forward to "discharging his debts . . . with the broad brush, meaning the destroying of the books and papers of the merchants."[87]

Meanwhile, on the other side of the globe, the East India Company was facing its own travails, caught between the general contraction of credit at home and a disastrous military campaign against Hyder Ali in Mysore that had already driven annual operating expenses to £1.7 million, up from a mere £700,000 seven years earlier.[88] As shown in Figure 1.2, total exports by the company to England and Scotland tumbled 22 percent in 1772 and 28 percent in 1773. By October 1772, its £300,000 cash account with the Bank of England had fallen "to so low an ebb" that the bank's directors refused any further credit "till the present debt is first liquidated," forcing the Company's directors to seek an emergency loan of £1.5 million, at 4 percent, from the government through the facilitation of Lord North.[89] Across the Channel, press reports in France and even Spain followed intently the Company's affairs, and those of its chairman, Sir George Colebrooke, who stood accused of duplicitously speculating in the shares of his own company.[90]

By May 1773, with its dividend slashed from 12.5 to 6 percent, its share price down 33 percent from June 1772, and some seventeen million pounds of unsold tea rotting in English warehouses, the Company finally persuaded Parliament to intercede.[91] In "An Act to allow a Drawback of the Duties of Customs on the Exportation of Tea to any of his Majesty's Colonies or Plantations in America; to increase the Deposit on Bohea Tea to be sold at the East-India Company's Sales; and to empower the Commissioners of the Treasury to grant Licenses to the East-India Company to export Tea Duty-free," popularly known in the American colonies as the "Tea Act," the government of Lord North removed British custom from East India Company tea destined for North America and permitted the Company to export directly to the colonies, with the aim of thereby enabling Company tea to effectively compete on price with smuggled Dutch tea.[92] The following month, by "An Act for establishing certain Regulations for the better Management of the Affairs of the East-India Company, as well in India as in Europe," Lord North's government furthermore granted the Company a bailout loan of £1.4 million, at 4 percent, with the Bank of England, wary of the threat to their own balance sheet should the Company collapse, agreeing to accommodate Treasury for the full amount of the loan.[93]

When news of the acts arrived in the North American colonies, smugglers and legitimate tea importers not named as consignees were outraged that directly imported East India Company tea would undercut their merchandise by a penny a pound, and successfully pressured consignees to refuse receipt of shipment. Tea ships bound for New York, Philadelphia, and Charleston therefore had no choice but to return to England with their cargoes. But in Boston, on the evening of 16 December, Governor Hutchinson's refusal to permit the tea ships *Dartmouth, Eleanor,* and *Beaver* to return to England without discharging their cargoes and paying customs duty prompted angry Bostonian merchants to disguise themselves as Mohawk warriors, board the three vessels, and over the course of three hours dump 342 chests of tea into Boston Harbor, in what would become known as the Boston Tea Party.[94] The political butterfly effects of a single bankruptcy in June 1772 were thus historic in import and magnitude.

But it was the personal toll, too, that rendered the financial crisis of 1772 so profoundly devastating. As shown in Figure 1.4, the total number of British bankruptcies in both 1772 and 1773 was higher than in any preceding year

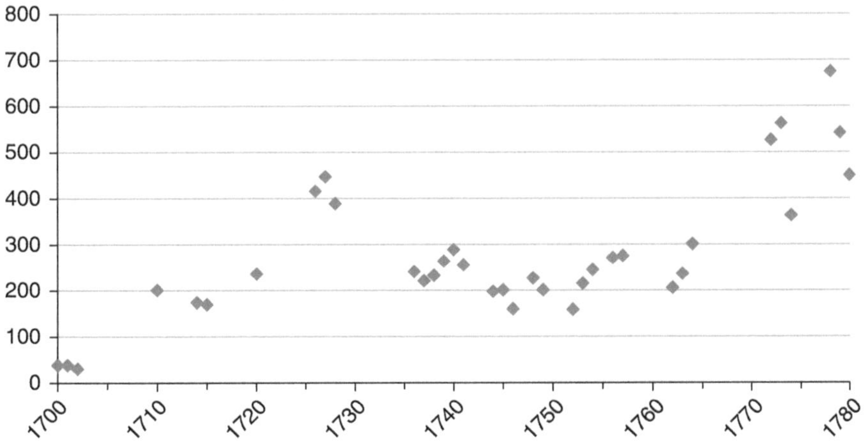

FIGURE 1.4. British bankruptcies, 1700–1780. Bankruptcy data from Chalmers, *Estimate of the Comparative Strength of Great Britain,* 291.

during the eighteenth century—including the years immediately following the collapse of the South Sea bubble—and for the entire period 1700–1780 was lower only than the disastrous year 1778, when the entrance of France and Spain into the American war rocked British financial markets. In April 1773, *London Magazine* reported the death of Henry Neale, late partner of Alexander Fordyce, "Of a broken heart," the standard euphemism for suicide.[95] Horace Walpole recounted that two other men, "Ruined by these failures," shot themselves, a fourth drowned himself, while yet another "flung himself out of window and broke his limbs."[96] In France, the *Journal Politique* reported such tragedies by writing that many, "Reduced to despair by the losses they have incurred on the occasion of this bankruptcy, have put an end to their existence in ways repugnant to humanity," while others, "more reasonable, rely on all the severity of the law to punish the perpetrators of their disgraces."[97]

On Threadneedle Street, meanwhile, the directors of the Bank of England, with their own gold reserves down to just £243,000 against a note circulation of £6 million, were hardly inclined to charity or magnanimity. When Douglas, Heron & Co. dispatched four of their wealthiest and most prominent shareholders—the dukes of Buccleuch and Queensberry, Archibald Douglas of Douglas, and Patrick Heron of Heron—to solicit the aid of the bank in order to "stop the present torrent," the directors balked.[98] Though the delegation assured the bank that "they understood themselves bound to the whole extent of their fortunes, for the operations of the Scotch bank; and were willing, for the further satisfaction of the Bank of England, to bind themselves in such further legal securities as could be reasonably required," the directors first demanded to know the full extent of Douglas, Heron & Co.'s outstanding liabilities. The delegates, whether through pretense or ignorance, offered a figure of £300,000, which elicited incredulity from the assembled directors, who were aware that the Bank of England alone held at least half that in Douglas, Heron & Co. paper. Though they eventually relented and offered to discount £300,000 in Ayr Bank bills, inclusive of re-discounting the £150,000 already held, the terms—immediate security of lands in England yielding £10,000 per annum, a deposit of government securities, and a bond from the firm for the entire amount of the advance—were thought so punitive that the delegates refused.[99] Four weeks later, however, realizing the desperation of their situation, the dukes of Buccleuch and Queensberry again entreated the bank, asking for a reduced credit of just £150,000, on the security of the firm's bond and bankers' acceptances alone.[100] This time it was the Bank of England's turn to refuse.

Indeed, though the Bank did ultimately come to the rescue of another Scottish bank, William Alexander and Sons (who, like Douglas, Heron & Co., had stopped payment at the end of the day on 24 June) with a £160,000 loan, it did so only on the security of the latter's sugar estates in Grenada, and because Alexander and Sons held the lucrative Scottish contract to export tobacco to the French farmers general.[101] To generate cash for retiring its outstanding debt, Douglas, Heron & Co., in contrast, was eventually compelled to raise £450,000 by a sale of annuities, at a staggering annual cost of nearly 15 percent, followed by £500,000 raised through the issuance of tradable bonds bearing 5 percent coupon, which required a special act of Parliament—all secured by the estates of the bank's proprietors.[102]

Third, history aside, on a more theoretical level the Ayr Bank crisis of 1772 ought to detain our attention on account of its implications for what George Stigler dubbed "capture theory," wherein statutory regulations or regulatory bodies ostensibly intended to serve the public interest in fact serve instead mainly to advance private concerns with concentrated interests in the regulated sector or industry.[103] The crisis itself presents a stark warning of the risks posed by regulatory capture, particularly in financial markets, and perhaps, for that matter, the risks of what former International Monetary Fund chief economist Simon Johnson has referred to as "intellectual capture."[104] As noted above, and as evinced in detail in Chapter 3, two of the salient pieces of regulation governing Scottish banking in the run-up to June 1772 were in reality the products of intense political lobbying by the largest and longest-established banks in Scotland. Not only did directors of the Bank of Scotland, Royal Bank of Scotland, Linen, Arms, Ship, and Thistle Banks each dispatch delegates to London with the explicit task of procuring in their favor an act of Parliament raising regulatory barriers to entry into Scottish banking, but also all of the Scottish Members of Parliament who formally proposed and shepherded the bill through both houses were themselves proprietors of the country's leading banks. Perhaps even more alarmingly, we find that the intellectual firepower of two of the most eminent Scottish economic thinkers of the time, Sir James Steuart of Coltness and Adam Smith, intimate friends both of directors at the Arms, Ship, and Thistle Banks, was enlisted to craft a sufficiently compelling, or at least persuasive, public-good argument on behalf of Scottish financial regulation.

This constitutes, or ought to constitute, a warning, because, as I also demonstrate in Chapter 3, the effects of the legal restrictions on Scottish banking implemented in 1765—regulations prohibiting the issuance of small-denomination notes and contingent debt—had the result not of mitigating financial instability but of intensifying it. In effect, the prohibition of small notes and banknote optional clauses in 1765 raised barriers to entry and lowered competition in Scottish credit markets, thereby both inducing banks to assume more balance-sheet risk and increasing the likelihood that portfolio losses in the event of an adverse financial shock would be transmitted to depositors and note holders through disorderly bank runs, suspensions of payment, and institutional liquidation. This, however, is precisely the result we would expect in instances of regulatory capture; by obtaining in their favor relative regulatory privilege, capturing agents are essentially incentivized to produce negative externalities. As we observe in the case of Scotland in 1772, these negative externalities can be especially costly when reduced competition gives rise to systemically important financial institutions.

Moreover, as Andrew Haldane, Director of Financial Stability at the Bank of England, has demonstrated, adding complexity to complex systems—such as highly interconnected financial networks—can exacerbate the risk that adverse shocks are amplified and propagated throughout the system.[105] Indeed, in Chapters 3 and 4, I find that the unintended and unforeseen higher-order effects of legal restrictions on Scottish banking, including not only prohibitions on small notes and optional clauses but also usury laws, elevated the level of systemic risk in Scottish financial markets. Attempts to regulate specific categories of financial activity can therefore generate not simply offsetting changes in bank behavior but changes that interact in often unpredictable ways with existing institutions, as well as with unanticipated changes in economic circumstances.

Although Simon Johnson's work, in particular, has compellingly illustrated that rent-seeking behavior by concentrated financial interests and the capture of legislator and regulator by the legislated and regulated are phenomena by no means exclusive to developing economies, the close resemblance of eighteenth-century Scotland—where noninclusive political institutions and official cronyism allowed an entrenched financial oligarchy to enjoy outsized legislative and regulatory influence—to current developing economies may perhaps render the Ayr Bank crisis especially germane to the political economy of development, as much as or more than it speaks to similar issues in developed contexts. To be sure, its relevance to contemporary development economics and new institutional economics owes not least to the fact that some, including Cameron and Kroszner, have suggested that Scotland under "free banking" may provide a model for financial reform in emerging economies today.[106]

At the same time, however, as I emphasize in Chapter 5, the regulatory changes lobbied for and implemented in 1765 were not purely and simply exercises in anticompetitive rent-reeking by Scotland's largest financial institutions and ought therefore to caution us against too simple a conception of regulatory capture. For the 1765 act was also the consequence of a genuine effort by the country's leading banks to impose order on a difficult macroeconomic situation—an effort that, as they saw it, was complicated by unrestricted entry of smaller banks and notes issuers. In the grip of a postwar balance of payments crisis, there was a strong sentiment among many, including Smith's Glaswegian banking friends, that *something* needed to be done. But with justifiable confusion as to the true sources of Scotland's macroeconomic challenges, the impulse to regulate was almost bound to result in misdiagnosis or, in the case of the optional clause, fixation on what was thought by the country's biggest banks to be an acceptably innocuous decoy for regulatory zeal.

The fundamental dilemma, I argue, was that after 1745, Scotland's was a rapidly emerging economy with a fixed exchange rate, large external debt, and a chronic current account deficit balanced by large but often highly volatile capital inflows. In particular, in 1756 and 1762–1764, large capital outflows due to exogenous political events relating to the Seven Years' War exerted immense pressure on the Scottish financial system, generating a massive excess relative supply of Scottish bills as investors scrambled to remit capital to London for speculation in the East India Company, Bank of England, and British government securities. The Scottish banks, and especially the large chartered banks in Edinburgh, bore the brunt of this imbalance, as interest-rate arbitrageurs sold bills on London at high premiums for Scottish banknotes, which they then immediately unloaded onto the Edinburgh banks for redemption in specie. Without recourse to higher deposit rates, due to a binding usury ceiling, the chartered banks responded exactly as the International Monetary Fund would likely have instructed them—by attempting to grind out a real exchange rate depreciation through a painful credit contraction. But for an economy already short on circulating media owing to the speculative external drain of specie, the consequent cash crunch invited numerous small-scale note issuers, Smith's "beggarly bankers," to plug the gap, which merely frustrated the Edinburgh chartered banks' efforts to defend the exchange rate.

Ultimately, the incipient balance of payments crisis was resolved only when the country's two leading banks, Bank of Scotland and Royal Bank of Scotland, resorted to imposing capital controls in the form of highly discriminate exercise of banknote optional clauses. Temporary capital controls between 1762 and 1764 appear, then, to have allowed time for the depreciation of Scottish bills of exchange to gradually pass through to relative prices and a current account recovery, without requiring a disruptive contraction of the money supply and accompanying deflation, thanks largely to the surrogate provision of money and credit by Smith's beggarly bankers. But from the perspective of the country's largest banks, the entrance of smaller-scale notes issuers had placed them in a difficult bind, confounding their efforts to, first, protect their own reserves and, second, manage the macro situation.

The intervening Bank Act of 1765 thus not only misdiagnosed the source of Scotland's macroeconomic troubles as one of too many bankers, but also did nothing to resolve the fundamental problem that Scotland's rapidly developing economy was vulnerable to large, speculative capital flows. Moreover, by effectively restricting entry, raising the minimum efficient scale of banking, and removing the voluntarily contracted option of selective capital controls, the act also undermined some of the strengths that had previously enabled the Scottish banking system to absorb such volatility. In other words, in the wake of 1765, you still had an unresolved perennial balance of payments problem, but now with the additional problems of bigger, more systemically important financial institutions, higher barriers to entry for new banks, and no contractual "circuit-breaker" to allow temporarily illiquid but otherwise solvent banks to liquidate assets without incurring fire-sale losses. The result was that when a major external financial shock hit in 1772, the flexibility and resilience that the system had exhibited in 1756 and 1763 was substantially diminished. Thus, while there were certainly macro-prudential motivations for Scotland's largest banks to lobby for regulatory intervention, the unintended second- and third-order effects were no less adverse on account of somewhat noble intentions. It is a cautionary tale of the risks of rushing to regulate *in the middle of* an ongoing financial crisis and *before* the causes of that crisis are sufficiently understood.

Fourth, and finally, however, the crisis of 1772 ought to interest us not just for the relevance of eighteenth-century Scottish banking to current issues concerning the reform of financial market institutions but also precisely for its uniqueness. From a historical perspective, though Scotland from 1716 to 1845 may not have constituted "free banking" in its pure, idealized form, it was certainly the closest practical approximation offered us by modern history. This is important because contemporary analysis of the effects of financial regulation is often plagued by the strong endogeneity of regulatory change, and by the fact that a regulatory apparatus with numerous simultaneously moving parts tends to leave outcomes hopelessly over-determined. In other words, it is the very scarcity of formal regulatory institutions governing Scottish banking during the "free banking" period that allows for a more precise identification of the determinants of institutional and regulatory changes, and the causal effects of those changes.[107]

The results of this empirical strategy are thus all the more striking for the relative simplicity of the historical context. What we discover, in Chapter 2, is that it was exactly the "great multiplication of banking companies" in Scotland and, contra Smith, the proliferation of what he derisively called "beggarly bankers," that rendered the Scottish financial system both intensely competitive and remarkably resilient to a series of severe adverse shocks, endogenous as well as exogenous, that buffeted the small developing economy before 1765. This resilience was due not to any prudential legal restrictions imposed on Scottish banking, but rather to the fact that, in the relative absence of regulatory complexity and associated expansion of the efficient scale of banking, the provision of financial services in Scotland was enhanced by relatively free and competitive entry and constrained by the market discipline of relatively competitive and nondisruptive exit.[108]

Moreover, as demonstrated in Chapter 3, while the regulatory restrictions imposed in 1765 at the insistence of vested banking interests clearly throttled some of this competitive flexibility and amplified both the assumption of risk by individual Scottish banks and the level of systemic risk in Scotland's financial sector as a whole, Scottish banking nonetheless retained much of its resilience. Indeed, as we shall see in Chapters 4 and 5, though litigation among Douglas, Heron & Co.'s unlimitedly liable shareholders themselves was still ongoing some six decades after the crisis of June 1772, creditors were fully restituted in 1774 by the issuance of eight-year, coupon-bearing bonds secured by the shareholders' personal estates. The subsequently rapid economic recovery in Scotland suggests that economies with flexible, decentralized financial systems and bank liability regimes that (unlike static, technical rules) *automatically* generate voluntarily contracted, *countercyclical* equity bail-ins, may in fact challenge Reinhart and Rogoff's conclusion that deep financial crises necessarily entail long, slow economic recovery.[109]

Indeed, I find that in the absence of a formal lender of last resort, the unlimited liability of shareholders in bankrupt Scottish banks essentially served that role, as sequestration of shareholders' personal estates effectively "bailed in" equity holders for more than their subscribed capital, thereby mitigating counterparty risk in the Scottish financial system and facilitating a more rapid recovery in the flow of credit. Once Douglas, Heron & Co. received parliamentary permission to issue the transferable bonds to their creditors, secured largely by the immense landed wealth of their 226 partners, the Scottish financial system and economy rebounded sharply. The fact that Scottish banks, unlike their English counterparts, could consist of more than six partners, moreover, meant that their equity base was generally sufficiently diffuse and diverse to absorb losses; of the sixteen banks that failed in 1772, I find that all but Douglas, Heron & Co. had fewer than six partners, while all three that failed and inflicted losses on creditors had fewer than six partners. For the entire Scottish free banking period, Acheson, Hickson, and Turner actually observe that all of the banks which failed and imposed losses upon creditors had fewer than seven partners.[110] The problem in 1772 was largely that Douglas, Heron & Co. at first conveyed ambiguous messages to the public concerning the liability of their partners, so that for a time there was considerable confusion as to whether they were, in fact, unlimitedly liable to the full extent of their personal wealth. Even after that question was clarified in the affirmative, the extent of the firm's debts was such that fully unfreezing Scottish credit markets necessitated the creation of a more liquid market for securities backed by the proprietors' estates, which required (due to the strictures of the Bubble Act) an act of Parliament expressly authorizing the bankrupt firm to issue tradeable bonds. The firm was thus essentially transformed into a "bad bank" whose sole function was to gradually work off its toxic assets and repay creditors while the immense landed wealth of its proprietors' personal estates provided a financial backstop.

Borrowing a term coined by Nassim Taleb, Lawrence White has even gone so far as to suggest that banking systems regulated by such market discipline rather than legal interposition, which often gives rise to moral hazard and "too big to fail" financial institutions, in fact historically seem to exhibit features not just of robustness or resilience, but of *antifragility,* or the property of gaining strength from stressors and failures.[111] As I summarize in Chapter 5, the evidence presented here certainly supports this case. The largely unregulated nature of Scottish banking, and the absence of regulatory complexity, gave rise to a highly competitive, flexible financial system that was able both to meet the considerable capital demands of the developing Scottish economy and, particularly in 1756 and 1763, to absorb a series of severe adverse financial shocks.

Moreover, contingent-convertibility debt contracts, in the form of the banknote optional clause, were, prior to their legislative ban in 1765, particularly instrumental in mitigating the risk of the kinds of disruptive, speculation-driven external reserve drains typical of rapidly emerging economies experiencing large "hot money" flows."[112] The combination of the optional clause with unlimited liability meant that contingent liability more generally was an essential stabilizing feature of the Scottish banking system, with creditors contractually at risk of being "bailed in" at each point of the capital structure; banknotes could be converted into interest-bearing promissory notes, deposits and bills into annuities or bonds, and subscribed shares into unlimited financial obligation. The financial crisis of 1772 is thus empirically salient, not as an indictment of Scottish banking, but rather of the specific regulatory changes that rendered a crisis in that system both more likely and more severe in the event of its occurrence. To be clear, the appropriate question is not why there was a global financial crisis in 1772, but rather why Scotland was so affected by and implicated in that crisis, and why it had heretofore weathered previous financial shocks, including one as recently as 1763, without remotely comparable distress.

To recapitulate, regardless of the *arguments* presented in this work, the *historical event* merits consideration. On a philosophical level, the financial crisis of 1772 stands out for its undeniable, if not entirely unambiguous, effect on the development of Adam Smith's thoughts concerning credit and banking, and for the questions it raises about the nature of money and the speed limits within which it may safely convey commerce. From a historical perspective, the crisis is noteworthy not only for its magnitude and personal consequence but also for its immense impact on global political, economic, and historic events, perhaps most notably with regard to simmering tensions in the North American colonies. On the theoretical front, meanwhile, it testifies to important problems in political economy regarding rent-seeking, regulatory, and intellectual capture as well, for that matter, as international macroeconomics. And, finally, in terms of methodology, the financial crisis of 1772 allows us to demonstrate the value of history in identifying and analyzing causal relationships of contemporary economic relevance.

One observer of the events of spring and summer 1772, a young man at the Merchant Taylors' School for boys, perhaps summed up their significance best in a poem entitled "The Moon" that he wrote and delivered on 21 October of that year. Noting that, while the rude viewer may look upon the moon and conclude that "the light which he admires, Flows from the radiance of her inbred fires," the sage "who studies Nature's laws, And from effects can trace the distant cause; Knows that the globe which thus attracts our sight, Possesses nothing of intrinsic light." The young poet then asks if the same is not also true of the "villain" and "specious man," who rely on "Mere outward show to hide some deep deceit; like the Moon, void both of light and heat." He continues:

> Whilst in your purse you keep the massy gold,
> It is in fact the thing which you behold.
> Turn it to paper, a new form appears,
> Which owes its value to the name it bears;
> 'Tis good or bad, as the contents declare,
> The Bank of *England,* or the Bank of *Air.*
> 'Tis plain such traffick varies like the Moon,
> Guided by Credit, the Commercial Sun.
> From that true centre it derives the force,
> Which hastens or retards its mazy course;
> Should Vice or Folly intercept its light,
> Commerce eclips'd, must sink in endless night.
>
> Thus, whilst the Moon, in her inconstant race,
> Shines with false beams, and ever-changing face,
> She gives this lesson to the incautious Man,
> With piercing eye each character to scan
> And, as new objects offer to his view,
> To separate the specious from the true.[113]

What I seek here is not only to sort "the specious from the true" of the "Air Bank" crisis itself but also to separate the fallacies and truths of financial regulation and crises more generally that the event allows us to reveal.

2

Beggarly Bankers

SMITH WAS CERTAINLY AWARE OF, and evidently discomfited by, the fact that the banking restrictions he advocated sat rather discordantly with his principle of natural liberty. "To restrain private people," he conceded, "from receiving in payment the promissory notes of a banker, for any sum whether great or small, when they themselves are willing to receive them; or, to restrain a banker from issuing such notes, when all his neighbours are willing to accept of them, is a manifest violation of that natural liberty which it is the proper business of law, not to infringe, but to support." Such violation, however, he concluded, is justified where the "exertions of the natural liberty of a few individuals, which might endanger the security of the whole society, are, and ought to be, restrained by the laws of all governments." He likened, therefore, "regulations of the banking trade" to the "obligation of building party walls, in order to prevent the communication of fire."[1]

Smith's concerns owed not simply to the collapse of Douglas, Heron & Co. in 1772, but also, and perhaps more decisively, to his experience of the tumultuous years from 1760 to 1765 in Scotland, during which time the Scottish economy was subjected to several severe adverse financial shocks, culminating in what I contend was a full-blown balance-of-payments crisis in 1762.[2] Blame for the country's monetary troubles—an acute scarcity of coin, an adverse exchange rate, a chronic drain of specie—Smith, then lecturing at the University of Glasgow, laid in large part upon an "excessive multiplication of paper money in Scotland," facilitated especially by the practice of issuing banknotes for "so small sums as twenty shillings," and by the insertion in those notes of "optional clauses" entitling the issuer to defer payment by six months, with interest. Had these "beggarly bankers" been "restrained from issuing any circulating banknotes, or notes payable to the bearer, for less than a certain sum" and "subjected to the obligation of an immediate and unconditional payment of such banknotes as soon as presented," the threat to the "safety" and "security of the public" posed by their trade would then have been greatly attenuated.

Although most subsequent economic historians, following Smith, conclude that this episode in Scottish financial history constituted a "small notes mania," fueled principally by the peculiarly Scottish banking practices of issuing banknotes for sums below £1 and inserting dilatory optional clauses in their notes, the reality was rather less straightforward. Smith, along with later Scottish financial historians, including Graham, Kerr, and Hamilton, seems to have here mistaken correlation for causation, or effect for cause.[3] Instead, I find not only that there is little evidence of a "mania," but also that the alleged banking offenses—namely, the issuance of notes in denominations below £1 and the adoption of optional clauses—were in fact rational and effective market responses to the very real monetary challenges confronting the Scottish economy.

Specifically, whereas in the decade before the Seven Years' War Scotland seems to have resembled a typical fast-growing emerging economy, with a current account deficit balanced by large capital inflows, upon the outbreak of hostilities the Scottish economy quickly swung to capital account deficit as investors rushed to speculate on the London exchanges. While these capital outflows were generally offset by current account surpluses driven by wartime demand, severe exogenous shocks in 1756 and 1762—harvest failure, increased remittances owing to wartime tax hikes, and intense speculation in government bonds following positive developments on the Prussian front—threw the economy into severe balance-of-payments crisis, with attendant external drains of reserves. In this context, the issuance of small notes by private banking companies was a rational response to an acute shortage of circulating media among Scottish merchants and traders, while the exercise of optional clauses—as it turns out, only rarely and exclusively against high-volume English speculators and arbitrageurs—was essentially a private application of capital controls on large "hot money" outflows. Resort to the optional clause, therefore, was rendered more likely by the inability of Scottish banks to respond to large capital outflows by raising deposit rates, owing to existing usury laws.

The organization of this chapter is as follows. First, I examine the history of the optional clause, finding that it was in fact originally adopted, not by Smith's so-called beggarly bankers, but by the oldest and largest Scottish banks as a strategic deterrent against hostile note raids by rival banks. I further demonstrate that the optional clause was only inserted in large denomination notes and was never invoked against ordinary note holders, or even against rival banks. Rather, the only evidence of option ever actually being exercised is by the chartered banks in Edinburgh against English interest-rate speculators betting on the discount spread between English and Scottish bills of exchange, in an effort to stem severe external drains of reserves. Even then it was invoked with extreme infrequency and exclusively against speculative arbitrageurs attempting to redeem large sums of large denomination notes. Second, I find that while there was a marked uptick in the number of note issuances, including several of 5s. and 10s. denominations, after 1760, this trend cannot be characterized as "manic" and produced no substantively different rates of inflation in Scotland compared to England. New issues of "small" notes, such as 5s. (£30.52 in 2014 prices), appear to have been issued largely by various merchants and tradesmen in response to the severe drainage of small denomination coin from the economy as English speculators arbitraged the discount spread between English and Scottish bills of exchange. These notes, moreover, were generally limited issues intended for narrow circulation among clients, employees, and suppliers, and were in any event readily discounted and exchanged by numerous single-proprietor notes exchanges and clearing houses.

Ultimately, the Scottish economy was exposed to a series of enormous exogenous shocks in the two decades leading up to 1765. Far from contributing, however, to consequent instability, the Scottish financial system actually exhibited considerable resilience and flexibility in absorbing those shocks and limiting transmission to the real economy. In this, contingent liability and small notes, the products of an intensely competitive banking sector, were instrumental.

WITHIN THE SCOTTISH FREE-BANKING LITERATURE, perhaps no item has generated as much debate as the optional clause. Figure 2.1

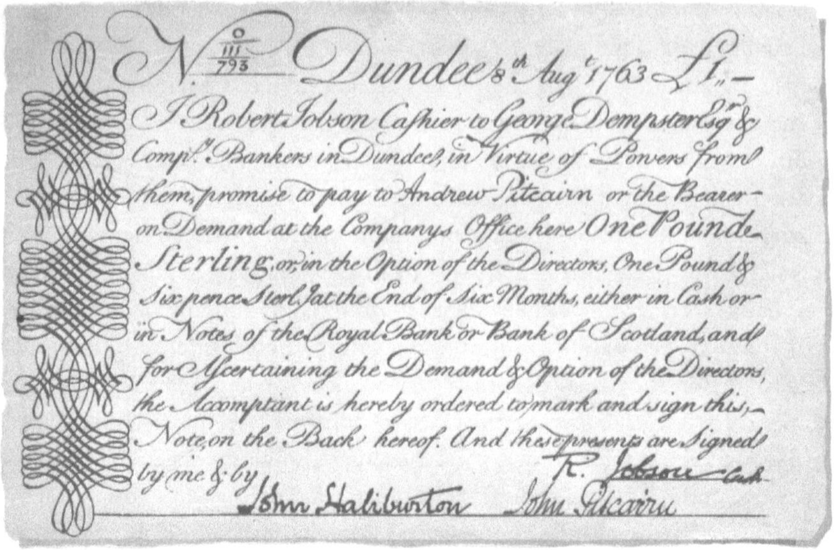

FIGURE 2.1. Dundee Banking Company note with optional clause. Graham, *One Pound Note,* 65.

reprints one such clause, inserted in a note of George Dempster & Co., the "Dundee Banking Company," in 1763, entitling the bearer to £1 sterling on demand or, "in the Option of the Directors," £1. 6d. six months hence, corresponding to an annualized rate of interest of 5 percent, the legal maximum. If this option was invoked, the cashier of the issuing bank was instructed to "mark" the note, indicating the date of presentation from which the six-month clock would begin to tick, during which time interest would accrue and the note would be unredeemable on demand by any bearer, though it could continue to circulate among accepting payees or in secondary markets. Early historians of Scottish banking, including Graham and Kerr, sided with Sir James Steuart and Smith in condemning the optional clause as inconsistent with "the nature of bank notes, whose legitimate character is that they should be convertible into specie on demand," and accordingly ascribed to the optional clause considerable blame for the alleged surfeit of notes and depreciation of Scottish bills between 1760 and 1765.[4] Graham called the device "objectionable," "odious," even "evil."[5] Without referring to the optional clause directly, Murray Rothbard criticized the "less-than-noble tradition of non-redeemability at Scottish banks."[6] Meanwhile Munn, though admitting that the optional clause was designed to preserve scarce specie, nonetheless concludes that it was "a disturbing and disruptive element in the commercial world."[7] Shah, similarly, doubts that the optional clause constituted "an effective and desirable mechanism for creating a stable free-banking system."[8]

On the other side of the debate, however, Meulen considered the optional clause a salutary and efficient innovation, a view echoed by subsequent advocates of free banking, including White, Selgin, Dowd, Cowen, and Kroszner.[9] Cowen and Kroszner hypothesize that "the option clause mitigated the instability caused by first-come, first-serve rules for payouts to depositors demanding specie." By providing, they argue, "for orderly suspensions with an interest 'bonus' for not being first in line, instability due to runs was reduced. Similarly, the option clause also decreased the likelihood of sudden large loan calls and the attendant costs imposed on bank borrowers." In other words, according to Cowen and Kroszner, the optional clause attenuated the risk that random noise could trigger bank run "bubbles" of the type demonstrated by Diamond and Dybvig.[10] Selgin and White concur, noting that though the optional clause was originally conceived as a defense against hostile note redemptions by rival banks, it could, in theory, have also served as a contractual "circuit-breaker," allowing temporarily illiquid but otherwise solvent financial institutions to liquidate assets without incurring fire-sale losses.[11]

Selgin and White are probably closest to the mark here. As they observe, the optional clause was adopted first and foremost as a defense against hostile note raids. But this in no way means that it could not also, in so doing, have minimized the capacity of such episodes and others to metastasize into broader threats to the stability of the greater Scottish financial system. Indeed, the discriminateness and selective frequency with which the optional clause was inserted and actually invoked meant not only that it provided an effective safety valve at moments of capital flight but also that it did so without imposing undue inconvenience on the vast majority of note holders, who generally seem either to have been entirely unaffected by the inclusion of option—which was universally limited to large denomination notes (at least £1, though often £5)—or else accepted option-bearing notes at par with demand notes. Indeed, the *Edinburgh Courant* in February 1765 noted that "notwithstanding this clause, specie continuing to be scarce, and the security of the different persons undoubted, the notes continued to circulate with the same facility as formerly."[12]

However, what even White and Selgin overlook, along with Gherity and Shah, is that though the optional clause was originally *inserted* into Scottish banknotes as a defense against hostile note raids by rival banks, it was in practice never *invoked* against other banks. Rather, all available historical evidence indicates that the only note holders ever actually subjected to exercise of option were interest-rate arbitrageurs, particularly from England, seeking to profit from the price differential between English and Scottish bills of exchange. In effect, then, the optional clause fulfilled two roles. First, it acted as a strategic deterrent against rival banks, a device whose exercise *within* the payments and clearing system would almost certainly have constituted an act of mutually assured destruction. But, second, it also served to attenuate the risk of runs owing to sudden *external* drains of specie as "hot money" sought higher investment returns in London and elsewhere.

Ironically, although later critics of the optional clause alleged that it was a device of "obscure" bankers of "doubtful credit" to delay due payment, the first bank to insert the clause in its notes was in fact none other than the august Bank of Scotland, often referred to simply as the "Old" Bank. Having endured relentless note raids by the recently incorporated Royal Bank, resulting in suspension of payments on 27 March 1728, the directors of the Old Bank resolved, on 6 November 1730, to issue new £5 notes (£684.10 in 2014 prices), payable to the bearer on demand or in the amount of £5. 2s. 6d. (corresponding to an annualized rate of 5 percent) six months after presentation, "In the Option of the Directors." Initially, the clause was restricted to £5 notes only, so as to avoid inconveniencing small- and medium-sized commercial clients, but two years later, under continued attack from the Royal Bank, Bank of Scotland on 12 December 1732 began issuing £1 notes with option.[13] The Old Bank's then remained the only option-bearing banknotes for fourteen years, until May 1756, when the two upstart Glasgow banks, the Arms and Ship, under aggressive assault from their now allied chartered rivals in Edinburgh and in the grip of a macro balance of payments crisis, finally resorted to likewise inserting optional clauses into their notes.[14] Next, however, were the other two chartered banks—the Royal and the Linen Banks—and the "aristocratic bank," the Thistle, in 1761–1762.[15] Ironically, then, it was six of the first banking institutions established in Scotland—coincidentally also the six largest, by subscribed capital—to avail themselves of the optional clause that would later lobby for its prohibition.

The origins of the optional clause, moreover, reveal that, far from providing an easy means for suspending payment, option was conceived precisely to avoid the necessity of suspending payment by allowing for the threat of discriminate and orderly suspension. When the Bank of Scotland suspended payments on 27 March 1728, following a demand for £900 by Andrew Cochrane, agent of the Royal Bank and Lord Provost of Glasgow, the directors of the Old Bank adopted a sort of proto-optional clause, pledging to resume payment in three months' time, with notes issued after 1716 to accrue interest at 5 percent during that interim.[16] Before resumption, in a public broadsheet, they then published a detailed account of the bank's balance sheet as it stood at the time of suspension and on 18 June 1728, noting, in italics and block capitals, that the free stock of the bank amounted to £40,466. 18s. 2d., and thus that they were fully ready to meet any demands that might be made upon them, inclusive of accrued interest.[17]

The following year, director Richard Holland first recommended formally inserting optional clauses into the bank's notes.[18] When his fellow directors eventually acceded to Holland's recommendation in late 1730, they took care to advertise "that they were resolved to make no use of this Optional Clause, in order to defer payment of any notes which should be presented in the ordinary course of business, but only to secure themselves from what they thought the unjust enterprizes of their rivals."[19] Evidently, their invention had the desired deterrent effect, as the Royal Bank's attacks thereafter abated, and Old Bank notes continued to circulate at par.[20] Indeed, it appears that after first inserting the clause into large denomination notes in 1730, it was another thirty-two years before Bank of Scotland actually invoked option by marking notes, and even then the decision was made conjointly, following lengthy discussions, with the Royal Bank.[21]

Even the private provincial banks, despite aggressive attacks from their larger public bank rivals, displayed considerable forbearance in exercising option. The ill-fated Banking Company of Aberdeen (Livingston & Co.), whose establishment, in 1747, gave the Old and Royal Banks cause to finally bury the hatchet, in fact never added the optional clause to its notes, most probably to its detriment. Founded by hosiers Alexander Livingston, William Mowat, William Bremner, and John Dingwall with a starting capital of just £600, the Aberdeen Company's venture into the note issuing business shortly aroused the antagonism of the two Edinburgh banks.[22]

Initially, the chartered banks were willing to tolerate the Aberdonians, and even accommodate them with cash credits of £500–1,000 to each of the founding partners. Their tolerance, however, endured only so long as Aberdeen confined itself to the business of discounting bills; once the provincials trespassed upon Edinburgh's presumed monopoly privilege of issuing notes, the Old and Royal Banks promptly withdrew all cash credits and deployed an agent to Aberdeen to conduct note raids.[23] The decision followed an extraordinary meeting between directors of both public banks on 19 July 1751, "With regard to the great circulation of paper credit occasioned by private persons erecting themselves into Banking companies," at which they effectively concluded a truce to conjointly suppress emerging private banknote issues in Aberdeen and Glasgow.[24] With its thin capital buffer, Aberdeen was ill-prepared for the combined onslaught. When, sometime in 1753, Edinburgh's agent presented for payment some £1,200 or £1,400 in Aberdeen Company notes, the Aberdonians, lacking the "mock Payments and dilatory Tricks" of later provincial private banks, had no choice but to make "Payment as fast as they could get Funds."[25] The following January, in *The Scots Magazine,* they announced their retirement from the banking business.[26]

Meanwhile, however, in Glasgow, the upstart Ship (Dunlop, Houston & Co.) and Arms (Cochrane, Murdoch & Co.) Banks proved tougher mettle, in no small measure owing to the optional clause.[27] Initially established, respectively, with the encouragement of the Old and Royal Banks to circulate their notes, the two Glaswegian private banks quickly ran afoul of their Edinburgh patrons through rapid expansion of their own note issues. The final straw seems to have been the withdrawal, in July 1751, of Glasgow's correspondents in Edinburgh, whose job it had been to retire Ship and Arms notes there; a clear indication to the Old and Royal Banks that the Glaswegian banks had their sights set on a much broader circulation than just Glasgow.[28] Pledging themselves to "a Mutual Friendship and harmony," the two public banks thus thereafter resolved to "mutually support, maintain and defend each of them their own, and the others interests against all attacks that may be made by other Societies that now subsist, or that hereafter may be set up or pretend to carry on the business of Banking in other parts of Scotland than Edinburgh, without lawful authority."[29] When the Glaswegians rebuffed Edinburgh's subsequent demands, submitted to Dunlop and Cochrane, that their firms discontinue the business of issuing notes, the Old Bank promptly curtailed the Ship's overdraft facility from £10,000 in June to £3,540 by October, and finally to zero from 11 January 1752, with the Royal likewise terminating their line of credit to the Arms.[30]

The two chartered banks also moved aggressively to crush their Glaswegian rivals via the courts. On 21 June 1756, John Watson, writer to the signet in Edinburgh, demanded £66. 2s. 6d. from a merchant in Leith, James Chalmers, for due payment of a bill of exchange. When the latter attempted to pay £50 of that sum in Glasgow banknotes, Watson refused and lodged a legal protest with the Court of Session for nonpayment. In reality, Watson's protest was merely a proxy battle; Watson himself was a director and large shareholder (to the extent of £1,193) of the Royal Bank.[31] The grounds for his protest—that Glasgow notes "were not the notes of any company established by act of parliament, royal charter, or any other legal way . . . nor had the solemnities required by law, and of consequence were intrinsically null"—could thus scarcely disguise the true motivation, namely, to have the Court declare private banking companies illegal. Revealingly, at the same time, the Royal Bank began adding the text "pursuant to Act of Parliament and Letters Patent under the Great Seal" to their notes, doubtless to underscore their allegedly superior legal foundation.[32] Yet despite Watson's concerted effort to tar the Glasgow banks as operating without legal standing or proper security, the Lords of Session unanimously rejected his protest, thereby confirming the right of private banking companies to issue legally binding promissory notes.[33]

Nonetheless, feeling the pressure, in late 1756 Glasgow attempted to negotiate terms of peace, proposing that they be permitted "to bank to the extent of £120,000" provided they confined their business to the counties of Ayr, Renfrew, Argyle, Lanark, and Stirling.[34] But with combined Arms and Ship note circulation probably amounting already to some £130,000, Andrew Fletcher, Lord Milton, deputy-governor of the Royal Bank, called this "no limitation at all," and demanded instead a limit of no more than £50,000, confined narrowly to Glasgow, Paisley, and Port Glasgow.[35] The Arms and Ship countered with an offer of £100,000, but by this point directors at the Old Bank had already soured on compromise and were reluctant to agree to any arrangement that would involve recognition of the Glaswegians' right to carry on as banks of issue.[36] In February 1757, at another joint meeting of directors, the two public banks thus effectively pulled the plug on further negotiation, their attention instead focusing "on what measures would tend to make these gentlemen [the Arms and Ship] weary of the Banking trade."[37]

Both banks, accordingly, shortly engaged the services of Archibald Trotter, formerly a partner of the private bank Coutts & Co., to act as their agent in Glasgow. Trotter's task was straightforward—to collect large quantities of Ship and Arms notes and present them for sudden redemption, with the aim of thereby forcing the Glaswegians into insolvency, as had befallen the Aberdeen

Company. His character was evidently well suited to the task, as Sir William Forbes recalls that contrary to his former partner, John Coutts, Trotter was "not possessing that liberality of thinking and acting in business for which the latter was so greatly distinguished . . . as neither his person nor manners were at all calculated to command their respect."[38] In Glasgow, however, Trotter, despite aggressive persistence, met with frustration. Not only were the Ship and Arms better capitalized than their erstwhile counterparts in Aberdeen, they also displayed considerably superior ingenuity. Trotter himself recounted one attempt to redeem notes of the Arms Bank:

> When their Notes were presented at the office for payment, a Bag of Sixpences was with great Deliberation produced and laid upon the table; the Teller then proceeded with ridiculous Slowness to open up the Bag and Count the Money. He would first Tell over a pound sterling, in single Sixpences ranked upon the Table, and then affecting to be uncertain about the Reckoning, he would gather this small money, and count it over again from One hand to the Other, sometimes letting fall a Sixpence for a Pretence to begin anew and count it over again; on other occasions he would make Time by ridiculous discourses upon the odd size or shape of Particular Sixpences, sound another upon the Table, to try if it was sufficient coin. And sometimes he would quit his occupation altogether upon Pretence of some sudden Errand or Call out of the Room. Very often they employed one Coggill, by his ordinary occupation a Porter, to act the Teller, and he lost time and blundered with great alacrity—being instructed to do his worst.[39]

During one thirty-four-day period, Trotter managed to obtain payment on just £2,893 of Arms notes, or £85 daily. On another occasion, in the course of an entire morning, he obtained a mere £7, in sixpences.[40] In May 1756, during one attempt to redeem £976, Trotter was turned away for appearing shortly after twelve o'clock noon, on the grounds that "the ordinary time of doing business for the forenoon was over."[41]

But procrastination was hardly Glasgow's only tactic. They also adopted the practice of meeting redemption demands, not with specie or public banknotes, but instead with thirty-day bills drawn on London correspondents. For instance, between 7 November and 4 December 1758, Trotter received in payment an average of just £36 per day from the Arms, leaving him still with £2,821 in Glasgow notes, which the cashier at the Arms offered to redeem with £1,000 in Old and Royal Bank notes, a mere £821 in silver, and £1,000 in thirty-day bills on London.[42]

More significantly, they also finally resorted to adopting the optional clause in their notes. Gherity, citing an article in *The Scots Magazine* from February 1765, incorrectly states that the clause was invoked by the two Glasgow banks in 1756. In reality, however, *The Scots Magazine* reports only that optional clauses were *inserted* into Arms and Ship notes at that time, on the occasion of "a run made upon them," in the middle of a war-induced balance of payments crisis.[43] Following the Bank of Scotland, printed option was payment in six months with 5 percent interest on an annualized basis, which the Arms and Ship later justified by referring to the Old Bank's precedent, noting that they "thought themselves at liberty to have recourse to the same expedient by which the Bank of Scotland had defended itself against the like enterprises of the Royal Bank."[44]

But it was in fact another six years before they may (according to an unpublished draft essay) have actually exercised the clause, during a second acute exchange rate crisis, and even then it was only *after* the Old Bank had already begun selectively marking notes; the Glasgow banks merely "followed their example."[45] The Scottish papers, however, make no mention of the Glasgow banks even ever invoking option. Moreover, far from provoking antipathy among their clients, the decision to insert the optional clause in 1756 as a defensive measure met with considerable public support among Glaswegians; *The Scots Magazine* reports that "there having been a run last week, by some persons from Edinburgh, on the two banking companies here, for gold and silver in exchange of the Glasgow notes . . . the inhabitants, with great readiness and alacrity, paid in large sums of specie to the two cashiers, and we are well assured, that the noblemen and gentlemen of this country have entered into a resolution to continue their countenance and support to these two companies."[46]

Crucially, as Gherity correctly notes, exercise of option was highly discriminate, as all delaying tactics, including option, were reserved only for "those who presented for payment any considerable sum in their own notes" and who refused to accept "smaller payments in specie" or "bills on London payable at long dates."[47] This included not only, and not even principally, hostile agents of rival banks, like Trotter, but also, more typically, interest-rate speculators. While Scotland had experienced large capital inflows in the decade following the Forty-Five, upon the outbreak of war with France in 1756 the economy swung to acute capital account deficit.[48] By summer, with speculative demand driving up government bond prices, particularly following the unexpectedly successful Prussian offensive in Saxony, English and Scottish investors alike were scrambling to remit specie to London. Though wartime demand meant the capital account deficit was balanced by current account surpluses in 1757–1761, a poor Scottish harvest in 1756 thrust the economy into a full-blown balance of payments crisis.[49] Bills on London surged to a premium of 4.5 percent or 5 percent over par, meaning a handsome profit could be made by drawing "fictitious" bills on London correspondents, often mere drawing posts, selling them at a premium for Scottish banknotes, immediately presenting those notes for redemption in specie, remitting the metal to London, and then repeating.[50]

Scottish newspapers teemed with accounts of such schemes, especially in 1762, when again the combination of crop failure, withdrawal of troops, and intense speculative demand for government securities (especially after the death of Empress Elizabeth on 5 January and Russia's subsequent retirement from the war), threw Scotland into severe balance of payments crisis for the second time in six years.[51] By the end of the year, 3 percent consols were up 36 percent, Bank of England stock 25 percent, and South Sea and East India shares up 38 percent and 41 percent.[52] Meanwhile, Scottish net exports plunged 31 percent in 1762, and a further 35 percent in 1763.[53] Defending the optional clause, one writer to the *Caledonian Mercury* asked readers to "watch the waggons to Newcastle, and smacks to London, and see the quantity of coin sent," arguing that "this mischief cannot arise wholly from the optional clauses, nor from the number of Banks, nor quantity of paper money, nor from scarcity of coin." Before the war, this writer recounted, specie was plentiful and "there was much English money invested in Scotland at 4 per cent., not less than £500,000 after the peace of 1748, because so much could not be got in England lent on heritable securities." But upon the outbreak of war, "Government gave high premium for money, the English withdrew their money from Scotland to invest it at home," while "Scotchmen using bank credits as much as possible, took money to London to dabble in the Stocks." As the exchange thus rose to "3, 4, and even 5 per cent. premium on London bills," moreover, wartime tax hikes led to an uptick in customs and excise remittances, while the emerging penchant of Scottish nobles to reside in London entailed larger annual remittances of rental income.[54]

A letter to *The Scots Magazine,* possibly by the same author, reiterates these claims, noting that before the war "there was a vast quantity of English money in Scotland at 4 per cent. as the English could not get such interest in their own country." However, "No sooner had the war broke out, and the government begun to give high premiums for money, than the English withdrew all their money out of Scotland," as too did many Scotsmen. "If any one will take the trouble," he therefore continued, "to look into the Newcastle waggon going from Edinburgh, or any of the Leith trading ships going for London, they will see such vast sums of specie going up as must surprise the most inattentive, and give every lover of his country reason to dread the inevitable consequences of such a perpetual drain of our specie from amongst us." "All these mischiefs," the author thus concluded, "can never surely be owing to the optional clause in the notes; nor to the delays, if any made, at the banks. No, no; these have a direct tendency to keep the money among us as it is plain to common sense, the more trouble any persons are put to in procuring specie, the less will they be able to either procure, or carry off with them."[55]

Yet another writer, similarly, suggested "the present call for money from England, is different from any other extraordinary demand. . . . In the present case, the demand is unlimited, and no provision the banks can make, can be of use; on the contrary, if they were to find a treasure, suppose of a million, it would only serve to increase it; because this demand arises from a profit on carrying money to London as a commodity, and not as the balance of trade."[56] Still another, writing under the initials "D.A.," even went so far as to suggest that Scotland's banks, in order to stem the drain of specie, "should be at pains to look after the stockjobbers in this country, and their assistants, and refuse them their credit." This he thought easy to do if simply "all their notes for the future may be made payable on demand, or, in the option of the banks, in six months with interest."[57] The editors themselves argued that "the only remedy at present seems to be for banks to mark their notes to be paid in six months. They will circulate as well, if not better than before, and so these rascals will be baulked."[58]

Writing in *The Edinburgh Advertiser* in January 1765, just as a bill for banning optional clauses was beginning to work its way through Parliament, Christopher Crabtree, a merchant in Aberdeen, likewise concluded that "the great and unusual demand for specie made for some years past, was principally occasioned by the premium on London bills getting up to three and four per cent.; and that again was chiefly owing to the sending money to London to be employed in the funds." He recollected the same scheme described by earlier writers, further noting that "London bills being got up to four per cent. premium, was the occasion of the first great run on the Edinburgh banks for cash," and that "this, no doubt, was the occasion of the Edinburgh banks using or taking the benefit of the optional clauses, to pay in six months; which certainly was a bold step, and, the world may see, was taken through mere necessity."[59]

It was, in fact, such interest arbitrageurs, even more than agents like Trotter, against whom the Scottish banks threatened exercise of option. Indeed, there is no evidence of Glasgow ever invoking option against Trotter. There is no mention of such action in the Glasgow or Edinburgh newspapers, and when in January 1759 Trotter submitted a formal petition to the Court of Session for alleged nonpayment of £3,447 in Arms Bank notes, his lengthy and detailed instrument of protest—wherein he painstakingly recounted each demand for payment he presented at the tell of the Arms Bank and the manner of payment or delay—made no mention whatsoever of option having been invoked at any time.[60] In both that document and a subsequent affidavit, complete with appendix, to the Court, Trotter listed with great precision the dates, hours, sums, note and coin denominations, teller and cashier names, and various dilatory tactics, including overzealous enforcement of bank hours, of his redemption attempts. Yet in no instance does he mention invocation, or even threat of invocation, of option.[61] This should perhaps not be surprising; with notes of the two chartered banks accounting for well over half of total circulation in Scotland and often used, as we have seen, as payment in lieu of specie, the Glasgow banks could ill afford to provoke the Old Bank into a retaliatory exercise of option. Such action, by instantly converting on-demand Bank of Scotland notes into six-month interest-bearing promissory notes, would have dramatically and adversely transformed the maturity profile of some 60 percent of Ship and Arms reserves, suggesting that the threat of mutually assured destruction likely deterred exercise of option within the bank clearing system.

Contrary to what Gherity, Selgin, and White aver, therefore, while it is true the optional clause was *inserted* into notes to deter hostile note raids by rival banks, there is little evidence that it was actually *exercised* against rival banks. Indeed, the only concrete indication of possible internecine invocation of option was in fact by the two chartered banks against one of the Glasgow banks. In the twilight of the clause's existence, rumors of an impending run on one or other of the two Edinburgh public banks by the aristocratic Thistle Bank reached directors at the Old and Royal, who resolved that "so soon as any such Demand for Specie is made from either of the Banks they shall give Orders to their Accountant and Teller to mark such Notes when presented."[62] This is the only such mention of contemplated exercise of option against other banks in the directors' minute books, and there is then no record of that resolution ever requiring execution.

Rather, option seems to have been invoked almost exclusively to deter what we might call the eighteenth-century equivalent of "hot money" flows; in essence, option constituted a form of capital control. For instance, it was in reaction to an external, not internal, drain of specie that the two public banks—which, owing to the reserve currency status of their notes, bore the brunt of capital flight—resolved on 1 April 1762 to mark notes presented in sums exceeding £50. With expectations of a victorious conclusion to the Seven Years' War resulting in a mass exodus of specie to take advantage of surging government bond prices and corporate securities—between January and March, government 3 percents rose 95 percent, while Bank of England stock was up 44 percent—the two public banks further pledged "to Support Each Other to the Last Shilling."[63] Under similar pressure in March 1764, the Old and Royal again resolved to "avail themselves of the Optional Clause in their Notes by marking such Sums as appear to be Called for with a view to make a profit of sending the Specie out of this Country."[64]

They had little choice; imports of specie were costing them dearly (in 1762 alone, Bank of Scotland had to import £100,000 of bullion from London, at a cost of 3.2 percent for exchange and 1.6 percent for transport), the Bank of England had refused them a £200,000 line of credit, and no one in Amsterdam would agree to a loan for less than 5 percent.[65] Their initial response was in essence to defend the nominal exchange rate through a policy of real exchange-rate depreciation; in early May, directors of the two public banks resolved to contract all credit by 25 percent, transfer specie between them as required, and fix deposit rates at the legal usury maximum of 5 percent for deposits of six months or more, and 4 percent on cash accounts.[66] But with Scottish merchants in desperate need of currency, let alone credit, private bankers quickly moved to satisfy excess demand for cash, which only exacerbated the public banks' challenge by in effect amounting to a highly unsterile sterilization. Notes issued by private banks could be mopped up by speculators in bills, redeemed for Old and Royal Bank notes, and then dumped on the chartered banks for redemption in specie. A standard market response would, of course, have been for the Edinburgh banks to discourage capital outflows by hiking deposit rates, but with usury laws imposing a binding ceiling of 5 percent, recourse to higher rates was legally denied them.

Under such circumstances, the chartered banks thus essentially had no alternative but to impose capital controls through exercise of option. Their action was reported in *The Scots Magazine* the following month, with the editors relating that "about the middle of March, the Edinburgh banks began to mark, instead of paying, the notes which they suspected to be the property of the selfish men." The magazine further noted with satisfaction that the action of the banks "obliged some of those wretches who had long preyed upon, and increased the distresses of their country, when thus disappointed of cash, to buy bills at a higher price than that at which they had sold, in order to enable their London correspondents to pay their draughts."[67]

More important, though, not only was option never *invoked* on small denominations and redemption amounts, it was not even *inserted* in smaller notes. The Linen Bank only printed option on notes of £5 or more.[68] The Old, Royal, Arms, Ship, Thistle, and Dundee banks all excluded option from notes below £1. Likewise, smaller note-issuing banks and quasi banks kept the optional clause out of their low denomination notes. John McAdam & Co., the "Old" Ayr Bank, reserved option for 20s. (£1) notes only; their 5s. and 10s. notes were without option. Glaswegian wine and spirit merchants George Keller & Co. issued option on 20s. but not 5s. and 10s. notes.[69] Even "obscure," single-proprietor trading firms that had ventured into limited issuance of small denomination notes, such as Alexander Wyllie, vintner in Aberdeen, James Smiton, coffeehouse keeper in Edinburgh, and the Wright Journiman Company in Perth issued their notes, typically of 5s. or less, exclusively on demand.[70] The brief and limited issuance of 5s. notes in 1761 by the prominent Edinburgh banking house of Mansfield, Hunter & Co. consisted entirely of notes payable on demand, that is, without option.[71]

At least some of the six banking companies that sprang up in Perth in 1763–1765, criticized by Graham and Kerr for "trading in small fish" and issuing notes of "trifling sums" (Rait's choice of word was "trivial") allegedly adopted the optional clause in several of their notes, but in the absence of surviving note specimens there is no reason to assume their reliance on option was substantively different from that of their provincial banking counterparts in Glasgow, Ayr, and Aberdeen. In fact, the one surviving note of the Perth bank of Blacklaws, Wedderspoon & Co., reported in *The Scottish Antiquary or Northern Notes & Queries,* was for the hardly "trivial" sum of £3 Scots, or 5s. sterling (£29.82 in 2013 prices), and was redeemable on demand.[72] Also in Perth, R. Robertson, merchant, on 5 February 1765 issued some 5s. notes, all without option.[73] Revealingly, despite Graham and Kerr's claims of "trifling" issues by the Perth banks, the smallest note issued by their successor Perth United Company was for one guinea, or 21s., in 1766, even though the Bank Act of 1765 permitted notes as small as 20s, which suggests that the Perth banks were hardly scraping the bottom of small-note issues.[74] Thus, the overwhelming preponderance of available evidence indicates that not only were the vast majority of note-holders positively discriminated against (i.e., spared any inconvenience) in the event of actual exercise of option, but also holders of small denomination notes were not even *exposed* to optional clauses—indeed, not even by the so-called beggarly bankers.

We can approximate the extent of optional clause adoption by tallying the number of new note issues bearing option. Figure 2.2 charts the number of *new* banknote issues with and without option in Scotland from 1725 to 1766, when the parliamentary prohibition of optional clauses took effect. The figures are compiled from numismatist James Douglas's 1975 catalog of Scottish banknotes. Douglas's inventory is no doubt incomplete, as several single proprietor note-issuing firms appear to have been omitted, likely because none of their notes survive (which could itself be indicative of limited issuance and circulation). Moreover, Douglas's record only permits us to evaluate the ex-

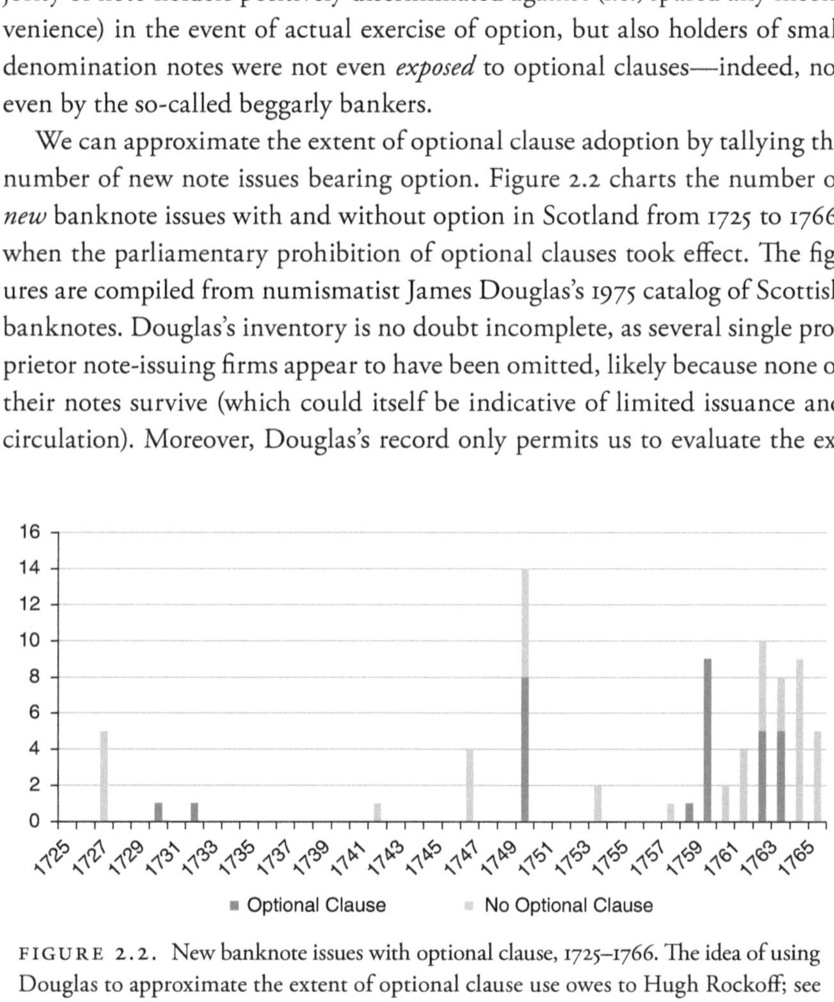

FIGURE 2.2. New banknote issues with optional clause, 1725–1766. The idea of using Douglas to approximate the extent of optional clause use owes to Hugh Rockoff; see Rockoff, "Upon Daedalian Wings of Paper Money: Adam Smith and the Crisis of 1772," *NBER Working Paper Series,* Working Paper 15594 (December 2009). I have re-tallied all sums directly from Douglas, having noted some slight discrepancies between Rockoff's figures and Douglas's catalog; Douglas, *Scottish Banknotes,* 54–55.

tensity of optional clause adoption (i.e., the number of note issues) rather than the intensity (i.e. the volume and run of each issue), let alone the frequency of exercise. Nonetheless, the catalog was exhaustively and meticulously compiled, and should thus, as Rockoff concludes, be considered broadly illustrative.[75]

By this gauge, it appears there was indeed an uptick in the inclusion of optional clauses in banknotes after 1760, though almost half of that increase is accounted for by one year, 1760—well before critics began clamoring for prohibition. Moreover, even during the "mania" years of 1761–1764, 60 percent of new notes were issued *without* the optional clause. Of the sixteen recorded issues below £1, only one bore an optional clause.[76] In other words, Douglas's catalog lends further confirmation to the observation that the optional clause was typically inserted only in larger denomination notes of £1 or more. Perhaps even more revealingly, almost all of the recorded issues with option—twenty-two of twenty-seven—are accounted for by the six largest banks, namely, the Old, Royal, Linen, Arms, Ship, and Thistle. To be sure, we might expect the largest banks by assets and circulation to account for the largest number of note issues generally. At the same time, their more extensive issuance of option-bearing notes would also be consistent with the status of their notes as de facto reserve currencies, and thus the necessity of maintaining a credible deterrent against external reserve drains by high-volume speculators.

THE OPTIONAL CLAUSE, however, constituted only half of Smith's criticism of Scottish banking during the 1760–1765 period. "Where bank notes are issued for so small sums as twenty shillings, as in Scotland," he also claimed, "many mean people are both enabled and encouraged to become bankers." This, he argued, was problematic, as "the frequent bankruptcies to which such *beggarly bankers* must be liable, may occasion a very considerable inconveniency, and sometimes even a very great calamity, to many poor people who had received their notes in payment."[77] Further, blame for Scotland's chronic scarcity of specie and frequent adverse exchange rate in the market for bills he laid directly on the shoulders not only of the optional clause but also on the "excessive multiplication of paper money in Scotland," facilitated especially by the velocity with which notes issued for "so small sums as twenty shillings, as in Scotland," would enter circulation.[78] The "suppression of ten and five shilling banknotes," by act of Parliament, he therefore concluded, "somewhat relieved the scarcity of gold and silver in Scotland; and the suppression of twenty shilling notes, will probably relieve it still more."[79]

That such "great multiplication of banking companies" generated a volume of paper currency "over and above what the circulation of the country could absorb and employ," to use the phrase oft repeated by Smith in *The Wealth of Nations,* has generally gone unquestioned, consistent as it is with the prevailing historical consensus that the period 1760–1765 in Scotland constituted a "small notes mania." Citing Smith, Graham, in a chapter titled "The Option Clauses, The Little Notes and the Lesser Notes of 1760–65," writes that "the ready means afforded for raising money by notes of bankers were taken advantage of by a number of extremely impecunious individuals in the capital, their example spreading like wildfire through the surrounding country, in a manner which has no parallel save in the North American note issues of 1780."[80] Though conceding that overissue of notes was not, in fact, a genuine or legitimate "grievance," thanks largely to regular and frequent note exchanges, Kerr nonetheless titles his chapter on the period "Note-Issuing Mania and the Act of 1765."[81] Munro, while concentrating almost exclusively on the perennial drain of specie during the Seven Years' War, likewise chose the title "Small Note Mania" for his chapter encompassing the 1760–1765 period.[82] Although Checkland and Munn appear hesitant to apply the term "mania," focusing instead on the macro pressures on the Scottish financial system, other recent scholars of Scottish banking, including Shah and White, more or less take it as given that the period was generally characterized by some degree of irrational exuberance for issuing notes.[83] Even those who are more skeptical, including not only Munn but also Rait and Saville, elect not to interrogate the assumption.[84]

Close inspection of the available historical evidence, however, casts considerable doubt on the supposition that 1760–1765 was characterized by a dangerously "great multiplication of banking companies" and paper currency, parliamentary restraint of which was purportedly salutary to Scottish finance. Again following Rockoff, we can obtain some sense of the timing of the alleged mania by examining the catalog of new issues compiled by Douglas.[85] Figure 2.3 graphs the number of new banknote issues recorded by Douglas from 1750 through 1782. On this basis, it would appear that during the supposed mania years of 1760–1765, enthusiasm for new issues peaked particularly in 1763–1765. Moreover, if we consider specifically the "small notes" element of the mania, the extensity of note issuance was even more concentrated, with

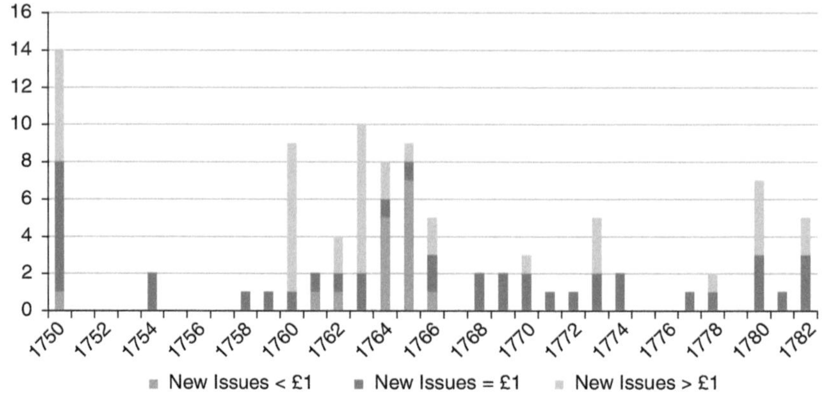

FIGURE 2.3. New banknote issues, by denomination, 1750–1783. *Data source:* Douglas, *Scottish Banknotes.*

1764–1765 accounting for 74 percent—fourteen out of nineteen—of recorded issues in denominations of £1 or smaller between 1760 and 1765. Because, as we shall see in Chapter 3, archival evidence reveals that directors at the two chartered banks were already discussing soliciting Parliament for a restriction on note issuance as early as late 1763, Figure 2.3 would suggest that opposition to private banknote issues actually preceded the most intense phase of the supposed mania. Indeed, considering that the two chartered banks together accounted for twelve of the fifteen new issues documented by Douglas between 1760 and 1763, their legislative appeal for note restriction appears rather more preemptive than reactive.[86]

To be sure, as noted above, Douglas's catalog almost certainly understates the number of note issues, particularly those of small denominations, largely because his catalog excludes many of the non-bank issuers of limited circulation promissory notes. But omitted note issues, too, seem to have been concentrated after 1763. Among those note issuers not listed by Douglas, for instance, is the aforementioned Wright Journiman Company in Perth, which in 1764 printed notes as small as one Scots shilling, or 1d. sterling—£0.51 in 2014 pounds sterling—for the purpose of paying its journeymen.[87] In Aberdeen, Alexander Wyllie and Robert Mitchell, both vintners, issued 5s. and 20s. notes, respectively.[88] Notes under £1 were also issued between 1763 and 1765 by the merchant houses of Martinson & Co., in Falkirk; William Yeaman & Co., in Dundee; James Scrimgeour & Son, in Borrowstounness; and the Mason Barrowman Company, in Edinburgh.[89]

Such notes, however, were rarely intended for broad circulation and were instead issued mainly to serve as promissory notes to suppliers or payrolls, often drawn on clients and correspondents. For instance, James More of Stoneywood evidently issued 5s. notes payable by Robert Byres, in Edinburgh, and advertised in *The Aberdeen Journal* that those notes continued to be honored in payment by Byres.[90] Alexander Fleeming & Co., in Kirkliston, issued 5s. notes for paying its journeymen.[91] We even find that James Smiton, a coffeehouse keeper in Edinburgh, issued notes obliging himself to pay the bearer "on demand, in money or drink, two shillings and sixpence sterling." These appear to have circulated among his coffeehouse clients, marked on the backs with receipts for mugs of porter or pints of beer or ale.[92]

Regardless, Douglas's catalog is still consistent with a contemporary estimate of *The Edinburgh Advertiser* that placed the number of banks of issue in Scotland in 1764 at sixteen.[93] Despite the above omissions, his catalog includes several quasi-banknote issues, including those under £1, and should thus be considered broadly reflective of the extensity of note issuance of various denominations. Listed for 1764, for example, are the Tannerie Banking Company in Perth, and George Keller & Co., wine and spirits merchants in Glasgow, who issued intricately engraved notes in 5s., 10s., and 20s. denominations.[94] According to *The Scots Magazine*, a meeting of Aberdonian magistrates on 1 January 1765 resolved to caution the public against accepting notes issued by several private note issuers, among them Keller & Co., alleging such notes were "under a very great suspicion." Keller, however, quickly struck back a week later with two advertisements in *The Edinburgh Courant*, assuring the public "that the few notes they have issued were intended for none of the purposes of banking, but to render their own plan of trade, which consists chiefly in the natural commodities of the country, more easy and convenient." They went on to add that the notes issued "contain no optional clause; and that hitherto every demand for the payment of them has been answered, and will continue to be so, with the greatest exactness and discretion," and further announced that they were pursuing legal action against the authors of the aforementioned allegations.[95]

Indeed, allegations of abuse in note issuance appear often to have been, at best, unfounded and, at worst, wholly manufactured. John Buchanan, in *Banking in Glasgow during the Olden Time*, observes that "some of the small merchants, jealous of the advantages which the issue of these notes conferred, endeavoured to excite public prejudice by printing and issuing lampoon-notes."[96] Of such parodies, there is certainly no scarcity of examples. One, dated 25 August 1764, was issued by the suspiciously comical "Ready Money Bank," of which there is no historical record of existence, for 1s., payable in "books, coffee, or ready money."[97] The likely satirical bank's hours were preposterously advertised as extending from just ten o'clock in the morning till noon.

A more malicious case is that of the Mason Barrowman Company. While a seemingly genuine note of this company—standard banknote size (6.5 inches by 3 inches) and clearly printed from a meticulously engraved copperplate, with standard anti-forgery features including handwritten script and intricate scrollwork—survives, signed by "William Johnston, Accountant," and "George Dunbar, Teller," a nearly identical note by the same company is dubiously signed by "Tim^y Credit" and "Barcklay Cash," accountant and teller. Both promise the bearer one Scots shilling (one penny sterling) on demand or with legal interest (5 percent) in six months at the option of the directors.[98] Either both were expensive fakes, or else one was genuine and the other a deliberate attempt to undermine the credibility and reputation of Mason Barrowman Company notes. If legitimate, the name of the company suggests they were in the business of transporting masonry stones and bricks, and thus likely employed numerous barrow haulers, whose wages they may have paid in company notes.

The most popular lampoon, however, was the so-called wasp note, which promised the bearer three pence sterling on demand or, "In the option of the Directors, Nine Ballads, Six Days after a demand."[99] One such note, supposedly issued by "Daniel McFunn, Duncan Buchanan & Co., is reprinted as Figure 2.4. A nearly identical note of the same date was issued by the fictitious bank of Andw. Whitecock, Duncan Dick & Co., and signed by "John Bragg, Cashier." This note is made out to "Thomas Tailor" in the amount of one Scots shilling, with option listed as "Three Ballads, Six Days after a demand."[100] Unlike genuine banknotes, which were printed from carefully engraved copperplates with handwritten script and often elaborate scrollwork, the wasp notes and similar lampoons were typically typeset by metal block and printed in cheap, simple style.[101]

Despite the parodies, genuine private banknotes were by no means illiquid. Even where legitimate note issuers printed notes for what critics called "trifling" amounts, intended for only limited circulation, numerous intermediary brokers set up shop to exchange goods or Edinburgh public banknotes for pri-

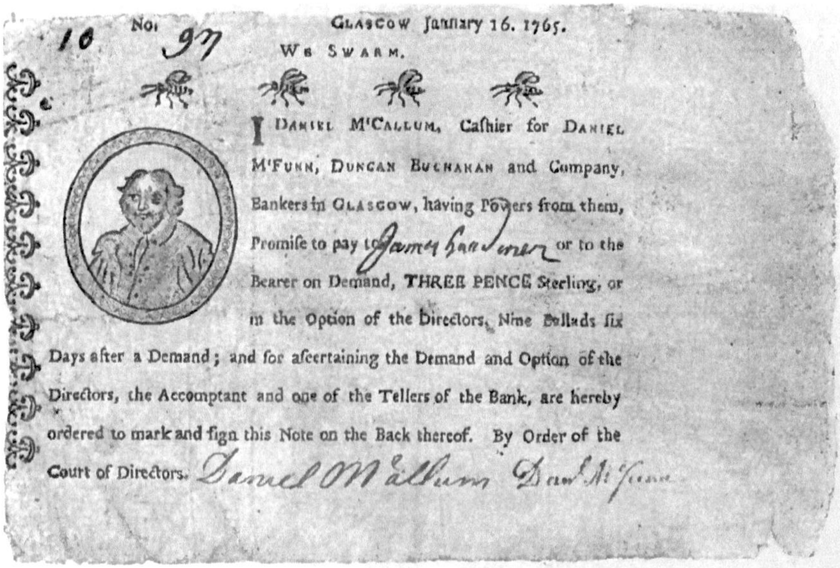

No. 10 97 GLASGOW January 16. 1765.

WE SWARM.

I DANIEL M'CALLUM, Caſhier for DANIEL M'FUNN, DUNCAN BUCHANAN and Company, Bankers in GLASGOW, having Powers from them, Promiſe to pay to [illegible] or to the Bearer on Demand, THREE PENCE Sterling, or in the Option of the Directors, Nine Bolluds ſix Days after a Demand; and for aſcertaining the Demand and Option of the Directors, the Accomptant and one of the Tellers of the Bank, are hereby ordered to mark and ſign this Note on the Back thereof. By Order of the Court of Directors. Daniel M'Callum [illegible]

FIGURE 2.4. "We Swarm" parody banknote, 1765. Stevenson, *Scottish Antiquary*, 72.

vate ones. For instance, in Edinburgh, "From a slender outsetting as a draper, old Mr. James Mansfield began to deal a little in bills of exchange, and by degrees founded a banking-house of the first celebrity in Scotland," the prominent private banking house of Mansfield, Hunter & Co. Similarly, the private bank William Cumming & Sons emerged out of the cloth shop of Patrick Cumming in Parliament Close, who gradually converted his business into a counting house, "Where he confined himself entirely to the transacting of money business." William Alexander & Sons, whose primary business was the purchasing of tobacco for the farmers-general of France, similarly became, in the words of Sir William Forbes, "Very considerable money-dealers." Samuel Foggo; Johnstone, Smith & Co.; Scott Moncreiffe & Ferguson; John Fyffe & Co.; and William Sinclair & Co., all private bankers, likewise entered the note and bill broking business without being themselves issuers.[102] *The Scots Magazine* reports that, as of April 1764, "no private bankers of Edinburgh issued notes, so far as we know, except Mess. Mansfield, Hunter, and Company; and they discontinued issuing, when such notes came to be thought prejudicial to the country," specializing instead in the intermediary functions of bill discounting and note broking.[103] Mansfield, Hunter & Co.

had indeed issued 5s. notes, payable on demand, on 1 June 1761, but the prominent bank could hardly be described as "beggarly."[104]

Whatever gripes there may have been about small notes issued by "beggarly" provincial banks, there was certainly no shortage of willing bankers and agents to exchange them. The Edinburgh newspapers teemed with advertisements by private bankers offering to exchange Old and Royal for provincial bank and quasi banknotes. Samuel Foggo offered to "retire the 5s. Notes of five of the Perth companies which issued them, namely, those of the Tannery Co. or Stewart, Richardson, & Co.; of the Craigie Co. or John Ramsay & Co.; of John Stewart &. Co.; of Blacklaws, Wedderspoon, & Co.; and of Mackeith, Rentoull, & Co." John Fyffe, private banker, exchanged all notes, from 5s. to £5, issued by George Dempster & Co. (the Dundee Banking Company), as well as the 5s. notes of William Yeaman & Co., also of Dundee. Robert Russell accepted notes issued by James Scrimgeour & Son, of Borrowstounness, while Joseph Lauchlan advertised that he exchanged those of Alexander Fleeming & Co., of Kirkliston.[105]

In Glasgow, meanwhile, according to Buchanan, "Merchants of known wealth and reputation dealt in bills of exchange, and received money from small traders and others, on deposit."[106] One John Blair, for instance, with a shop in Glasgow's Saltmarket, placed an advertisement in the *Edinburgh Evening Courant* advising that "all persons who have occasion to buy or sell bills of exchange, or want money to borrow, or have money to lend on interest, or have any sort of goods to sell, or want to buy any kind of goods, or who want to buy sugar-house notes, or other good bills, or desire to have such notes or bills discounted, or who want to have policies signed, or incline to underwrite policies in ships or goods, may deliver their commands."[107] Another merchant, David Watson, advertised in *The Glasgow Journal* that his firm "takes in Ayr, Dumfries, Perth, and British Linen Bank notes, at a discount of one penny a pound; or, if there is a hundred pounds of one kind, at a discount of a quarter per cent., and pays the value in Edinburgh or Glasgow notes."[108] Several joint-stock companies, including many involved in the lucrative Virginian tobacco trade, also branched out into other businesses, which naturally involved them in note broking and clearing, including, for example, the "Soaperie," the Wester, Easter, South, and King Street Sugar-works, Bell's Tannarie, and the "Old Tannarie."[109] In other words, a considerable ecosystem of quasi banking and clearing institutions formed around the issuance of small commercial banknotes. They also constituted a vital check on overissue; while notes of reputable banks were exchanged at minimal charge, notes of lesser known or questionable issuers could involve exchange commissions of up to 9d. on every 20s, or 3.75 percent.[110] Combined with periodic exchanges of notes among banks themselves, the rate of note clearing was thus quite high. As even Kerr admits, although "freely stated," an overissue of notes, "with the system of periodical exchanges, which even then was pretty systematically carried out," was in fact "impossible except to a small extent."[111]

In any event, if the issuance of banknotes had been as excessive and profligate as contemporary and subsequent critics alleged, we would expect to observe a pronounced effect on inflation. In fact, however, no such outsized effect is discernible in available Scottish price data. Figure 2.5 plots aggregate grain price levels in London, Edinburgh, and Glasgow from 1700 to 1790, indexed at 1700 = 100. This inflation proxy must be treated with extreme caution, as food prices are, of course, highly volatile, especially during years of adverse harvest shocks, as occurred in 1756 and 1762. As we can see, price level movements in Edinburgh and Glasgow closely tracked changes in London prices, with a 76 percent correlation between Edinburgh and London and a 78 percent correlation between Glasgow and London. To be sure, though during the "mania" years of 1760–1765 inflation in the two Scottish cities un-

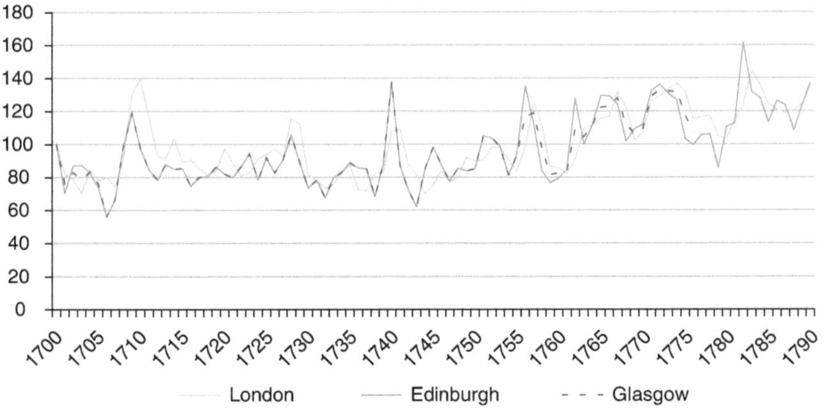

FIGURE 2.5. Consumer price index, 1700–1790. Base 100 = 1700. London price data is from Gregory Clark, "The Price History of English Agriculture, 1209–1914," *Research in Economic History* 22 (2004): 41–124. Edinburgh, Glasgow, and Perth data are from A. Gibson and C. Smout, *Wages and Prices in Scotland, c. 1580–1780* [computer file] (Colchester, Essex: UK Data Archive, June 1995), SN: 3302.

doubtedly outpaced that of London, the disparity was not vastly disproportionate; over those five years, prices rose cumulatively by 61 percent and 73 percent in Edinburgh and Glasgow, respectively, versus 43 percent in London, corresponding to average annual inflation rates of 12.2 percent and 14.7 percent, versus 8.5 percent. But nearly 60 percent of the gap is accounted for by just one year, 1762, *before* the note-issuing mania had supposedly gotten seriously under way, and more likely the result of an unusually bad Scottish harvest, which caused Scottish grain prices to spike temporarily.[112] Indeed, even in Perth, subject to the harshest criticism and where at least six new issuers of small banknotes popped up between 1763 and 1765, inflation only mildly exceeded that of Edinburgh and Glasgow; from 1763 through 1765, consumer price inflation in Perth averaged 4.6 percent, versus 4.2 percent in Glasgow and 2 percent in Edinburgh.

Smith himself even conceded, in *The Wealth of Nations,* that the "great multiplication of paper money in Scotland," had not, in the 1750s at least, resulted in any appreciable augmentation of the "money price of commodities." In fact, he noted, "In 1751 and 1752, when Mr. Hume published his 'Political Discourses,' and soon after the great multiplication of paper money in Scotland, there was a very sensible rise in the price of provisions, owing, probably, to the badness of the seasons, and not to the multiplication of paper money." Corn, he observed further, is "upon most occasions, fully as cheap in England as in France; though there is a great deal of paper money in England, and scarce any in France."[113]

While some contemporary and later critics would point to the resolutions of Commissioners of Supply—local administrative bodies responsible for tax collection and public revenue—in several provincial towns to accept in payment only Edinburgh banknotes as evidence of a genuine problem of excess money supply, the reality is rather more complicated. In 1763, the Commissioners of Supply in Aberdeenshire, Linlithgowshire, Roxburghshire, Haddingtonshire, Selkirkshire, Dumfriesshire, and Inverness-shire variously resolved that from December 1763 or January 1764 they would cease accepting all notes save those issued by the Bank of Scotland, Royal Bank, and British Linen Company. The Heritors in Edinburghshire similarly held a meeting at Inner Session House, on 4 October 1763, and resolved that

> Taking into consideration the pernicious consequences which may arise to this country from the multiplying of paper money now circulating, both

> in regard to the uncertainty of their security, and the facilitating of frauds and forgeries on the ignorant and unwary; and likewise considering, that they are the cause of so little specie remaining in this country; do resolve—That, from and after the 1st of December next, they will not receive in payments Notes of any company whatever, except those of the Edinburgh Banks, established by public authority.[114]

In correspondence with directors of the Bank of Scotland and Royal Bank, the "Gentlemen of the Town and County of Aberdeen," including the sheriff, magistrates, and "principal Gentlemen and proprietors within the County," were rather more blunt, indicating that their resolution was "in order to suppress the Circulation of Private bank notes in the Town and County of Aberdeen and to introduce in place thereof the two Edinburgh Bank Notes," and, ultimately, "to rid the said Town and County of the Notes of Private Banking Companys."[115] At least two of those present at the meeting were shareholders and directors of the Bank of Scotland, Royal Bank, and Linen Bank—Alexander Garden of Troop and Alexander Udney of Udney.[116]

Two years later, in January 1765, Garden and James Ogilvy, Earl of Findlater, approached Garden's fellow directors of the Old and Royal Banks to suggest a similar initiative in the county of Banff. The directors were keen to go along, on the condition of Ogilvy "procuring a Resolution of the Noblemen and Gentlemen of Banffshire" to accept only Old and Royal Bank notes in payment.[117] On 25 March, Alexander Gordon, Duke of Gordon, and James Duff, Earl of Fife, both shareholders and directors of the Bank of Scotland, answered proposals from these "Noblemen and Gentlemen" of Banff. Both directors were themselves substantial landowners in Banffshire. They approved the proposals "for checking the Circulation of the Notes of Private Bankers in place of cash, as the Country in general must be unacquainted with the Credit of these Private banks," though evidently the rest of Banff's principal proprietors had not been quite as eager to "rid the county" of private banknotes. Having flatly rebuffed the earl of Findlater's proposal to accept only Bank of Scotland and Royal Bank notes in payment, they agreed instead merely to discount private banknotes by 5 percent of face value, provided, moreover, that the two public banks pledged to "impress their own Notes and a sufficiency of Cash for taking up the other Notes . . . and supplying the Circulation of the Country."[118] Nonetheless, the joint committee of the public banks quickly affirmed Duff and Gordon's approval and immediately recommended sending

£4,000 (£3,600 in notes and £400 in silver specie) to Banff for "taking up the Notes" of the Thistle, Arms, and Ship Banks, as well as those of "the Banking Company at Ayr" and George Dempster & Co., the Dundee Bank.[119]

An analogous initiative to suppress private banknotes in Renfrewshire was thwarted entirely, probably in no small measure owing to the fact that the meeting of "the Justices, Freeholders, and Commissioners of Supply" was chaired by none other than Sir James Maxwell, founding partner of Maxwell, Ritchie & Co. (i.e., the Thistle Bank). The gentlemen of Renfrewshire, with Sir James presiding, concluded that "limiting the circulation of paper money to the Banks of Edinburgh would be highly prejudicial to the landed and commercial interests of this part of the United Kingdom, by creating a dangerous monopoly to these Banks, in a branch of business so very important." They further launched a spirited defense of private banking companies, asserting that the private banks were "established upon as firm and solid foundations as either of the Banks in Edinburgh," primarily because "both the stock of the former, and the estates, real and personal, of the partners, are jointly and severally bound for every Note they issue"; that is, they were unlimitedly liable.[120]

Rather, in an adroit and perhaps deliberately calculated deflection of attention from the proposed public banknote monopoly, they laid blame for "the high exchange between England and Scotland, the boundless extension of paper money, and the great scarcity of gold and silver coin in Scotland" not on private bank money but rather entirely on "the use of optional clauses in Scots Bank Notes." "These optional clauses," the Renfrewshire proprietors alleged, "have given rise to such dilatory and evasive payments as are unknown to bankers of credit in any other part of Europe; and while these clauses, and the arts they have introduced, are continued and practised, the same inconvenience will arise from all Notes, whether issued by public Banks or private Banks."[121] Faced with aggressive and concerted lobbying for an effective public bank monopoly in municipal payments, it seems, Sir James was keen to generate a diversion. A contemporary writer to *The Scots Magazine* was particularly perceptive, remarking of the recent resolution in Renfrewshire that fixation on the optional clause "diverted the people's attention: and they did not care what notes they took, if the optional clause was to be taken away; and upon these two words, *optional clause,* the gentlemen of Aberdeenshire have just now laid the foundation of all our calamities."[122] But the true problem, he argued, was neither optional clauses nor excess paper currency, but rather the ongoing speculative drain of specie by interest arbitrageurs, to which the aforementioned devices were merely remedial responses.

In any event, the proceedings in Aberdeen, Banff, and Renfrew thus suggest that these "public" resolutions to refuse acceptance of private banknotes were hardly owing to genuine appeals to the public good, but rather were merely political extensions of the intense rivalry between the Edinburgh public banks and the provincial private banks. Having failed in their attempts to crush the Glaswegians, as they had the hapless Banking Company of Aberdeen, through aggressive commercial practices, and having similarly failed to shut them down through the courts, the Edinburgh banks now turned their attention to the fiscal and regulatory apparatus of the state. Munn essentially concurs, noting that the initiatives seem "to have been very much a matter of country versus town where the landowning heritors and commissioners who, almost certainly, had connections with Edinburgh banks found themselves in a conflict of interests with the town-based merchant class who formed their own banks to provide for their monetary needs which had been largely ignored by the Edinburgh bankers."[123] Boase, likewise, writes that, confronted by an acute scarcity of legal coin, "Many traders had copper coins struck, of the value of pennies and halfpennies, bearing such device as pleased their fancy, along with their names and trades, so serving as advertisements as well as an accommodation in transacting their business," while "others made Notes for 5s. and smaller amounts, which in general circulated readily among tradespeople, at least in the places where they were issued." "But the country gentlemen," he observes, "led on most probably by some who visited Edinburgh occasionally, and there picked up theories on religion, politics, and commerce, of a very unpractical character, were in hostile array against these 5s. Notes (some were against paper money altogether)."[124]

Not surprisingly, then, note resolutions were in practice difficult to enforce and largely ineffective, quite simply because, in Boase's words, "The zealous curators of the country's welfare did not perceive, that these 5s. Notes were welcomed because crown pieces were scarce."[125] The same writer to *The Scots Magazine* who appreciated that condemnation of the optional clause was a red herring wrote that while banning all but Old and Royal Bank notes might have been "more convenient for the lieges," one "very good reason why these resolutions proved abortive was, that the trading part of the world were glad to accept of any notes in payment, rather than lie out of their money, and run the risk of losing it altogether."[126] A letter to the *Caledonian Mercury* in

October 1764 echoes these sentiments, maintaining that the circumstances of scarce coin and credit "being well known, and the dependency of several trading towns on the banks of Edinburgh being cut off, induced the people to think of erecting banks of their own." "These schemes," the writer continued, "the scarcity of cash, and the impossibility of carrying on trade and manufactures without them, have encouraged, and seem still to multiply with the increasing wants of the people." Thus, "to these banks," he concluded, "trivial as they are, we owe at present the preservation of commerce in several considerable towns."[127] Hardly testimony to the alleged pernicious influence of private paper currency.

THE OVERWHELMING VOLUME of historical and statistical evidence, therefore, demonstrates that Adam Smith's claims that the issuance of banknotes "for so small sums as twenty shillings" invariably encourages "many mean people" to become "beggarly bankers" who "must be liable" to frequent bankruptcies and sometimes "very great calamity," and that the optional clause was singularly responsible for the adverse exchange with England in the market for bills, simply do not withstand scrutiny. The much-maligned optional clause was employed with extreme infrequency, and even then with strict discrimination, invoked only against interest-rate speculators and "hot money" seeking to redeem large sums of large denomination notes; in essence, as a form of capital control against large exogenous drains of specie in the face of a fixed exchange rate and binding interest-rate ceiling. Crucially, the vast majority of note holders and indeed notes, including virtually all those under 20s., were entirely unaffected by option. While there was, to be sure, a marked uptick in the number of note issuances, including of 5s. and 10s. denominations, after 1760, this trend was less a symptom of "mania" than it was a rational market response to an acute capital account deficit and the requirements of trade. Inflation was, in fact, not markedly different in Scotland than it was in England, and even where an exceptional multiplicity of private note issuers elicited the scorn of later economic historians, there was no contemporary shortage of private quasi bankers willing to engage in the business of note exchange, discounting, and clearing.

Further reflection suggests, pace Smith, that these results should perhaps not be terribly surprising. For, contrary to Smith's fears of excess circulation of paper money well beyond the capacity of the country's specie base to support it, excess circulation was precisely what the highly competitive Scottish banking system before 1765 was so effective at inhibiting and counteracting. Note issuers, of whatever scale, could hardly afford to expand their circulation too far beyond reserve levels, as the assiduity—or, more accurately, aggressiveness—with which rival issuers or their agents would present them for redemption rendered such a strategy exceedingly risky. The legion of note exchangers and employed agents, moreover, meant the velocity of note clearing, or "reflux," in contemporary parlance, upon issuers was quite high. No banker, meanwhile, could risk inconveniencing his regular clients by arbitrarily and indiscriminately exercising option, nor could he invoke the privilege against rival banks without risking retaliation, and probably mutually assured destruction.

Moreover, both contingent liability, in the form of the optional clause, and emergence of small-note issuers seem to have been key to enabling the Scottish financial system to absorb severe, adverse macroeconomic shocks in 1756 and 1762–1763. In both instances, acute balance of payments crises owing to exogenous external shocks were resolved only when the country's two leading banks, the Bank of Scotland and the Royal Bank of Scotland, resorted to in effect imposing capital controls through highly discriminate adoption and, on the latter occasion, exercise of banknote optional clauses. The largely unrestricted entrance of small-note issuers in concert with temporary capital controls between 1762 and 1764 appear, then, to have allowed time for the underlying macro-imbalances to sort themselves out through nominal adjustments in the bills of exchange market, without the requirement of a disruptive major contraction of the money supply and accompanying deflation. Indeed, after tumbling 30 percent in 1762 and 35 percent in 1763, net exports surged by 90 percent in 1764 as the depreciation of Scottish bills delivered a tremendous fillip to Scottish exporters, while at the same time dampening imports.[128] By the end of 1764, total exports were already 7 percent above their pre-crisis peak in 1761.[129] The abundance of these "beggarly bankers" and "subversive" clauses was not, therefore, as Smith would have it, a source of systemic vulnerability, but rather of systemic robustness, even "anti-fragility," as each subsequent crisis induced institutional changes that rendered the Scottish banking sector as a whole better able to withstand such shocks.

3

Procuring an Act

IRONICALLY, THE EXCESSIVE ISSUANCE OF LIABILITIES by Douglas, Heron & Co., so harshly criticized by Smith, was the precise banking practice that the legislation of 1765—of which Smith was a staunch supporter—had ostensibly been designed to prevent. Indeed, the bill brought forward "for regulating the Currency and due Payment of Notes and Bills issued by the Banks, Banking Companies, and Bankers, in that Part of Great Britain called Scotland" was explicitly promoted as a remedy for the "inconveniencies" arising from the alleged overabundance of paper money. Smith himself championed the regulations introduced by the 1765 act as safeguards "against that excessive multiplication of paper money which ruins the very banks which issue it."[1]

The logical question to ask, therefore, is whether legislation purportedly implemented to restrain, or at the very least attenuate, overissuance of private banknotes was in fact effective in so doing and, in the event it was, whether that was even a salutary outcome. We have already observed in Chapter 2 that the small notes "mania" that served as ostensive impetus for regulatory intervention was not quite as manic as some contemporaries, and most subsequent historians, claimed it to be. Nonetheless, insofar as the profusion of paper currency, however exaggerated it may have been, constituted the raison d'être of the Scottish Bank Act of 1765, it is reasonable to evaluate the extent to which it fulfilled its stated purpose, as well as the efficacy of that result in mitigating financial instability.

Analyzing the conception, enactment, and effects of the banking legislation of 1765, however, what we find is that while the regulatory constraints thereby imposed did indeed curtail the issuance of private banknotes—or, more accurately, the number of private banknote issuers—they did so at the cost of exacerbating the vulnerability of the Scottish financial system to adverse shocks. Specifically, by raising barriers to entry, lowering competition in the provision of short-term credit, and increasing the efficient scale of banking, the prohibition of small notes and optional clauses substantially amplified the level of systemic risk in Scottish credit markets—in other words, the risk that a single large financial institution, such as Douglas, Heron & Co., could jeopardize the entire Scottish financial system. We discover, moreover, that this result should hardly come as a surprise, for though the stated intent of the Bank Act was to prevent excessive issuance of paper currency, in reality its underlying purpose was to achieve precisely what it did achieve, namely, to raise barriers to entry and limit competition in the Scottish banking sector.

The organization of this chapter is thus as follows. First, I trace the legislative history of the 1765 Scottish Bank Act, highlighting the extent to which all of the principal parties involved in drafting, promoting, and enacting the bill had substantial vested interests in banking sector consolidation in Scotland. Second, acknowledging that even collusively conceived regulation could still have attenuated financial instability, I analyze the effects of the 1765 legislation on the Scottish banking system. I demonstrate that in the seven years from the passage of the act to the crisis of June 1772, there were discontinuous changes in average bank size, new bank formations, and frequency of bank failures. More precisely, the additional capital requirements imposed by the prohibition of small and contingent liability notes meant that, after 1765, there were fewer new entrants into Scottish banking, the average size of new entrants increased more than tenfold, and the number of bank failures rose from an average of less than one per decade to more than eight. Finally, I show that by effectively raising minimum capital requirements and eliminating the flexibility of the optional clause, the 1765 act both induced banks to assume more balance-sheet risk, and increased the likelihood that portfolio losses would be transmitted to depositors and note holders through disorderly bank runs and institutional liquidation.

AS WITH THE ADOPTION and exercise of the optional clause, considerable confusion attaches also to its demise. While most historians point wholly at the public banks—Saville even asserts, incorrectly, that "there was opposition from the Arms, Ship and Thistle banks, but they lacked influence at Westminster"—Gherity and Munn accurately observe that several of the private provincial banks, too, evidently lobbied Parliament in support of prohibition.[2] In truth, the optional clause seems to have been employed by both the public and the larger provincial banks essentially as a strategic bargaining chip for securing more favorable terms in the proposed bill. Specifically, the public banks considered optional clause prohibition as a possible necessary concession for obtaining competitive advantage through legislation, while the private bankers endeavored to affix blame for Scotland's monetary troubles exclusively on the optional clause, with the aim of thereby blunting the chartered banks' arguments for exclusive note-issuing privileges, as well as the efforts of English commercial interests to ban both optional clauses and banknotes under £5 in Scotland. As we have seen, though chartered and nonchartered banks alike had inserted optional clauses into their largest denomination notes, the former alone had never actually invoked option, and even then did so sparingly, discriminately, and only with reluctance under extreme circumstances.

Although the optional clause was the subject of considerable public debate between 1762 and 1764, the Old and Royal Banks appear to have initiated the formal campaign that ultimately resulted in legislative prohibition, despite the fact that a comprehensive ban was not their primary objective. At a series of closed-door meetings in late December 1763 and early January 1764, directors from the two chartered banks resolved to appoint four delegates from their respective boards to conjointly "solicit the aid of Parliament" in restricting the business of banking in Scotland. Armed with £463—£400 in bills on the Bank of England and sixty guineas in specie—the delegates, John Inglis and Alexander Tait of the Old Bank and John Young and Alexander Gray of the Royal, were under detailed instructions to "procure in Favour of the two Banks," ideally, an "exclusive Privilege of Banking and of issuing printed Notes" in Scotland.[3] Failing that, "If it shall be thought proper to admit any general toleration of banking," they were "to endeavour to procure an Act of Parliament declaring that it shall not be Lawfull to any Person or society of Persons in Scotland to Bank or issue printed Notes for any Sums whatsoever except such as are or shall be authorized by Law to that effect."[4]

Only if that initiative, too, failed to gain political traction were they then instructed to be "First Movers" in an effort to "procure an Act of Parliament" prohibiting the optional clause *and* declaring "that no Company but such as were established by publick authority should be permitted to issue Notes under the value of Ten pounds sterling."[5] It was largely a nod to the necessity of political horse-trading. Noting that, "as the optional clause inserted in the several notes of the banking companys in Scotland has been complained of and only became necessary by the multiplication of banks in that country and as it is now proposed that this evil shall be restrained," the directors concluded it would be best, in order to secure their primary objective of a restriction on notes issue, to appear the mature first mover in any legislative campaign for optional clause prohibition. As they clearly viewed the exercise of option as having been necessitated by the "multiplication of banks," prohibition of option in conjunction with a monopoly on note issuance, or at least a ban on small notes, seemed a small price to pay, especially as legislative prohibition would resolve any first-mover disadvantages to exclusion.

In exchange for exclusivity in note issuance, the banks were willing, first, to accede to some sufficiently distant date "from and after which all private Banks in Scotland are to be abolished" as would permit "said private Banks and all concerned with them to wind up their affairs in the best manner they can and so as to prevent any Distress upon the Country." Second, if objections should be raised in Parliament that the city of Glasgow's commerce required a banking presence (or, more bluntly, if representatives of Glasgow's banking interests were to propose receiving authorization of their own chartered bank), the delegates were to commit to the establishment of a branch at Glasgow. And finally, if legislative support was still not forthcoming, the banks were willing to offer, as "encouragement to the Manufactures" of Scotland, an unspecified fixed annual contribution to the Trustees for Improving Fisheries and Manufactures of Scotland, of which the deputy governor of the Royal Bank, Andrew Fletcher, Lord Milton, was chair.[6]

The accompanying memorial drafted for parliamentary circulation was effusive, arguing that banks "established by publick authority, under proper Restraints and Regulations, have been found by Experience to be of Great publick utility." To the "legal Foundation, great Security and utility of these public Banks," the directors contrasted the "manifest detriment and ruin" inflicted on the Scottish economy and Scottish credit markets by "illegal" private banking companies.[7] In rendering their case, they pursued a two-pronged strategy, appealing both to legality and to the general welfare.

On both fronts, their claims were tenuous. The legal contention was that the business of banking was an enterprise that could be undertaken only with express parliamentary authorization, either directly or by parliamentary sanction of a royal charter. The charters by which the Old and Royal Banks were established, they argued, demonstrated that the "Power of Banking or Carrying on a Banking Trade in Scotland cannot by the Common Law of the Kingdom be Assumed by any Companys or undertakers or lawfully Exercised without the Sanction of such Publick Authority." Nor, they claimed, was this a mere technicality; the separate statutes establishing the two public banks deemed their notes protestable by summary diligence, provided for perpetual corporate succession, and prohibited the proprietors from employing any part of their stock in "Trade or hazardous adventures" apart from the "Trade of lending and Borrowing money upon Interest and negotiating bills of Exchange."[8] These provisions, it was asserted, rendered the public banks substantially more secure and reliable to note holders and creditors than their private counterparts.

But the memorial also argued for regulation on the grounds of general public welfare. Criticizing the alleged aggressiveness with which the private banks pushed their notes, particularly those of small denominations, into circulation, the public bankers claimed that those notes "are almost universally received by low ignorant and poor People, who are most lyable to imposition by bad Security," and for this reason proposed "that the Power of Issuing Notes under Ten Pounds Sterling shou'd be limited to the Publick Banks only and that . . . it shall not be lawfull for any private Persons or Companys to Issue Notes for Circulation in the Banking way under the Sum of Ten Pounds Sterling."[9] Appealing again to the presumed financial illiteracy of small-denomination note holders, they further suggested that "Many ignorant country People are incapable to make any distinction" between the supposed inferior security of privately issued banknotes and "the Publick Bank notes with great safety and credit" to which they were "accustomed." With the superior security of their notes thus apparently not self-evident, the "publick Evil" of excess private banknotes could not be remedied "without the juxtaposition of Legislative Authority."

It would be misleading, however, to conclude that legislation was thereby obtained only, in Royal Bank historian Neil Munro's words, "Through the insistence of the two Edinburgh Banks."[10] For word of the delegation evidently spread quickly, and the provincial banks were hardly idle in seeking their own parliamentary accommodations. Before the decision to formally petition Parliament had even been resolved by the public banks, Archibald Ingram, Lord

Provost of Glasgow, prominent tobacco merchant, and partner in the Glasgow Arms Bank, wrote to his friend James Stuart-Mackenzie, Keeper of the Privy Seal of Scotland and Member of Parliament (M.P.) for Ross-Shire, expressing concern over reports that "a deputation from the Banks of Edinburgh are gone to London" with intent "to apply to Parliament for an exclusive privilege to this branch of business, or to be indulged in some preference."[11] He further implored, "I beg leave, therefore, to request that your lordship will use your interest to promote a continuance of the Banks here, and, also, that they may be put on an equal footing with the Banks at Edinburgh." This latter appeal was a direct attempt to invalidate one of the main arguments of the public banks for the purportedly superior security of their notes, namely, that they were protestable by summary diligence.

"At the instance of" Glasgow's merchant community, Ingram included with his letter a memorial of their own, dated 4 February 1763, "Respecting them, as members of the Banking Companys erected in this place."[12] Despite documenting the extreme infrequency and selectiveness with which Scottish banks had ever actually invoked the optional clause, the memorial's authors nonetheless then proceeded to ascribe all of Scotland's monetary troubles, particularly the deterioration in the Scottish exchange rate in bills and outflow of specie, to the optional clause, arguing that the clause's inclusion rendered Scottish notes inferior to English. It was a strained argument, contending that the reason bills on London could only be had in Scotland at a premium was owing, not to Scotland's adverse balance of trade with England, and thus an excess relative supply of Scottish bills, but rather because bills on London sold in Scotland were sold in exchange for Scottish banknotes, which were purportedly inferior on account of the fact that some included optional clauses. Noting further the first-mover dilemma of voluntary exclusion, "An Act of Parliament," they concluded, "is the proper remedy for all these inconveniences," duly including a draft petition to that effect.[13]

While Gherity interprets the existence of Ingram's memorial as evidence of provincial bank support for optional clause prohibition, the picture is in fact a bit murkier. The overriding fear of all three principal Glasgow banks was that ostensibly remedial legislation would in fact simply grant the public banks the monopoly they sought. The implicit argument of the memorial, therefore, is not so much a genuine indictment of the optional clause, as it is a diversion of blame for Scotland's monetary challenges from allegations of overissue of private banknotes, the principal claim on which the case for chartered privilege was premised. Indeed, to preface the memorial, Ingram also included an essay, undated and authors unknown though with notes by Sir James Steuart, under the heading "Thoughts Concerning Banks, and the Paper Currency of Scotland."[14] After outlining the advantages conferred upon an economy by the provision of paper money, the memorial then translates that case into an argument against monopoly privilege in note issuance. Supposing all paper notes, save those issued by the two Edinburgh public banks, were to be suppressed by decree, the authors ask "whether or not it wou'd be equally for the interest of the country, as a measure here to be suggested, or only for the particular benefit of the two Banks at Edinburgh."[15] The present "degradation of paper money," they replied, would in no way be remedied by a duopoly of the two public banks, as duopoly would hardly "insure the publick that the two Banks will not, as much as formerly, triffle [*sic*] in their payments" or avail themselves "of the liberty assumed by the Optional Clause to defer payment for six months with six months' interest."[16] It is an all the more compelling argument in light of the fact, elaborated in Chapter 2, that the public banks seem to have been alone in ever actually exercising option.

Accordingly, by adroit deflection, the authors conclude: "It is apprehended that it is to this Optional Clause that all the real evils that have arisen in Scotland from paper money are owing, and that its removal will be a security not only against an increase of these evils, but all return of them to the degree already felt." In other words, if a remedy was sought to the strains on Scotland's monetary system—the chronic drain of specie, the depreciation of paper currency relative to coin, and the adverse exchange between English and Scottish bills—it ought to consist not of prohibition of note issuance by private banks but rather of elimination of the optional clause. "Paper money," they insisted, "is a publick benefit when under proper regulation, but may be a public grievance when not properly regulated."[17] These arguments, we should recall, strongly echo the defensive response of Sir James Maxwell of the Thistle Bank to efforts by Old and Royal Bank allies among the Renfrewshire Commissioners of Supply to secure a monopoly of the two chartered banks in public payments. Alarmed by the very real possibility—the Old and Royal had, after all, already obtained similar resolutions from Commissioners in Aberdeenshire, Linlithgowshire, Roxburghshire, Haddingtonshire, Selkirkshire, and Dumfriesshire—of a chartered bank stranglehold on official receipts and expenditures, Sir James had resorted, on 13 December 1763, to a spirited assertion of the "firm and solid foundations" of private banking companies, the "highly prejudicial" consequences of limiting the circulation of their notes, and, finally, for any and all legitimate complaints that may be raised against Scottish banking, a narrow indictment of the "dilatory and evasive" practice of inserting optional clauses in banknotes.[18]

Indeed, if the singular indictment of the optional clause for all Scotland's monetary troubles was authentic, it is odd that the three Glasgow banks were by no means unanimous in their advocacy of prohibition. While the aristocratic Thistle Bank appears to have been in favor of petitioning Parliament, the directors of the trade-oriented Arms and Ship Banks were more hesitant. In early January 1765, with a Scottish bank bill likely to be taken up during the next parliamentary session, John Glassford, founding partner in both the Thistle and Arms, wrote fellow Thistle Bank founding partner Baron William Mure of Caldwell to report on a meeting between himself, fellow partner James Ritchie, and Provost Andrew Cochran, founding partner of the Arms Bank, and Colin Dunlop, founding partner of the Ship Bank, concerning a memorial proposed to be conveyed to London.[19]

The dominant subject of the meeting was whether or not to include in the memorial an additional clause soliciting prohibition of notes under £1. While both banks sought a reduction in the issuance of small notes, the floor they sought was substantially lower than that solicited by the two public banks. Whereas the Old and Royal Banks sought a floor of £10, the Thistle and Ship desired a much lower floor of just £1. Their concern, however, was that "it may be dangerous to bring in this clause into the House of Commons, as, when they are once possessed of a bill, they may fill up the blanks in what manner they please, and make the smallest note perhaps £5, (which is the highest of the Glasgow notes at present,) or at least £3, or £2."[20] Banning optional clauses and requiring that all notes be subject to summary diligence, they hoped, would be less blunt instruments for bringing about the desired curtailment of note issuance by "obscure" issuers.[21] Provost Cochran in fact even made a point to note the Arms and Ship's reluctant support for optional clause prohibition, calling it the Thistle's "own scheme," which the Arms and Ship were only "going alongst with" conditional on the Thistle agreeing to "go alongst with them in their scheme" of soliciting a ban on notes of less than £1.[22] Ultimately, it appears, they elected to compromise by appending a codicil to the memorial noting the difference of opinion on the question of prohibiting notes under £1.

The Glasgow banks' support for a note minimum was likely based on two considerations. The first was a desire to curtail competition from the numerous small banking companies, often single-proprietor trading enterprises—corn brokers, tanners, vintners, scriveners, woolen and linen merchants, sugar dealers—that had, in response to the balance of payments crisis of 1762–1764, ventured into the business of issuing currency and promissory notes to suppliers and clients.[23] The smaller denominations of these notes—typically 10s. and 5s., or approximately £61.04 and £30.52, respectively, in 2014 prices—meant capital requirements for note issuance were comparatively low. Equally important, however, was that small notes constituted a relatively low-margin business for the larger Glasgow banks. The profit earned by banks on the issuance of notes is an increasing function of the length of time during which they can keep their notes in circulation, unredeemed. The typically higher redemption rates, or "reflux," of lower-denomination bills, therefore, meant a *proportionately* greater volume of reserves had to be held against notes outstanding, which naturally meant reduced scope for seigniorage. A satirical poem printed in *The Scots Magazine* in January 1763 illustrates the point:

> With 5s. and 10s. notes first we'll begin
> Which tradesmen will take without scruple;
> To 20s.'s with option we may next proceed;
> Our Profits will then be quadruple.[24]

Given, however, the liquidity constraints in the Scottish economy, there was a distinct first-mover disadvantage to unilaterally evacuating the small notes business, a problem that multilateral regulatory prohibition would resolve.

In any event, the appeals of early 1764 quickly elicited political movement. On 22 February, Sir Gilbert Elliott, M.P. for Selkirkshire, wrote Baron Mure from London on the subject of Scottish banking legislation. He had evidently had several conversations concerning Scottish banking regulation, including with ambassadors from the Thistle as well as with Lords Elibank—himself a prominent shareholder in the Royal Bank and future cofounder, in 1766, of Alexander Johnston, Hugh Lawson, & Co., also known as the Dumfries Bank—and Eglinton.[25] Lord Eglinton, he noted, seemed "determined to bring in some bill or other against Optional Clauses and small notes," which to Sir Gilbert did not seem to be the "proper object of Parliamentary interposition." Moreover, he doubted the efficacy of the proposed legislation, writing, half correctly, that "the Optional Clause and the small notes have certainly given a facility to convey the silver and gold more effectually out of Scotland, but they are not the *cause* of this distress," the true cause being simply "the superior advantage to be made of money" in England. He further cautioned that the sudden removal of small notes and accommodative credit as substitutes for scarce coin could occasion considerable economic distress.[26]

Nonetheless, the Glasgow bankers appear to have still been apprehensive of a more blunt response from Parliament, with perhaps some justification. On 19 January, the directors of the two public banks received word from Alexander Tait, one of the commissioners tasked with soliciting Parliament, that it would be advantageous to specify a precise sum for the "encouragement of the manufactures" that would be annually paid by both banks to the Trustees for Improving the Fisheries and Manufactures in exchange for exclusivity in note issuance. The directors resolved that £3,000 annually, or £1,500 each, was the price they were willing to pay for monopoly privilege.[27] Whether or not the Glaswegians were aware that Edinburgh had just upped the ante, they clearly conveyed their concerns to the Lord Privy Seal, Stuart-Mackenzie, who replied that their fears were overblown. "As to the affair of the Banks," he wrote Mure, "which you, the people of Glasgow, and many others, seem to apprehend greatly, you need not, I assure you; for, in the first place, their demands are by no means what they have been represented; and, in the next place, I believe 'tis impossible for the Legislature to apply a remedy." Though he entreated Mure not to publish these sentiments, beyond hinting that "the great alarm taken has mighty little or rather no foundation at all," his expectation was that "things will remain pretty much in status quo."[28]

Regardless of whether their alarm was warranted, though, the Glaswegians were playing both offense and defense, with the optional clause as their main bargaining chip.[29] Sometime in January or February 1764, the proprietors of the Thistle, in their own words, resolved to distinguish "themselves by being the first movers for leaving out the Optional Clause," conditional, however, on His Majesty granting them "a patent for carrying on the business," which they clarified was intended "to extend no further than to erect them into a Company that can sue and be sued, and that their notes might be signed by their Secretary or Cashier, in place of the tedious manner now used by two Partners and that officer likewise."[30] In other words, the Thistle was offering up the optional clause in exchange for, to recall Lord Provost Ingram's earlier words to the Lord Privy Seal, an "equal legal footing" with the chartered banks.

Unbeknownst to Glasgow, though insinuated by Sir Gilbert and the Lord Privy Seal in their letters to Baron Mure, the Privy Council had in fact already rebuffed the public banks' petition for a monopoly in note issuance. Matters relating to Scottish banking had been delegated by the King-in-Council to a committee of three Scotsmen—the Lord Privy Seal, Sir Gilbert, and James Oswald, M.P. for Dysart Burghs.[31] Not only were Oswald and Sir Gilbert friends of both David Hume and Adam Smith, but Oswald was furthermore from Kirkaldy and a childhood friend of Smith, who was himself intimate friends with James Ritchie, Baron Mure, and Glassford of the Thistle Bank and Andrew Cochran and Provost Ingram of the Arms.[32]

As Checkland notes, Smith was in London at the time with the young Henry, Duke of Buccleuch, just before their departure for France on the duke's grand tour, and evidence strongly suggests that he met with the Lord Privy Seal. In his letter to Baron Mure of 2 February, the Lord Privy Seal mentioned that "Mr. Smith tells me that his recommendation of Mr. Young was merely to teach his class this winter, and nothing more," implying the two had recently spoken.[33] Checkland thus calls it "an intriguing conjecture whether Smith was consulted about Scottish banking," while Gherity justifiably writes that "in view of the fact that the appointment of Mr. Young was hardly a topic of such public importance as to call for a meeting with the Lord Privy Seal, I am led to conclude that the occasion of the meeting was another topic of greater importance."[34]

In any event, the Privy Council's dismissal of the public banks' demand for monopoly privilege was brusque. On 26 January, the delegation of John Inglis, John Young, Alexander Tait, and Alexander Gray wrote the directors of the two chartered banks to report that they had met the preceding day with the Lord Privy Seal, Oswald, and Sir Elliot, to whom they had previously provided copies of the banks' memorial. The delegation was "very sorry to say" that redress, in the form of monopoly privilege, was not likely to be forthcoming. The Privy Council had informed them that "the Trade of Banking is a matter not of Public favour but of *Right* to every subject in common."[35] Echoing Glassford's plea for equal footing, their Lordships continued that not only was it the case that there was "no Difference betwixt Established Banks and Private Bankers except the formers being incorporated," but also that in the consideration of public opinion "nothing that would have the appearance of an exclusive privilege in favor of the Banks wou'd be listen'd to by the people of this Country."[36]

The delegation was thus forced to convey that abolition of the optional clause and prohibition of small notes was as far as the Privy Council was willing to go, and even then the measures would have to apply equally to all banks, public and private. Further, the Privy Council suggested a minimum denomination of £5, consistent with the 1704 and 1708 acts of Queen Anne in England.[37] This put the chartered banks in a bind. Their memorial had called for a prohibition of notes under £10, but only for private banks and with retention of the optional clause. The combination of a universal £5 minimum simultaneously with loss of the optional clause would, they feared, given the acute shortage of specie in the Scottish economy, occasion severe financial distress. "The present situation of this Country with Respect to Specie," the directors concluded, "is such that if the Optional Clause be taken away every Bank in Scotland may be easily shut up and the Necessary uses of Individuals cannot be answer'd without the Currency of Small Notes."[38]

The directors' conclusion constitutes a striking revelation of the disingenuousness of their opposition to the optional clause and, for that matter, small notes. In essence, they were acknowledging that the optional clause and small notes were reactions to, rather than causes of, Scotland's chronic specie drain. Legislative options thus apparently exhausted, the team of Inglis, Young, Tait, and Gray were to return from London at their convenience, unless there was a probability of the proposed "or any other Regulation" being brought forward, in which case they were to remain and "take Care that nothing be done to the prejudice of your Constituents."[39]

But momentum had already developed, and in any case the British Linen Company had not been standing idly by. Lord Eglinton—Alexander Montgomerie, 10th Earl of Eglinton—whom Sir Elliot had mentioned to Baron Mure as "determined to bring in some bill or other against Optional Clauses and small notes," was in fact one of the founding partners and largest shareholders in the Linen Bank.[40] That bank had been one of the last of the major banks to resort to adopting the optional clause, finally capitulating in 1761. "The very great scarcity of silver," concluded their directors at the time, "having induced the directors of the Royal Bank to issue notes with the like option clause contained in those of the Bank of Scotland, and all the private banking companies; this measure of the banks has occasioned an unusual demand for specie for the company's notes, and made it not only advisable, but necessary, to take the same precautions the banks and other companies have done."[41] Even then, though, they appear to have inserted it sparingly, and only on larger-denomination notes. Like the Old and Royal Banks, moreover, the Linen Bank evidently avoided the small notes business altogether; James Douglas's record of Scottish banknotes records no Linen Bank issues under £1 or 20s. after 1750.[42]

Indeed, as early as January 1763, it seems, Scottish bank regulation was at the top of Eglinton's mind. In his diary entry for 5 January 1763, the young James Boswell recounted that he and his friend, Andrew Erskine, had visited Lord Eglinton in London, who was also entertaining the Lord Advocate for Scotland, Sir Thomas Miller, as well as his nephew, Sir James Macdonald. "Erskine and I," Boswell wrote, "were most amazingly bashful and stupid. The conversation was all about the banks of Scotland."[43]

With Eglinton thus lobbying hard for a bill, on 13 March the directors of the Old and Royal Banks wrote again to their lobbying team in London, advising them to agree to the prohibition of optional clauses and notes under £1, but only after an unspecified future date, and also to accept a provision for summary diligence on all banknotes, an indication that they had abandoned any hope of securing monopoly privilege in note issuance.[44] The directors again further added that if any other provisions were brought into the bill "with a view to limit or Restrain private Banking Companys in Scotland, that they be always so Calculated as not to affect the Rights and Privileges of the Established Banks."[45]

Ultimately, rather than risk the abrupt shock of prohibition, it seems the banks opted to run out the clock. When Privy Councilor James Smith-Stanley, Lord Strange, brought forward a bill "for regulating the Manner of issuing and paying Bills, Notes, or other Tokens" in Scotland, seconded by Sir Alexander Gilmour, on 19 March, it was blocked by the Lord Advocate, Sir Thomas, whose brother was a proprietor of the Old Bank.[46] Parliament was thus prorogued on 19 April without having passed a bill.[47] Nonetheless, negotiations continued during the recess, such that by November Glassford was able to report to Adam Smith that "the Members for Scotland seem now resolved to carry the Bill for abolishing the optional Clause in Bank and Bankers notes this ensuing Session which you know was drop'd in the Last."[48] Two weeks later, directors of the Old and Royal Banks again met jointly and unanimously agreed "that as an application will be made to Parliament to abolish the Optional Clause in Bank notes, that the two Banks shou'd be the Movers thereof," and accordingly assigned four directors—two from each bank—the task of preparing a draft bill.[49]

Parliament reconvened on 10 January 1765, and several of the Scottish M.P.'s promptly met to thrash out a draft bank bill. On 15 February, George Dempster, M.P. for Perth Burghs and founder of the bank George Dempster & Co. (the Dundee Banking Company) wrote his fellow partners to report that several of the Scottish Members had resolved "1st, To abolish all optional clauses in Bank Notes; 2d, To suppress all Notes of five shillings; 3d, To allow of summary diligence on Bank Notes."[50] As Munn suggests, this might have been a bargaining ploy, as most of the Scottish banks represented in the House favored a higher floor than 5s. but were perhaps inclined to leave room for negotiation with the English financial lobby, which favored a £5 minimum.[51]

In any event, three days after Dempster's letter, leave was given by the House "to bring in a Bill regulating the Currency and due Payment of Notes issued by the Banks and Banking Companies" in Scotland.[52] The Members tasked with preparing and bringing forward the bill constituted a virtual "who's who" list of Scottish banking. There was the Lord Advocate, Sir Thomas, M.P. for Dumfries Burgh, whose brother Patrick was in fact not only a proprietor of the Bank of Scotland but also a partner in the Edinburgh bank of Mansfield, Ramsay & Co. Sir Thomas's father-in-law, moreover, was John Murdoch, founding partner of the Glasgow Arms Bank. There was James Coutts, M.P. for Edinburgh and partner in the prominent private banking firm of James & Thomas Coutts. There was Lord Frederick Campbell, M.P. for Glasgow Burghs, a cousin of Baron Mure of the Thistle and son of the 4th Duke of Argyll, one of the largest shareholders in the Linen Bank.[53] Sir Gilbert Elliot, a cousin of the Coutts, in addition to a close friend of Mure's, was again involved, as was James Oswald, who not only addressed Baron Mure as "Willy," but also whose brother, Richard, was a shareholder and future deputy governor of the Linen Bank and whose cousin, George Oswald, was a founding partner in the Ship Bank.[54] In May, they were joined by Dempster, Stuart-Mackenzie, and Sir Archibald Edmonstone, whose cousin, John Edmonstone, was a director at the Bank of Scotland.[55]

With such political and financial firepower behind it, a draft bill was quickly hammered out, with the proposed notes minimum restored to £1, and presented to the House by the Lord Advocate, Sir Thomas, on 7 March. After a second reading on 12 March, the bill was formally brought to a vote on 1 April, with the House amending the language slightly to refer to the "practice" that had developed in Scotland of issuing small notes and inserting optional clauses, in place of "custom." With these minor amendments, "An Act for regulating the Currency and due Payment of Notes and Bills issued by the Banks, Banking Companies, and Bankers, in that Part of Great Britain called Scotland; and for restraining the Practice of issuing notes and Bills for Sums less than Twenty

Shillings, by such Banks, Banking Companies, and Bankers" passed, and the Lord Advocate was instructed to carry it to the House of Lords for their concurrence.[56]

Sir Thomas delivered the bill to the Lords the following day, when it was promptly read for the first time in that House. Upon a second reading two weeks later, however, the bill began to encounter headwinds, with the Lords resolving to commit the bill to committee.[57] The holdup, it seems, was pressure from English traders to Scotland who, "Being the principal Merchants and Traders to Scotland," were "taking Notice of a Bill depending in this House, for the better Regulation of the Paper Currency in that Part of Great Britain called Scotland" and accordingly submitted their own petition to the upper House craving specific Scottish bank regulation. The English traders were essentially seeking to lower the cost of converting and remitting Scottish currency earnings, and consequently lamented the "inconvenient and troublesome" delays in redemption that attended Scottish banknotes, which they alleged imposed "a very considerable Expense" on their commerce. Indeed, the very reason Scottish banks had resorted to small notes and the optional clause in the first place—namely, to conserve scarce specie—was precisely why the English merchants desired their prohibition; the English wanted to be able to convert large sums of Scottish currency into specie with minimal cost and delay. Hence, they sought not only summary diligence on Scottish banknotes and a ban on optional clauses, but also a much heftier £5 note minimum.[58]

Their petition, along with the Commons bill, was referred to committee and, upon yet another reading, again referred. In committee, however, the "witnesses" summoned to give evidence hardly constituted a representative cross-section of interested parties. Testimony was given by John Inglis, shareholder and director of the Bank of Scotland, as well as father of the bank's former deputy governor, David Inglis, and one of the original four sent by the two chartered banks to "procure an Act"; John Young, director at the Royal Bank and also one of the initial four lobbyists for the chartered banks; John Campbell, shareholder, director, and cashier at the Royal Bank; and John McCall, prominent Glaswegian tobacco merchant and founding partner of the Thistle Bank.[59]

The committee reported its amendments to the Lords in early May. Though demands for the higher £5 note floor were rebuffed, the committee had nonetheless tightened and toughened the bill. First and foremost, they explicitly clarified that the bill's provisions were to apply not only to "any Person or Persons," but also to "whatsoever Bodies Politick or Corporate." To obviate any potential wiggle room for quasi banks, they further stipulated that summary execution was to proceed not just on "the Payment of all Notes, Accepted Bills, Post Bills, Tickets, Tokens," but also on "other Writings for Money, of the Nature of a Bank or Banker's Note." Finally, while optional clause prohibition was to remain deferred until one year hence, the ban on notes under £1 was brought forward twelve months, to the first of June 1765.[60] The amended bill passed the Lords on 8 May and was conveyed back to the Commons the same day, where, after review by committee, it was approved with only slight modifications on 15 May. With the Lords' concurrence, it became law one week later.[61]

THE EFFECTS OF THE BANK ACT were substantial and immediate. Indeed, before the act had even been passed, the directors of the Dundee Banking Company resolved to circumscribe their note circulation and suspend any new cash accounts until the full impact of the regulations became clear. Two months later, just after the bill passed the House of Commons, they instructed their London agents "to collect for the Bank, as fast as they can, the following specie:—£300 in nine shilling pieces, £100 in thirteen shilling and sixpenny pieces, £200 in four shilling and sixpenny pieces." To their Edinburgh agent, John Fyffe, they similarly issued instructions "to pick up what gold he can under a guinea," and directed the bank's cashier "to order more small gold from time to time." The directors further resolved to cease accepting Perth banknotes and, later, Glasgow notes. In August, they also took advantage of the twelve-month deferment of optional clause prohibition by issuing new notes with option, deemed essential as they replaced 5s. and 10s. notes with larger-denomination £1 or 20s. notes.[62] Five months later, in January 1766, they issued a capital call of 10 percent on existing shareholders, followed by a second call of 10 percent in March.

Indeed, this latter response is indicative of the most dramatic consequence of the Bank Act, namely, a pronounced increase in the efficient scale of banking. As shown in Figure 3.1, between 1749 and 1765, the average starting capital of new Scottish private banks was £9,040, and the average bank consisted of fourteen partners. From the passage of the act until the crisis in June 1772, however, average starting capital jumped more than ninefold, to £84,667,

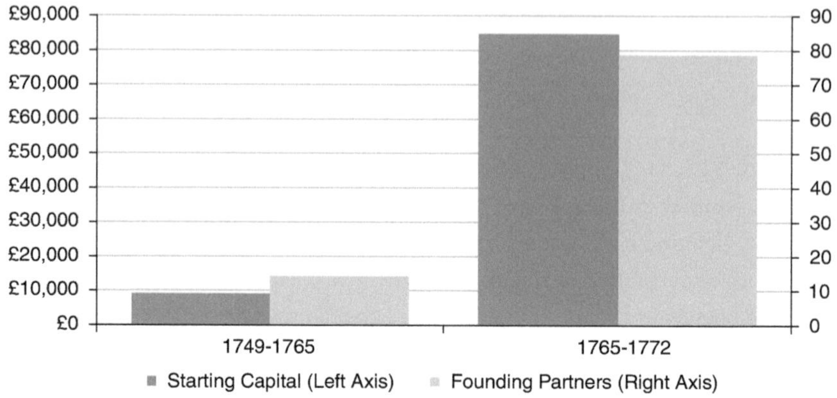

FIGURE 3.1. Mean starting capital and founding partners, 1749–1772. *Data sources:* Balance sheet and cash books, Lloyds Banking Group Archives; Sederunt books, Royal Bank of Scotland Group Archives; "Bank of Scotland Family Tree," Lloyds Banking Group Archives; *The Royal Bank of Scotland: A History* (Edinburgh: Royal Bank of Scotland, 1998); Boase, *Banking in Dundee;* Checkland, *Scottish Banking;* Kerr, *Banking in Scotland;* Malcolm, *History of the British Linen Bank;* Munn, *Scottish Provincial Banking;* Munro, *Royal Bank of Scotland;* Rait, *Union Bank;* Saville, *Bank of Scotland.*

while the average number of partners rose nearly sixfold, to 79. Even if we include the three chartered banks in the pre-1765 sample, average starting capital more than tripled after the act's passage, while the average number of partners more than doubled. Per partner, the average upfront capital call thus rose from £639 before 1765 to £1,077 after. Scottish banks, in other words, got bigger—much bigger.

We can also observe this effect in bank consolidations. In Perth, the recently formed private banking houses of Stewart, Richardson, & Co., John Ramsay & Co., John Stewart & Co., Blacklaws, Wedderspoon, & Co., John Bruce & Co., and Mackeith, Rentoull, & Co. all immediately ceased issuing 5s. notes, retired any outstanding 5s. notes, and shortly combined into one firm, the Perth United Banking Company. One of the original partners in the newly formed bank was in fact none other than George Dempster, one of the Scottish M.P.s behind the bill. The unified bank had a starting capital of £32,000—more than twice the starting capital of the largest pre-1765 private bank—and was comprised of eighty-one partners—likewise more than double the largest pre-1765 private bank.[63] Whereas there were no recorded mergers prior to 1765, the seven-year period from 1765 to June 1772 witnessed three. In addition to the amalgamation of the six Perth banking companies in 1766, the year 1771 saw both the Dumfries bank of Alexander Johnston, Hugh Lawson & Co. and McAdam & Co. of Ayr absorbed by Douglas, Heron & Co.[64]

Similarly, numerous quasi-banking operations that had ventured modestly into the note-issuing business during the specie-scarce years of 1762–1764 exited the market altogether. George Keller & Co., wine and spirit merchants in Glasgow, who in 1764 had issued 5s. and 10s. notes without option and 20s. with option, recorded no further note issues from 1765.[65] Likewise in Kirkliston, the firm of Alexander Fleeming & Co., which on 24 September 1764 had issued "a few" 5s. notes for paying their journeymen, announced on 10 July 1765 that they would be retiring any outstanding notes.[66] In Aberdeen, Alexander Wyllie, vintner, who had previously issued 5s. notes, redeemable in silver at the Exchange Coffee House, also evidently quit the note-issuing business.[67] The minutes of the Dundee Banking Company mention the brief issue of bank notes by the merchant houses of Martinson & Co., in Falkirk, and William Yeaman & Co., in Dundee, in 1764–1765, while Kerr reports the issuance of notes under £1 by James Scrimgeour & Son, in Borrowstounness, in 1763–1765.[68] All three houses ceased issuing notes after 1765.

Of course, a possible alternative explanation is that after 1765 there was a discontinuous surge in large-scale capital investment in Scotland that required a commensurate increase in the average scale of banking enterprises. This, however, is implausible, given that both before and after 1765 Scottish banks were not engaged in direct financing of capital investment, but rather limited their business to providing working capital through cash accounts and discounting bills of exchange. Observed changes in the scale of banking in the immediate aftermath of 1765 were thus unlikely to have been demand-side driven, as there was no discontinuous shift in demand for large-scale mobilization of capital by banks. From a supply-side perspective, on the other hand, the increased minimum scale of banking observed in the wake of the 1765 legislation should hardly be surprising. Optional clause prohibition limited banks' flexibility in the face of large redemption demands, and at the very least removed the deterrent against such demands, thereby requiring the maintenance of larger reserves and capital buffers. On 1 April 1769, for instance, the *Glasgow Chronicle* reported that the Bank of Aberdeen, in an ongoing note-picking battle with the Thistle Bank, made a demand on the latter for £41,700 sterling, which the Thistle "immediately paid in gold and silver specie."[69] In 1771, the Bank of Scotland presented £5,400—91 percent of which consisted of £1 notes—to the Dundee Bank for redemption in gold and simultaneously made similar demands upon the Perth United Company. In retaliation, the Dundee Bank made a £5,000 demand on the Old Bank, which responded a few months hence with a £9,800 demand. The Perth United Company was even forced to borrow £1,000 in gold from Dundee to meet one such note raid.[70]

Similarly, the ban on small notes generally meant larger, or "lumpier," average note redemptions, further raising minimum capital requirements.[71] These effects, moreover, were amplified by an additional provision of the act mandating that banks be open continuously for note redemptions from nine o'clock in the morning till three o'clock in the afternoon, constituting an approximately 33 percent increase in the number of hours during which notes could be presented.[72] As none of the Scottish bankers had advocated such a stipulation, it was almost certainly added at the insistence of English commercial and financial interests, who frequently lamented the tactics employed by Scottish banks to conserve specie, including restricted teller hours.

While the average size of Scottish banks was thus increasing, however, the net number of new banking companies dropped off precipitously after 1765. In other words, banks were, on average, getting bigger, and there were fewer of them. Figure 3.2 charts the total number of new bank formations and bank

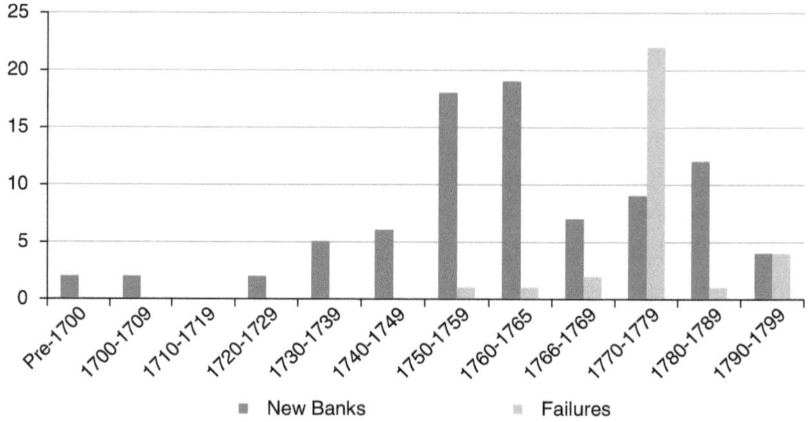

FIGURE 3.2. Bank formations and failures, 1700–1799. *Data sources:* Boase, *Banking in Dundee;* Forbes, *Memoirs of a Banking House;* Buchanan, *Banking in Glasgow;* Kerr, *Banking in Scotland;* Munn, *Scottish Provincial Banking;* Munro, *Royal Bank of Scotland;* Rait, *Union Bank;* Saville, *Bank of Scotland.*

failures—that is, exit owing to institutional insolvency—for each decade from 1700 to 1800, with the decade 1760–1769 divided at 1765. As we can see, the years from 1750 to 1765 were marked by high entrance rates into the banking sector. Moreover, the entire period before 1765 records only two bank failures—the firm of Adam and Thomas Fairholme in 1764 and the Banking Company of Aberdeen in 1753 (though the latter was wound up voluntarily following aggressive attacks by the two Edinburgh public banks, and all creditors, including note holders, were paid in full).[73] Whereas the five years to 1765 saw the formation of no fewer than nineteen banks, with only one failure, the five years following 1765 witnessed the establishment of just seven new banks, with two failures—the firms of William Hogg and Sons and Ebenezer McCulloch & Co., both in 1769.[74] Two years later, Alexander Johnston, Hugh Lawson & Co., in Dumfries, and McAdam & Co., in Ayr, had to be acquired by Douglas, Heron & Co., as both were effectively insolvent.[75] In all, then, compared to just two failures in the entire period until 1765, the fifteen years after 1765 claimed a total of twenty-two banks, with sixteen of those failures occurring in 1772. In contrast, not even the 1762 collapse of the Leith Sugar House Company—to which several of the Edinburgh banks were considerably exposed, as both creditors and partners—had resulted in a single bank failure.[76]

Curiously, the elevated rate of bank failures did not correlate with higher levels of financial leverage. Figure 3.3 plots average leverage ratios for both public and private banks from 1752 until 1782, inclusive. Throughout the entire period, leverage ratios were higher for the private banks than for the chartered banks, reflecting the latter's incentive toward equity over debt financing provided by the privilege of limited liability. The Bank Act, though, coincided with a dramatic convergence in leverage ratios between the private and public banks. Moreover, before 1765 the private banks appear to have effectively sustained leverage ratios in excess of six, eight, and even eleven to one—again, with only two instances of failure. Inasmuch as balance sheets were beginning to get a bit stretched by 1762–1763, ratios had already come down off their peaks by 1764, *before* the passage of the Bank Act, though they were still north of five to one. But subsequent to 1765, failure rates rose significantly in spite of the maintenance of drastically lower leverage ratios—on average, just 2.32 to one between 1766 and 1772. In fact, not even the Ayr Bank, levered 7.46 to one when it collapsed in June 1772, attained leverage ratios regularly sustained by private banks prior to 1765.

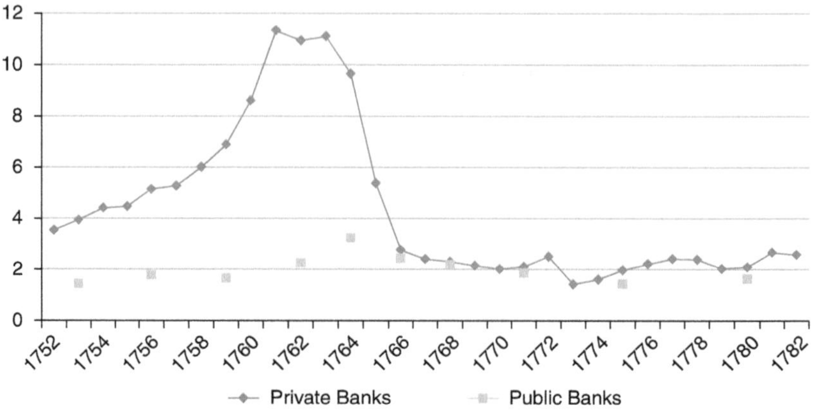

FIGURE 3.3. Average leverage ratios, 1752–1782. Leverage ratios calculated here are liabilities divided by subscribed, or nominal, capital. In practice, only a fraction of subscribed capital was actually paid up, so operating leverage ratios were probably higher. However, given that the percentage of subscribed capital that was actually paid up at any given time was not often published, for consistency I only calculate leverage ratios using total subscribed capital. *Data sources:* Balance sheet and cash books, Lloyds Banking Group Archives; Sederunt books, Royal Bank of Scotland Group Archives; Boase, *Banking in Dundee;* Checkland, *Scottish Banking;* Munn, *Scottish Provincial Banking.*

Reserves tell a similar story, as shown in Figure 3.4. While average reserve ratios for the public banks hardly changed after 1765, those of the private banks rose, on average, 33 percent from their pre-1765 average levels, from 15 percent to 20 percent. That is, after 1765, the private banks were considerably more conservative than before in holding specie and Edinburgh banknotes in reserve against outstanding notes. The public banks, on the other hand, as they had never been in the business of issuing notes below £1, appear to have less affected by the 1765 law.

The profusion of failures in 1772 occurred, therefore, despite the private banks being substantially better capitalized and maintaining larger reserves than before 1765. While this may at first seem paradoxical, it should perhaps not come as a surprise. For, by effectively raising minimum reserve requirements and lowering sustainable leverage ratios, the regulations of 1765 were hardly neutral with respect to the maturity and risk profiles of bank assets. Ceteris paribus, less leverage and higher reserve requirements imply lower profitability. In order to maintain profit levels, therefore, banks must either

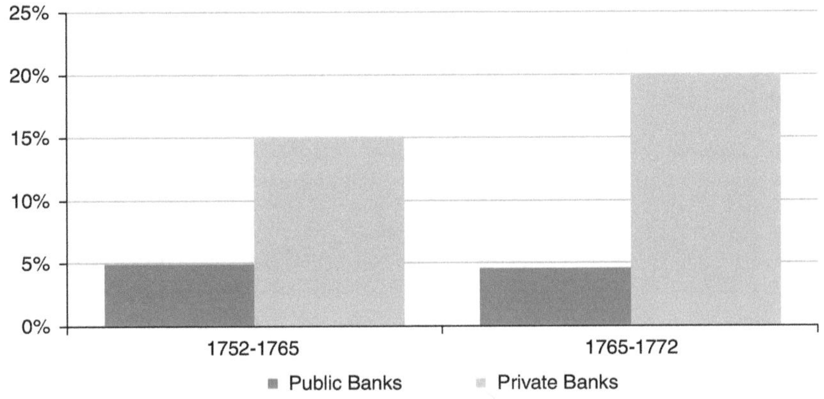

FIGURE 3.4. Average reserve ratios, 1752–1772. *Data sources:* Balance sheet and cash books, Lloyds Banking Group Archives; Sederunt books, Royal Bank of Scotland Group Archives; Boase, *Banking in Dundee;* Checkland, *Scottish Banking;* Munn, *Scottish Provincial Banking.*

aggressively cut costs—difficult to effect when the principal cost is the cost of capital, including equity and reserves, the sum of which has just risen substantially—or else raise the average yield of their assets, which means increasing the average maturity and/or risk level of their loan portfolio (at least so far as possible in the presence of usury ceilings).

We observe all three effects in available balance sheet data. Figure 3.5 plots the share of total assets accounted for by bills of exchange and cash credits. Before 1765, commercial bills of exchange—overwhelmingly of thirty days' maturity—constituted, on average, 40 percent of bank assets, while cash credits accounted for 48 percent. After 1765, bills of exchange plummeted to an average of less than 17 percent of assets, while cash credits jumped to 60 percent, with the change occurring abruptly between 1764 and 1766. In other words, there was a dramatic shift in the composition of bank assets, away from short-term bills, typically backed by inventory or goods receivable, toward perpetual overdraft facilities, which were essentially revolving loans secured only by cosignatories.[77] This result is especially significant in light of Smith's advocacy of the "real bills doctrine." If Smith's aim was to reduce the proportion of bank credit *not* directly employed in financing real commercial transactions, the regulations he promoted in 1765 achieved precisely the *opposite* effect. Indeed, cash advances actually accounted for 67 percent of

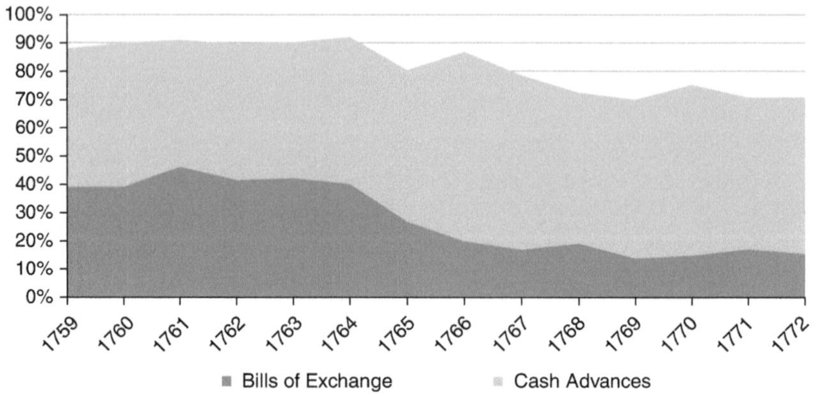

FIGURE 3.5. Bill of exchange and cash advance share of total assets, 1759–1772. *Data sources:* Balance sheet and cash books, Lloyds Banking Group Archives; Sederunt books, Royal Bank of Scotland Group Archives; Boase, *Banking in Dundee;* Checkland, *Scottish Banking;* Munn, *Scottish Provincial Banking.*

Douglas, Heron & Co.'s assets, more than any other bank, public or private, and well above the pre-1765 average of 48 percent.

Moreover, the regulations evidently had a profound effect on the composition of bank reserves. Though, as we have seen, banks did, after 1765, hold more reserves, a greater percentage of those reserves were held in the form of the notes of other banks. While disambiguated private bank data is unavailable, the records of the Bank of Scotland, as shown in Figure 3.6, indicate that whereas prior to 1765 the notes of other banks accounted for, on average, 81 percent of reserves, that figure spiked after 1765 to an average of 91 percent between 1765 and 1772. In fact, on the eve of the financial crisis, banknotes accounted for 94 percent of reserves, thereby constituting substantial counterparty risk at the heart of the bank's balance sheet, and a serious threat to the functioning of the Scottish payments system in the event of an institutional bankruptcy or general liquidity crunch.

Given limited sample size, formal causal inference here is, unfortunately, not possible. Two pieces of evidence, however, are worth noting. First, the £1 floor on banknote issues was undoubtedly binding. The balance sheet of the Dundee Banking Company is instructive. As shown in Figure 3.7, a year before the legislation of 1765, 5s. and 10s. notes accounted for a full 20 percent of total outstanding banknotes by face value. Even as late as early 1765, with the new regulations pending, 18 percent of the Dundee Bank's notes were

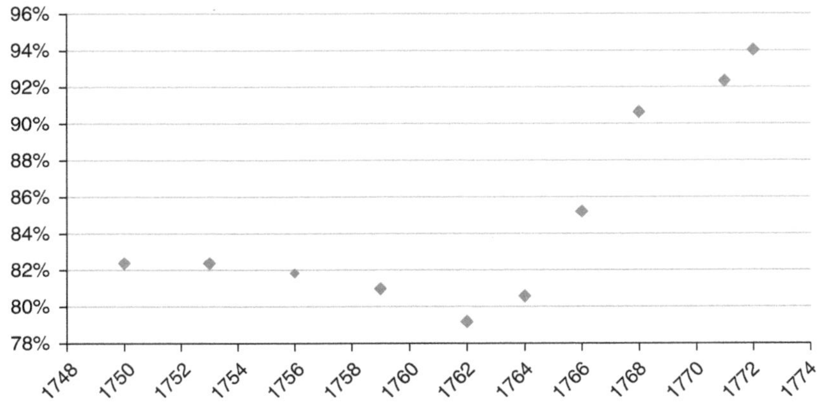

FIGURE 3.6. Banknotes as a percentage of reserves, Bank of Scotland, 1750–1772. *Data source:* Ledger Books, Lloyds Banking Group Archive.

below £1. Six months after the ban had taken effect, 13 percent of all outstanding Dundee notes were still under £1. Only by January 1767 had the bank been able to retire the majority of its 5s. and 10s. notes. Thereafter, £1 or 20s. notes typically accounted for 97 percent of the Dundee Bank's total outstanding notes by value, indicating there was little demand for larger-denomination notes.

Even the public banks, it seems, were affected at the margin. At a 17 December 1765 joint meeting, directors of the two banks, "Having under Consideration the Expediency of Issuing Guinea Notes," concluded that "Issuing Guinea Notes [twenty-one shillings] and discontinuing the Twenty Shillings Notes wou'd be detrimental to both Societys."[78] Though the Old Bank did eventually, nearly three years later, print a number of guinea notes on 2 May 1768, the Royal Bank did not follow suit until 1777.[79] In fact, of the fourteen new note issues recorded by Douglas between 1765 and 1772, only three were for denominations larger than £1, of which one was a guinea.[80] So desperate, in fact, were they for smaller denomination notes, that many Scottish traders actually adopted the practice of cutting up 20s. notes into quarters in order to settle accounts.[81] The editors of *The Scots Magazine* thought it worthwhile to note, suggestively, in their July 1774 issue that "tickets of three, five, and seven shilling pieces, payable at sight the same as bank notes, are issued out by a capital person of most towns in England, which pass current, and are a

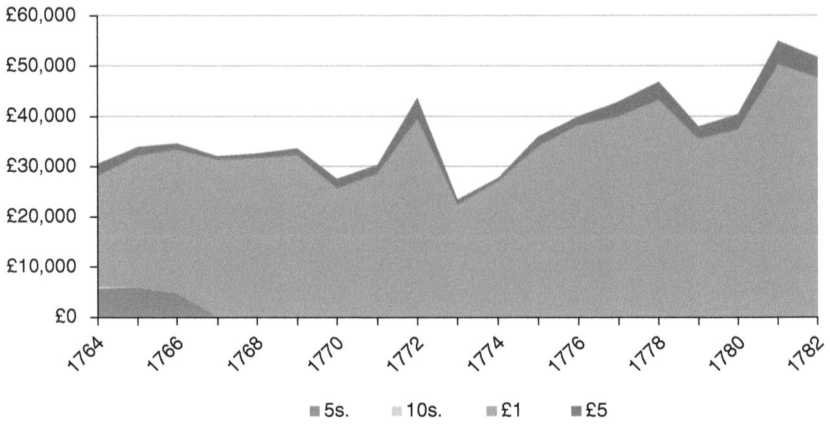

FIGURE 3.7. Dundee banknotes in circulation, by denomination, 1764–1782. *Data source:* "Annual Balance Sheets of the Dundee Banking Company," in Boase, *Banking in Dundee.*

great relief at this time to tradesmen, especially when gold, particularly quarter guineas, is so much scrupled by the farmers and country people."[82]

The effects of optional clause prohibition on macrostability are somewhat more difficult to assess, since, as demonstrated in Chapter 2, there is no evidence of option having ever been exercised except in rare instances of large, exogenous external specie drains by English arbitrageurs. We can only speculate, therefore, as to whether, in the face of both external and internal reserve withdrawals in 1772, Scottish banks would have invoked option and, if so, whether such action would have made any material difference in halting the cascade of bank failures.

The pattern of bank closures during the crisis is, however, perhaps revealing on this question. Specifically, facing large internal and external drains of specie in June 1772, several Scottish banks attempted to replicate the optional clause through temporary suspension of payment with pledges of compensatory interest. The Merchant Banking Company of Glasgow, for instance, facing overwhelming demands for specie, shut its doors on 9 July. Shortly thereafter, however, it advertised that its partners, numbering "more than seventy" and "whose real and personal estates are wholly engaged for the payment of the company's debts," were possessed of ample means to cover all of the bank's liabilities, and that it would thus resume business on 9 October—exactly three months after closure. It further announced that upon reopening it would pay 5 percent interest on all outstanding notes as compensation for suspension, secured by a bond registered in the borough court books of Glasgow.[83] The bank duly resumed business on 9 October and survived the crisis.[84]

In Edinburgh, similarly, the private banks of William Alexander and Sons and John Fyffe & Co. temporarily closed their doors, on 24 June and 20 August, respectively, but later reopened, the former just a few weeks later, on 13 July.[85] Of Fyffe & Co., Sir William Forbes recounted that "John Fyffe, from a principle of high honour, suspended his payments in 1772, because he was fearful of the effect of those numerous bankruptcies which he saw daily happening around him. But, on a more narrow inspection of his affairs, he found no reason for apprehension, and very soon went on again."[86] Such temporary suspensions were in fact reminiscent of the clause's immediate precursor; two years before it became the first to include the optional clause, recall, Bank of Scotland had suspended payments on 27 March 1728, resuming exactly three months later, on 27 June, following placement of a public advertisement pledging 5 percent interest to be paid on all suspended notes issued after 1716.[87]

Perhaps most notably, Douglas, Heron & Co. attempted to staunch the bleeding in June 1772 by temporary suspension of payments, coupled with a pledge of compensatory accrual of interest. After their advertisement of a reward for the identity of any source of rumors concerning their solvency, which they colorfully attributed to "some ill-grounded rumours raised by foolish or malicious persons," failed to halt the hemorrhaging of reserves, the directors were compelled to close their doors.[88] On the morning of 26 June, they issued a circular announcing that "the company of Douglas, Heron & Co., Bankers in Air, taking into their consideration the present state of the credit of this country, and the uncommon demands that have been made upon them for specie, owing to causes sufficiently well known, have come to the conclusion to give over for some time paying specie for their notes." The directors added, however, that as the country "cannot entertain the smallest doubt of the solidity" of the bank's foundation, "it is hoped that on occasion of a national emergency of this kind, the holders of their notes will not be under any alarm." Moreover, "In order to give full satisfaction to the public," they further declared that they "will pay five per cent interest for such of their notes as remain in the circle, until paid, after 26th June current."[89] The bank resumed payments on 28 September, almost exactly three months after suspension, announcing its intention to recommence in an advertisement released ten days before.[90]

Although we possess no counterfactual scenario in which the Scottish banking system was subjected to a shock quite of the magnitude of June 1772 with the handicap of the optional clause to which we might contrast the actual historical episode, we can nonetheless compare the orderliness of payment suspension under the optional clause before 1765 with the disorderliness of ad hoc suspension through sudden stoppage after 1765. Whereas invocation of the optional clause had been discriminate, with banks always continuing to redeem smaller denomination notes while marking larger notes presented by high-volume speculators, suspensions in June 1772 were indiscriminate, implying a more comprehensive disruption to the flow of credit and an amplification of the incentive to be first in line for large redemptions. In particular, indiscriminate suspension of payment in 1772 generated significant contagion effects, as suspension by any one bank immediately rendered illiquid those of its notes held as reserves by other banks. Thus, several banks that failed were subsequently determined by bankruptcy trustees to "have carried on their business with such regularity, diligence, and frugality" that their failure owed purely to "their connection with other houses which have stopt payment."[91]

In contrast, on the occasion of the failure of Adam and Thomas Fairholme on 23 March 1764, for example, at a critical moment when the balance of payments had once again turned against Scotland and arbitrageurs were inundating the banks with demands for specie, the Old and Royal Banks had resolved to "avail themselves of the Optional Clause in their Notes by marking such Sums as appear to be Called for with a view to make a profit of sending the Specie out of this Country."[92] Smaller sums of banknotes, in other words, remained convertible on demand, and even marked notes could continue to circulate among accepting payees and in secondary markets. Interbank note clearing, meanwhile, remained unaffected.

Similarly, two years before, in the face of an overwhelming specie drain and speculative attacks by "hot money," the two public banks had instructed their cashiers to mark notes for any single redemption demand exceeding £50 (£6,334 in 2014 pounds sterling), and a day later further reduced the threshold to £20.[93] Though, bearing the brunt of the attacks, the public banks were compelled also to temporarily curtail cash accounts, the fact that many of their lower-denomination notes remained in circulation and generally redeemable on demand meant the private banks quickly took up the slack, often offering Old and Royal Bank notes or bills on London as payment in lieu of specie.[94] And, in any event, by the end of 1763 Bank of Scotland's note circulation was already 32 percent higher than at the start of 1762, while cash credits were

40 percent higher.[95] In contrast, in June 1772, even the public banks had no choice but to transmit portfolio losses indiscriminately to all note holders and depositors. Faced with a 52 percent drop in reserves, the Bank of Scotland was forced to curtail credits by 29 percent between the end of 1771 and the start of 1773, while notes outstanding contracted 13 percent by mid-1772. Even two years on from the June 1772 crisis, the Old Bank's outstanding notes stock was 50 percent lower than in December 1771, and cash credits 25 percent lower.[96]

Among private banks for which a comparison between 1764 and 1772 is possible, the contrast is similarly stark. Figure 3.8 plots weekly note circulation and specie reserves of the Dundee Banking Company from 17 December 1763 to 19 August 1764 and 16 March 1772 to 15 February 1773—that is, from thirteen weeks before the first bank closure in each crisis episode, to, respectively, twenty-two and thirty-five weeks after. As we can see, the collapse of Adam and Thomas Fairholme on 23 March 1764 did little to halt the expansion of the eight-month-old Dundee Bank's note circulation. After a temporary pause of approximately four weeks, the bank's directors resumed expansion of their note supply by 22 April. Moreover, at no point were they compelled to contract outstanding notes or restrict cash credits. In contrast, as the bank burned through specie reserves during the summer of 1772—a

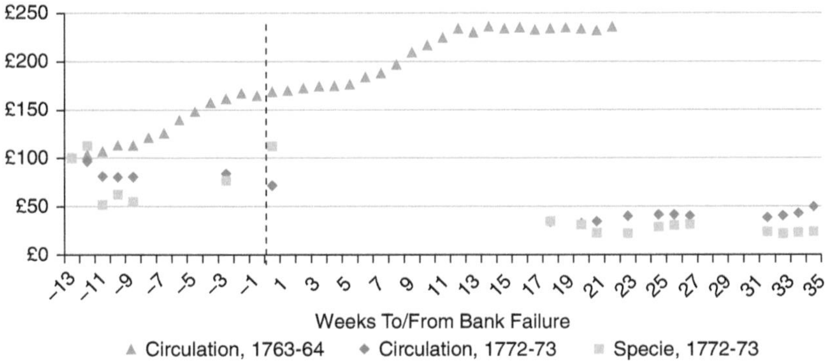

FIGURE 3.8. Dundee banknote circulation and specie reserves, December 1763–November 1764 and March 1772–February 1773. Unfortunately these are the only weekly figures available. Weekly specie figures for 1763–1764 are unavailable. Figures are indexed to Week -13 = 100, with the dotted line at Week 0 indicating the week of the first bank failure. *Data source:* Boase, *Banking in Dundee,* 50, 87.

recently bolstered cushion of £19,867 on 15 June plummeted 69 percent, to just £6,132, by 19 October—it correspondingly had to contract note circulation by a staggering 53 percent. Nor were cash accounts spared; on 2 September, the directors resolved to restrict all cash accounts to four-fifths of their overdraft limits.[97]

To be sure, comparing March 1764 to June 1772 is not a comparison of like with like, the latter crisis being several orders of magnitude greater. Nonetheless, the collapse of the Fairholmes was by no means a minor event; at the time of stoppage, their liabilities amounted to a substantial £107,000.[98] A severe financial crisis in the summer of 1763, resulting in the failures of thirty-two merchant houses in Amsterdam and fifty-four in Hamburg, with numerous bankruptcies occurring also in Stockholm, Bremen, Berlin, Altena, and Leipzig, similarly seems to have been absorbed by the Scottish banking system without considerable disruption.[99] While there is no evidence of the public banks again invoking option against English interest-rate speculators on this occasion, they certainly issued the credible threat of doing so.[100] Indeed, for the entire period before 1765, we ought to be alert to the possibility of the dog that did not bark. Though in England the financial crisis of 1763 may not have been on par with those of 1772 or the South Sea, it was certainly considered as severe by contemporary Dutch and German financial observers.[101] The failure of the 200-year-old Dutch bank of de Neufville for 330,000 guineas on 29 July 1763, following by a few days the collapse of Arend, Joseph & Co., for 50,000 guineas, was noted with considerable alarm in the English and Scottish presses.[102] The bankruptcies in Amsterdam alone were estimated to total some 60 million Dutch florins, or £5 million. In Prussia, meanwhile, Frederick the Great's bankers, Gottskowsky and Strucksus, came under such pressure that the king advanced to them emergency lines of credit totaling 325,000 crowns. Even the turmoil of the War of the Austrian Succession and the capture of Edinburgh by Prince Charles Edward in 1745 seem to have passed without notable financial disruption in Scotland.[103]

The adverse impact on the payments system of disorderly suspension in 1772 thus cannot be overstated. Far from legally obligatory convertibility on demand attenuating the risks of bank runs and disruptive institutional liquidation, the ad hoc nature of suspension and resumption in 1772 attached considerable uncertainty to the execution of ordinary payments, and thereby accelerated redemption demands.[104] Whereas previously marked notes might have continued to circulate, albeit at discount, on account of the specific assurance of repayment in six months with interest, suspension in 1772 typically occurred with no specified resumption date, meaning that suspended notes effectively ceased to be accepted in payment. Thus, even the Carron Company, with a capital of £100,000, formerly reliant on the Ayr Bank to meet weekly operating costs of £500, found itself unable to pay its wages and debts by the end of June. The company was rescued only when the two public banks, in late July, agreed to weekly rediscount £250 each in ninety-day bills, corresponding to a stunning annualized rate of 63 percent, inclusive of commission.[105] De jure convertibility, therefore, was no guarantee of de facto convertibility, with important implications for the functioning of the payments system. Moreover, while we cannot know whether the various small-notes issuers that exited the banking business after the 1765 act would not have done so anyway as the balance of payments crisis of 1762–1764 subsided, the absence of their reentrance in 1772 meant that as the larger banks retrenched, there was no offsetting increase in the provision of currency and short-term credit by smaller quasi banks, such as had mitigated the effects of earlier financial shocks.

But there is perhaps a much broader point to which the sum of evidence presented here overwhelmingly points. That is, the scarcity of specie and "pusillanimity" in the provision of credit to which Smith attributed the great "clamor" for a new bank in 1769 were, pace Smith, conditions exacerbated by the very regulatory apparatus he promoted.[106] In other words, the legislation of 1765 amplified a credit vacuum which a large-scale venture, such as Douglas, Heron & Co., was able to fill with spectacular speed and to remarkable extent. Moreover, the result was one clearly foreseen by contemporaries with a keener comprehension than Smith's of the true source of Scotland's monetary travails—namely, that Scotland was a small open economy with a fixed exchange rate during a period of extreme international macrovolatility. Large capital inflows could thus quickly reverse direction as exogenous external shocks sucked reserves from the Scottish financial system, with consequent contractionary pressure on the country's money supply.

Indeed, even as the Bank Act's parliamentary promoters were shepherding it through the Commons, Edinburgh papers teemed with proposals to petition the two Edinburgh public banks to issue 5s. and 10s. notes.[107] In early January 1764, one writer to *The Scots Magazine,* writing on behalf of "the retail-dealers of Edinburgh, especially those who deal in vivres, such as bakers, fleshers, vintners, grocers, &c.," implored the Old and Royal Banks to issue 5s. notes, and even suggested that, should the two chartered banks refuse, then "the best of the private banking companies should be requested to do it."[108] Another, baffled by hostility toward the optional clause, wrote that "for my part, I cannot conceive how a thing so evidently calculated to keep the specie among us, should have met with such dislike at present." He further noted that whereas it might be easy for the "country gentleman" to refuse any but Old and Royal Bank notes, the "man of business" could hardly afford to be so selective.[109] One writer to the magazine, signing his letter "a lover of Scotland," even proposed that "our banks should issue paper-tickets of 5s not payable in specie but in bank-notes, a twenty-shillings note to be given on demand for four of them."[110] Four years earlier, still another writer had recommended to the country's banks that "ten and five shilling notes may be issued; And, if likewise necessary, six-penny, three-penny, and penny pieces may be cast off on brass, or thick white iron, shaped and sized like the national coin, and having a curious device upon them, difficult to be imitated."[111]

Similarly, the *Annual Register* for 1765 documented several objections to the Bank Act, warning that abolition of the optional clause could "occasion runs on all the banks, which they are by no means in a position to answer." They further cautioned that "the limiting of the quantum of these notes to sums not less than 20s. will spread an universal distress all over the country," adding that "in the remote parts of Scotland, the seat of the linen manufacture, the want of silver had become a great interruption to business, which was in a great measure remedied by these little notes." After all, they concluded, "The value expressed in every note is due by somebody to the bank; if the banks are called upon to pay such notes, they have no other method of answering the demand than by forcing it out of their debtors; so that it is not the banks, but the inhabitants of the country that will suffer the distress."[112]

Sure enough, the alleged overpopulation of banks and overabundance of banknotes in 1763–1764 on which basis the promoters of the 1765 Bank Act justified its regulatory provisions quickly gave way, after 1765, to complaints not just of scarce specie but of scarce currency, with the banks receiving harsh public criticism for inadequate provision of credit and circulating media.[113] It was thus that the foundation of Douglas, Heron & Co. in November 1769 was welcomed by *The Scots Magazine* with an assertion that "the utility and advantage of a bank of this kind to the country is too obvious to require any commentary." Its "influence upon the commercial part of this nation," along with "the evident tendency it must have to forward the improvement of the country, and the aid and support which it must naturally afford to its manufactures, were the inducements of those concerned to establish it, and are the benefits expected to be derived from it—events wished for by all who are lovers of their country."[114]

4

Prodigals and Projectors

In the "party walls" that Smith advocated so as to ensure that banks and bankers might conduct their trade "with safety to the public," it is curious to note that he made no reference to the considerable stabilizing effects of one institutional feature of Scottish banking, or to the potentially destabilizing effects of another—namely, unlimited shareholder liability and usury laws. In *The Wealth of Nations,* only in passing does Smith mention that individual shareholders in Scottish private banks faced joint and several unlimited liability for the debts contracted by their bank, while he dedicates several pages to supporting a legal restriction on lending in the form of a 5 percent interest-rate ceiling.

I find, however, not only that unlimited liability was a vital source of stability in the Scottish financial system, but furthermore that it was the key factor in the recovery of Scottish credit markets after the crisis of 1772. In particular, I argue that in the absence of a formal lender of last resort, the unlimited liability of the partners in Douglas, Heron & Co. in effect served that role. Upon declaring bankruptcy in August 1773, the firm was essentially transformed into a "bad bank" whose sole function was to gradually work off its toxic assets and repay creditors while the immense landed wealth of its proprietors' personal estates provided a financial backstop. A £500,000 bond issue, secured by £3,000,000 in mortgages to the shareholders' estates, allowed the firm to satisfy creditors, at 5 percent interest, as the company's assets, and those of its partners, were gradually liquidated. Only after an act specifically authorizing the bond issue passed Parliament in early 1774 did Scottish credit markets begin to thaw.

In addition, I contend that the collapse of Douglas, Heron & Co. highlights a tension between the benefits of scale, in the form of a larger equity base and greater asset and liability diversification, and the drawbacks of consequent higher monitoring costs. Unlike English private banks, which were often severely undercapitalized owing to the six-partner rule implemented to protect the Bank of England's privileged status, Scottish banks generally enjoyed a broad capital base, with an average of forty-one partners. This diffuse ownership effectively spread risk over a larger and more diverse set of shareholders; in fact, of the sixteen banks that failed in 1772, all but Douglas, Heron & Co. had fewer than six partners. Of the three banks that failed in 1772 *and* inflicted losses on creditors, all three had fewer than six partners. On the other hand, Douglas, Heron & Co., with 226 partners, seems to have struggled to enforce managerial accountability and suffered from serious deficits in shareholder oversight of elected directors. One of the principal advantages of unlimited liability—namely, a strong incentive for owners to effectively monitor management—appears therefore to have been undermined in part by the bank's unwieldy size and the insufficient flow of information to shareholders.

Finally, I suggest that the collapse of Douglas, Heron & Co. indicates potential interaction effects both with the legislation of 1765 and with existing laws concerning usury. By increasing the efficient scale of banking, the 1765 act rendered more likely the emergence of a large, systemically important financial institution such as Douglas, Heron & Co., with attendant difficulties of effective monitoring. Moreover, the problem of insider lending—rampant at the Ayr Bank—was potentially exacerbated by a binding interest-rate ceiling of 5 percent, which necessitated credit rationing by non-price mechanisms. The allocation of credit by insider lending, in particular, critically compromised the dispersion of risk on Douglas, Heron & Co.'s balance sheet and concentrated the firm's assets in the very "prodigals and projectors" whom Smith thought a reasonable usury ceiling would exclude.

It is certainly conceivable that Smith felt no need to discuss the implications of unlimited liability in Scottish banking for the simple reason that it was not a liability regime unique to Scotland; aside from the Bank of

England, whose charter granted its proprietors the privilege of limited liability, bank shareholders in England, too, were liable to the full extent of their personal wealth. But this simple explanation is unconvincing owing to the fact that not only was the issue of unlimited versus limited liability a salient one in Scottish banking circles, it was even deployed as an argument for private banking, and against a monopoly by the Edinburgh public banks, by Smith's friends at the Glasgow Arms, Ship, and Thistle Banks.

In Provost Ingram and John Glassford's January 1764 memorial to the Lord Privy Seal, with notes by Sir James Steuart, the Glasgow private bankers had gone on the offensive, writing that "If 'tis alledged that the security of the Banks [Bank of Scotland and Royal Bank of Scotland] is better than that of any private Companies, it is admitted that their security is very good, altho' the proprietors are not bound to the publick further than the extent of their respective shares of the Bank stock." They further argued that "without detracting from the security of the two Banks in Scotland, that given to the publick by the Glasgow Companies is thought noways inferior to that of either of these Banks; these Companies having given to the country, not only the security of the stock advanced by the Partners, but to the whole extent of the fortune of each Partner." And, underscoring the point, they noted that in each of the private Glasgow banking companies "there are several gentlemen of well known, good, and unentail'd estates, who are Partners, and bound as above mentioned."[1]

It was an argument they had in fact already advanced in print, in a November 1763 essay in *The Scots Magazine* that Gherity has contended Smith had some hand in drafting.[2] "By the constitution of a bank ESTABLISHED BY AUTHORITY," they there remarked, "the proprietors are no further bound, than to the amount of their respective shares of the bank stock; whereas every partner of a private banking-company, is not only bound to the amount of the stock advanced, but is farther liable to the whole extent of his fortune, for every obligation that is contracted."[3] Establishment by public authority, carrying the privilege of limited liability, they thus argued, "Makes a difference very material in favour of the bank-proprietor, and as material against the public." For, the proprietor in such enterprises "in all events risks no more than the stock he trades on, and the public can look to nothing beyond that stock for its security." In contrast, "A private banking company, uncovered by any such legal protection, is obliged to interpose the whole estates, real and personal, of every one of its members, in satisfaction of its engagements to the public." Surely, they then concluded, "That banking society certainly stands upon the firmest basis, whose capital, pledged to the public, bears the greatest proportion to its circulation. It is much to be questioned if either of the public banks would venture to be weighted by that standard against several of the private ones."[4]

Nor, moreover, was the argument employed solely by the Arms, Ship, and Thistle. In an advertisement printed in the 30 April 1765 issue of the *Edinburgh Advertiser,* the proprietors of the recently established Dundee Banking Company (George Dempster & Co.) announced that they had issued notes for £5, 20s., 10s., and 5s., payable to Andrew Pitcairn or the bearer and signed by Robert Jobson (cashier) and two partners. "That the public," they continued, "may be enabled to judge how far they are safe in receiving these notes, there is subjoined to this, a list of the persons concerned in that company, *who have by a security granted at the commencement of their business, and registrated in the borough-court books of Dundee, bound themselves, conjunctly and severally, to retire the above-mentioned notes.*"[5] They then listed the names, residences, and occupations of all sixty of the company's shareholders, with the eight landed gentlemen in the company listed first.

The following month, in an anonymous letter to the publishers, one writer commended the Dundee Bank's advertisement, writing that "the making this public in the newspapers is a right measure for all concerned, as it satisfies even the most scrupulous, that they are safe to take such notes." He further noted that such action "must also be of advantage to the proprietors, as they will be able to circulate a greater number than formerly, and will have a preference over other banking companies, who neglect to give this satisfaction to the public."[6] Urging other banks to follow suit, the writer contended that "I see no way of giving this satisfaction but by following the example of the Dundee bank; that is, to give public notice in the newspapers, upon what foundation the company or bank stand, and the names of all concerned." He also suggested they specify whom they had appointed as agents in Edinburgh to retire outstanding notes.

Sir James Steuart, in his marginal comments to Ingram and Glassford's memorial, had earlier made the same point. "In order to be able to judge fairly," he wrote, between those banks "established by authority," and the private bankers, who "are bound to the whole extent of their estates, real and personal," it was essential that "these estates should be known; and not only that, but they should be pledged in warrandice for payment of their notes, with a preference to all contractions of debt by the proprietors." In the absence of these two conditions, he concluded, "They cannot be with propriety weighed in the balance against the stock of a Bank established by authority."[7]

But the issue of unlimited liability ought to have been even further to the forefront of Smith's mind in the wake of the crisis of June 1772. As noted in Chapter 3, after suspending payment on 9 June, the Merchant Banking Company of Glasgow subsequently advertised that its seventy partners, personally liable to the full extent of their wealth, were possessed of ample means to cover all of the bank's liabilities and would therefore resume business on 9 October, exactly four months after closure. The bank duly resumed business on that day, paying compensatory interest at 5 percent on suspended notes, and ultimately survived the crisis.[8] According to *The Scots Magazine,* by July "many persons in Glasgow and other places engage to take the Merchant company's notes in payments, being fully satisfied of their security; and at a meeting of the partners, July 14, measures were agreed to, which will enable them to open sooner than the time mentioned in the advertisement."[9]

William Alexander and Sons, similarly, were able to reopen on 13 July after obtaining a £160,000 line of credit from the Bank of England, on the security of Alexander's own sugar estates in Grenada, in addition to his exclusive contract to export tobacco to the French farmers general.[10] Further, Douglas, Heron & Co. agreed to extend a £30,000 loan to William Alexander and Sons, on the security of £20,000 in heritable securities to the latter's estates at Blackhouse, Clermiston, and Langside, and breweries in Edinburgh.[11] In Perth, meanwhile, the Perth United Banking Company stemmed the panic by raising a subscription on the security of the estates of the firm's eighty-one partners.[12] Douglas, Heron & Co., too, initially tried to staunch the bleeding in June 1772 by taking out public advertisements in the Scottish papers listing the names, residences, occupations, and subscribed capital of their 226 partners, with the firm's most prominent landed aristocrats, including the Dukes of Buccleuch and Queensberry, listed first and foremost. But whereas the Merchant Banking Company of Glasgow had made sure to advertise that the partners' "real and personal estates are wholly engaged for the payment of the company's debts," Douglas, Heron & Co. were somewhat circumspect on this point. Though noting that they and their heirs, executors, and successors were jointly and severally bound, they avoided a more explicit statement of their unlimited liability, perhaps under the mistaken belief that advertisement of a subscribed capital of the unprecedented sum of £150,000 would be more than sufficiently assuring.[13] It was a potentially costly point to slur, given that as recently as April 1772 even the Bank of Scotland had thought it necessary to seek clarification from Douglas, Heron & Co.'s directors as to whether their partners were, in fact, jointly and severally liable (the secretary of the bank's board of directors, Alexander Lockhart, had responded on 21 April in the affirmative).[14]

Even for banks that ultimately had to be wound down, unlimited joint and several liability mitigated short-run panic and fire-sale liquidations. For instance, another bank that had suspended payment during the crisis, Johnstone & Smith, partially resumed payments after opening their books to creditor scrutiny and raising a subscription on the security of the proprietors' estates.[15] The trustee appointed by the firm's creditors, Walter Coffer, gave notice by public advertisement in the Scottish papers on 26 September that he had "examined the books of those gentlemen [Johnstone & Smith] with care, and is fully satisfied, that they have carried on their business with such regularity, diligence, and frugality" that their failure owed purely to "their connection with other houses which have stopt payment." The trustee further added that "some friends and creditors" of the firm, "observing the great uneasiness which they are under upon account of the notes so issued by them, many of which may probably be held by poor people, who can ill afford to wait the future dividends of their estate, have generously completed a subscription, by which the trustee will be enabled to pay a composition at the rate of 15s. in the pound on all their notes still in the circle," regardless of the situation of the trust-estate. In other words, confident in the security of its proprietors, several friends and creditors of Johnstone & Smith were willing to fund composition with creditors while the firm and proprietors' estates were gradually liquidated, in the expectation that, for those creditors willing to wait, distribution would be at least equal to 15s. in the pound.[16]

Meanwhile, the firm of Gibson and Balfour, who had failed on 24 June, ultimately settled its debts in full through four equal installments, with interest, over four years. As interim security, creditors, including Douglas, Heron & Co., received heritable securities backed by the proprietors' personal estates.[17] Garbet & Co., which also failed on 24 June, likewise discharged all its debts in full through installments spread over five years, on the security of the proprietors' estates, though final resolution, with interest, among the partners themselves took nearly forty years.[18] There was some initial confusion as to whether an earlier partner, John Roebuck, retained partial ownership of the firm and thus remained liable for debts incurred, while efforts to remit money from Samuel Garbet's son-in-law and partner Charles Gascoigne's Russian investments were evidently still ongoing in 1811.[19] Nonetheless, creditors were fully secured through £27,000 in heritable securities to Gascoigne's Dalderse estate and £12,000 of £50,000 in Carron Company stock owned by Garbet, with Garbet himself ultimately having to liquidate his shares in factories at Prestonpans and Trent.[20]

In fact, of the sixteen Scottish banks that ultimately collapsed in the wake of Black Monday, only three failed to eventually pay their creditors in full. In addition to Johnstone & Smith, the firms of Fordyce, Malcolm & Co. and Charles Fergusson & Co. reached composition settlements with creditors for 6s. 6d. and 5s. in the pound, respectively.[21] Both, however, seem to have constituted highly irregular cases. First, the largest creditor to both firms was none other than Douglas, Heron & Co., meaning the loss was ultimately borne primarily by shareholders of the Ayr Bank.[22] Second, Douglas, Heron & Co. acceded to the composition in a borderline negligently hurried and opaque fashion: the directors involved claimed that the deed of composition had been signed by "many" of the creditors of Fordyce, Malcolm & Co. and Charles Fergusson & Co., though it is unclear how many were "many." Considering that the report from the 24 August 1772 meeting of creditors of Fordyce, Malcolm & Co., reprinted in that month's issue of *The Scots Magazine,* noted that "John Fordyce and Andrew Grant are possessed of very considerable landed property, subject to the legal attachments of creditors," it would be surprising if a majority of other creditors, like Douglas, Heron & Co., acceded to a composition of just 6s. 6d. in the pound less than one month hence.[23] Barely a month after acceding, Douglas, Heron & Co. actually extended a new £29,000 to Fordyce, Malcolm & Co. to cover composition payouts, on the security of partner Andrew Grant's estate at Torrerie as well as lands owned by Fordyce at New Grange near St. Andrew's and two houses in Edinburgh.[24]

The directors who authorized the bank's London representatives to accede to both compositions were in fact harshly criticized in the report of the committee of inquiry into Douglas, Heron & Co.'s demise. Recognizing that they lacked authority to accept any composition settlement, the four directors present in London to negotiate a sale of heritable annuities had on 5 September referred the proposals of Fordyce, Malcolm & Co. and Charles Fergusson & Co. to their fellow directors in Ayr. Absent a quorum of directors from the Edinburgh office, however, directors from the Ayr and Dumfries offices elected on 18 September to effectively pass the buck to Edinburgh, resolving that "*in regard* they have not an opportunity to inspect the state of the affairs of the said Charles Fergusson and Company themselves, *as the same is not before them,* they do remit the consideration of this affair to the Edinburgh Directors."[25] Six days later, a meeting of directors "was *pretended* to be held at Edinburgh," comprised of just two directors, John Campbell and Archibald Cockburn, and a third extraordinary director. Though such a meeting, under the contract of copartnery, had no power to accede to such settlements as were under consideration from Fordyce, Malcolm & Co. and Charles Fergusson & Co., the three directors nonetheless resolved to instruct the firm's London representatives to accept the offers of 6s. 6d. and 5s. in the pound.

Writing to the directors in London, Campbell and Cockburn admitted they were suspicious of the propriety of the settlements, noting that "we are perfectly convinced, that there is something at the bottom, both of the affairs of Charles Fergusson and Company and of Fordyce, Malcolm and Company. But we cannot make matters better by standing out; so, out of necessity, we must concur." The commission of inquiry later concluded that

> It does not appear, that the two Directors who authorized this important transaction acted from any proper knowledge of the affairs of Charles Fergusson and Company, and Fordyce, Grant, and Company, or indeed that any satisfactory state thereof was so much as laid before them, when they came to this hasty and inconsiderate resolution, by which they were at once to squander or annihilate upwards of [£]30,000 of the funds of the Company. One thing seems sufficiently plain, that they had neither the time nor opportunity, nor the necessary materials, for examining the matter with any accuracy, or judging the expediency or inexpediency of acceding to the proposed composition.[26]

In light of such a damning assessment, we must be careful not to assume that the figures of 6s. 6d. and 5s. in the pound constituted final restitution for all, or even most, creditors of the failed houses. Indeed, one disgruntled shareholder of Douglas, Heron & Co. noted of the composition with Fordyce, Malcolm & Co. that "several of the creditors in fact never acceded," and asked his fellow partners whether they would not have suffered less had they followed the lead of those nonacceding creditors "who will," he asserted, "without doubt render their whole debts effectual."[27] The committee of inquiry seemed to concur, observing that "some of the creditors of these houses did recover a much higher composition than that which was paid to this Company," and concluding that, in any event, several of the creditors to both houses did not accede to the composition offers, and that "we cannot discover any great loss which our Company could have sustained, if our Managers had also refused to accede."[28]

Two institutional features, in particular, seem to have played critical roles in facilitating the overall effectiveness of unlimited joint and several liability in mitigating the transmission of adverse financial shocks to depositors and other creditors of failed banks. First, sequestration of the personal estates of bankrupt partners, through application to the Court of Session by creditors, was swift. Already by 25 June, the estates of the partners of Arbuthnot & Guthrie, Gibson & Balfour, Fordyce, Malcolm & Co., Garbet & Co., and Johnstone & Smith had been sequestered by the Court, followed on 9 July by Simson, Baird & Co.[29] Lists of sequestrations were regularly printed in the Scottish papers, as well as the *London Gazette,* along with dates, times (twelve noon being standard), and location (typically Parliament House in Edinburgh) of upcoming meetings of creditors or their nominated agents.[30]

Creditors could then vote to proceed under sequestration, or else to elect a trustee to manage liquidation and distribution of the bankrupt estate(s), along with a committee to advise and supervise the designated trustee. Trustees were typically instructed to adhere to a strict timetable for soliciting creditor claims, assessing the assets of the trust-estate and distributing liquidated assets to creditors, and were further directed to keep creditors apprised through regular advertisements in the Scottish papers.[31] As late as 1793, trustees were posting assets for liquidation by public auction at the Old Exchange Coffee House in Edinburgh.[32]

That sequestration and distribution of bankrupt estates proceeded with such order was partly a stroke of luck. Just one week before Alexander Fordyce's failure a new act of Parliament for regulating bankruptcy in Scotland had received royal assent.[33] The act put an end to the inequitable system of bankruptcy distribution preceding, wherein the first creditors to lay arrestments on a debtor were able to secure for themselves claims to the debtor's estate for sums owed, to the exclusion of others.[34] Two years prior, in the wake of several commercial bankruptcies, including two for the quite substantial sums of £70,000 and £60,000, one writer to *The Scots Magazine* had lamented the injustice of current arrangements, noting that it was not uncommon for "eminent" bankrupts to hastily reach accommodations with favored creditors. The writer had thus advocated, among other reforms, "An act of parliament setting aside all preferences, and giving to every person an equal share or distribution of the bankrupt's effects with the least expense."[35]

These and several other bankruptcies in 1769, ranging from £1,000 to £16,000, seem to have provided the impetus for consequent legislative initiative. The resulting act not only established new procedures for sequestration and the appointment of factors for equitable distribution among all creditors but also mandated that appointed factors keep creditors apprised of proceedings through regular advertisements in the *London Gazette* as well as in an Edinburgh paper to be appointed by the Court of Session.[36] As one commentator in *The Scots Magazine* thus put it in early August 1772, "The British legislature seems in some degree to have been inspired by a spirit of prophecy, in framing the late statute concerning bankruptcies in Scotland." He called it "a most fortunate antidote" against "those numerous evils, which the late failures would infallibly have occasioned, had the diligences of creditors been regulated by the law as it formerly stood."[37]

Nonetheless, in an operation the size of Douglas, Heron & Co., opportunistic looting was almost inevitable. On 13 and 15 June—after news of Neale, James, Fordyce & Down had reached Edinburgh but before Douglas, Heron & Co. had stopped payment—the Edinburgh directors allowed David Campbell, a fellow manager holding four shares, to exchange £11,000 to £12,000 of his bills for the same value in the company's bills. Eight thousand pounds of Campbell's bills eventually defaulted.[38] Even more flagrantly, a receipt for a £2,500 credit to the London bank of Mayne and Needham was given to John Bushby, one of the four directors in London to negotiate the sale of annuities, in exchange for £2,500 in already protested bills held by Bushby.[39] As the committee of inquiry observed, "Mr. Bushby was in one hour raising money upon annuities, in name of the Company, at the King's Arms tavern, and the next hour was carrying the proceeds to Jermyn street, and applying them in payment of his own engagements."[40]

Mayne and Needham, meanwhile, appear to have taken full advantage of the chaos at the Ayr Bank by engaging themselves in some £46,500 worth of transactions, all drawn on Douglas, Heron & Co. Though Mayne and Needham's accommodation with Douglas, Heron & Co. had been for a mere £10,000, the latter's representatives in London nonetheless covered them to the full extent of their engagements with £15,400 in bills and a further £31,100 in cash raised via the sale of annuities. The representatives of Douglas,

Heron & Co. thus used funds raised at exorbitant cost to cover Mayne and Needham for having massively exceeded their credit limit, as all the while Mayne and Needham continued to discount Douglas, Heron & Co. bills. In other words, the company was gifting Mayne and Needham the very funds which the latter then used to lend back at steep cost.[41] Meanwhile, a further £9,000 deposited in the cashier's account in London and £6,220 raised by annuity seem to have disappeared entirely without trace.[42]

The cost of such negligence, however, was borne, not by note holders and creditors, but by fellow shareholders. The sale of redeemable annuities referred to above was a desperate attempt to keep the bank afloat in the wake of the Bank of Scotland, Royal Bank of Scotland, and Bank of England's refusals to extend emergency lines of credit. It was an exorbitant price to pay. On the security of the proprietors' personal estates, a total of £457,750 was raised by sale of single- and double-life annuities promising payments of £100 in every £700 for a single life and £100 in £800 for the longer of a double life, corresponding to 14.3 percent and 12.5 percent per annum, respectively. Stating the obvious, *The Scots Magazine* called the terms "the most advantageous, as is observed, that ever were offered." The subscription was, not surprisingly, filled before the end of July.[43] Alarmed by the staggering cost, a worried David Hume wrote to Adam Smith in October 1772 noting that "as far as I can learn, the Duke of Queensberry alone signs the Bonds of Annuity in his own Name; but it is imagind that the Duke of Buccleugh, Mr Douglas etc., have enterd into an Agreement to bear their Share: Otherwise it were Madness in him; and indeed not very wise in him and them in any case."[44]

Claims by Munro, Munn, Sechrest, Cowen and Kroszner, Saville, and Rockoff that the Bank of England and the Edinburgh chartered banks provided crucial lender of last resort functions during the crisis, or Karrlander's assertion that a lender of last resort was absent, are quite simply false.[45] Not only did the Old and Royal Banks rebuff Douglas, Heron & Co.'s entreaties for a bailout in June 1772, and the Bank of England offer an advance only on unacceptably extortionary terms, but the latter even demanded personal bonds of the Dukes of Buccleuch and Queensberry, as well as of Archibald Douglas of Douglas and Patrick Heron of Heron, just to roll over Ayr Bank bills they already held.[46] Indeed, far from extending fresh credit on that collateral, the governor and company then further stipulated a strict timetable for tapering their purchases of Ayr Bank bills. Like every other Scottish bank, meanwhile, the eminent banking house of John Coutts & Co. refused even to accept Ayr

Bank notes, though through the facilitation of David Hume, managing partner Sir William Forbes reluctantly agreed to take Adam Smith's off his hands as a special favor.[47]

Nonetheless, there was a lender of last resort: the shareholders of the Ayr Bank. Kerr, Munn, and Saville misleadingly suggest that the decision of the Old and Royal Banks to take up £80,000 of the estimated £129,000 of outstanding Ayr Bank notes after July 1773 was, in Saville's words, a sign of "considerable maturity" in stabilizing the situation.[48] But examination of the Old Bank's letter and ledger books reveals that the two public banks accepted Ayr notes only after a personal appeal by the Duke of Buccleuch, and then only on the security of ninety-day bills drawn directly on Douglas, Heron & Co.'s most prominent shareholders.[49] Throughout the latter half of 1773 and early 1774, numerous bills in even denominations of £50, £400, and £2,500, signed by Thomas Hogg, cashier, or George Home, director in Edinburgh, were drawn on, among others, partners John Hamilton, John Campbell, Robert Riddick, and John Bushby, as well as high-quality bills drawn on Patrick Lord Elibank and John Lord Garlies, Earl of Galloway. Personal bonds of Archibald Douglas of Douglas and Patrick Earl of Dumfries, in the amount of £2,500 each, moreover, were deposited as security.[50] As these bills came due, new ninety-day bills of the same value were redrawn and deposited as security.

It was the sale of annuities, meanwhile, that had allowed the bank to resume payment at its Ayr office on 28 September 1772, from which time it soldiered on until finally conceding defeat in August 1773.[51] Shortly thereafter, a committee of fifteen shareholders was appointed to wind up the company's affairs.[52] Desperate to extricate themselves from the heavy burden of paying almost 15 percent per annum on life annuities, the committee quickly proposed a £480,000 bond issue in London for redeeming the annuities sold barely more than a year prior. Essentially, the bond issue was to be used to repurchase the annuities so as to enable Douglas, Heron & Co. to pay down its debts at more reasonable interest as the bank's assets and the estates of its shareholders were gradually liquidated, the proceeds from which would then be employed to repurchase the bonds in four equal payments from 1778 to 1782.[53] Essentially, therefore, Douglas, Heron & Co. was to become a mere shell company, a "bad bank" whose sole function was to gradually work off its toxic assets and repay creditors while the immense landed wealth of its proprietors' personal estates provided a financial backstop.

The terms were generous: £750 in bonds for each single-life and £850 for each double-life annuity, bearing the legal maximum of 5 percent interest per annum, paid half yearly. In addition to the security of the company's assets and the estates of its shareholders, amounting to more than £3,000,000, the committee also proposed to mortgage specific unentailed estates in Scotland generating annual rent of £32,000.[54] The legal hitch, however, was that such a transaction might place Douglas, Heron & Co. in contravention of the Bubble Act, which restricted the issuance of transferable stocks to chartered corporate entities.[55] In any event, the committee concluded that "said Bonds cannot be issued and transferred, and the Proposals before recited carried into Execution, without much Difficulty, Trouble, and Expence, unless aided by Authority of Parliament," not least because they wished endorsed bonds to be exempt from stamp duty and therefore solicited the aid of their Westminster connections to bring forward a bill authorizing an issue of up to £500,000.[56]

Despite support from the majority of annuitants, the bill met with substantial opposition in the Commons. The problem was that the proposal that the issued bonds be "rendered to all Intents and Purposes negotiable and vendable, like East-India Bonds, Navy and Exchequer Bills, or any Effects of a similar Nature," but paying 5 percent coupon, compared to the 3 percent then offered on East India bonds, aroused the concern of the directors of the East India Company, who feared the new issue would depress prices of their own securities.[57] The company mounted an aggressive opposition, even submitting a petition of "Merchants, Bankers, and Traders, of the City of London" asserting that "if the said Bill should pass into a Law, it will be highly injurious to the trading Part of this Country, and depreciate the Value of the National Funds," and therefore urged that it be defeated.

The three members who spoke against the bill, moreover, all had close ties to the East India Company or were themselves active traders in government securities. Robert Henley Ongley, M.P. for Bedfordshire, was the son of a former director of the company, and not only held substantial shares in the company himself, but was further known to have "frequently dabbled in Government stock, as subscriber or purchaser, usually in partnership with City men." Richard Fuller, M.P. for Stockbridge, owned £1,000 in East India and £20,000 in Bank of England stock, and was also known as "a considerable speculator in Government stock." Charles Wolfran Cornwall, M.P. for Grampound, had long been intimately involved in East India Company affairs, both as a supervisor and as a close friend of Robert Clive and George Colebrooke.[58]

Douglas, Heron & Co., and in particular the Dukes of Queensberry and Buccleuch, however, had their own friends in the Commons, including the Lord Advocate for Scotland, James Montgomery, Sir Lawrence Dundas (governor of the Royal Bank of Scotland), Alexander Wedderburn, George Dempster, Charles Fox, and Lord Beauchamp, all of whom spoke in support of the bill.[59] In the end, under the careful stewardship of the Lord Advocate, the bill passed the Commons by a vote of 176 to 36 on 28 March, with the House of Lords affirming on 30 March and the king offering royal assent the following day.[60]

As with the sale of annuities, demand for the new bonds was considerable. Premiums quickly rose to 6 percent, even 7 percent over par, implying that not only did investors desire the higher coupon rate, relative to East India and government three percents, but also that they actually viewed Douglas, Heron & Co. bonds as offering superior security to alternative assets.[61] So keen, in fact, were the directors of the Bank of Scotland to obtain Douglas, Heron & Co. bonds that they effectively strong-armed the company's directors into transferring additional bonds in exchange for a loan. After two months of intense negotiations, Bank of Scotland agreed to lend Douglas, Heron & Co. £30,000, but only on the condition that the latter also agree to sell them £40,000 of the new bonds at par. In other words, at a moment when Ayr Bank bonds were trading at least 3 percent over par, Douglas, Heron & Co. was obliged to withhold £40,000 of them for sale to the Old Bank at face value.

Barely a week after the agreement was concluded on 28 June, Edinburgh director George Home had to write to fellow partner Alexander Machonochie in London to facilitate the bond sale, to inform him that "the Bank of Scotland are very anxious to have these bonds, and as now that the bargain is concluded, it is best for us to do what we can to oblige them." He added, in a separate note on 11 July, that "until they be delivered, we will have difficulty to get [Bank of Scotland] even to make out the securities which are to entitle us to the £30,000." Two weeks later, with half of the £40,000 already having been delivered, Home again wrote Machonochie to impress upon him that "it is unnecessary for me to repeat that the directors of the Old Bank are anxious for the delivery of *all* the bonds they are to receive in terms of our agreement." Machonochie, frustrated by the harsh terms, replied by noting that, though he probably had a sufficient number of bonds to fulfill the remaining sum, he wished to remind Home that "as the premium is 3 per cent, remember you borrow at that expence."[62]

In the end, not only was Douglas, Heron & Co. compelled to sell the £40,000 at par for the £30,000 loan, but also £10,000 more, again at par, for an additional £10,000 advance from Bank of Scotland.[63] As the committee overseeing the liquidation of Douglas, Heron & Co. would thus later allege, "The Bank of Scotland were anxious to get the Bonds in question even at a premium," and therefore "the Committee were forced to give them the whole £50,000 without a premium to obtain a loan of £40,000 which they were under a necessity to borrow even on these very hard terms to prevent the Affairs of the Company from going into Confusion, while the redemption of the Annuities was going on."[64]

For partners of the Ayr Bank the end result was carnage. Already by August 1775, 112 of 226 partners were insolvent.[65] For each £500 share, the average shareholder of Douglas, Heron & Co. ultimately paid out a staggering £2,935, or nearly six times his initial investment.[66] As of 1788, the Duke of Queensberry still owed almost £45,000 for his four shares. The Duke of Buccleuch, with just two shares, owed some £15,000. By the same date, Sir Adam Fergusson, four-time M.P. for Ayrshire and Edinburgh, had paid £3,578, and still owed £822.[67] The following year, still solvent partners were called upon for a further £1,400 per share. An earlier attempt by one partner, Alexander Hair, to resist an additional call of £200 per share in August 1773 by claiming the bank could not compel any partner to pay into the company's stock more than the precise sum to which he had subscribed had been roundly rejected in court. In the case of *Douglas, Heron and Company v. Hair,* the Court of Session ruled on 24 July 1778 that the call was not for an addition to the company's stock, "But for money to answer debts beyond what the stock can pay," for which all partners were jointly and severally liable.[68]

Among Ayrshire gentry thus ruined by the bank's collapse were Patrick Douglas of Cumnock, Hugh Logan of Logan, Robert Kennedy of Pinmore, Archibald Crawfurd of Ardmillan, John Christian of Kinning Park, George McCrae of Pitcon, Sir John Whitefoord of Ballochmyle and Blairquhan, and David McLure of Shawood.[69] Crawfurd suffered the ignominy of having to sell his Ardmillan estate to an uncle, Thomas Crawfurd.[70] John Carruthers's single share cost him his family's estate at Holmains, making him the last Baron of Holmains. John Campbell, M.D., with two shares, lost almost everything and was forced to sell his Wellwood estate, while John Hamilton of

Rozelle and Carcluie had to sell the latter 312-acre estate to the Countess of Crawford.[71] Christian, formerly cashier at the Ayr branch, lost lands in Cuningpark, Windyhall, and Gairholme. The two shares of William Logan of Camlarg, one of the bank's directors in Ayr, eventually cost him his Camlarg estate in 1780, as his "merciless uncle," from whom he had borrowed money to improve the estate, refused to bail out his nephew.[72]

The uncle, John McAdam of Craigengillan, had founded the late John McAdam & Co., the "Old" Ayr Bank, which, recall, had effectively failed just one year before the crisis and had to be absorbed by Douglas, Heron & Co. In the words of McAdam's grandniece, Georgina McAdam:

> While John McAdam was making money on all hands came the disastrous failure of the Ayr Bank—it was entirely set going by the landed proprietors of the Counties round—and the effect was far worse than the present state of Ireland with the encumbered estates. Estates changed hands for *nothing!* They were engulfed and wherever our Ralph Nickleby held the smallest mortgage he squeezed the last drop of blood out of the victim, between himself and the bankruptcy, Barbeth—where his granddaughter Mrs McAdam Cathcart now lives—became his, Camlarg and many large estates. Uncle Gilbert's estate went at last with this shock and meantime Mammon was silently acquiring Waterhead.[73]

As Georgina's account indicates, John's younger brother, Quintin McAdam, was an original subscriber to Douglas, Heron & Co., with two shares, and ultimately had to sell holdings in Barbeth and Barleith to his older brother to cover his liability. Another brother, Gilbert McAdam, was also ruined by the bank's collapse, such that by 1780 he too had been forced to sell his estates in Merkland and East Auchinlongford.[74]

William Donald, who had purchased the lands of Cockhill and Mosshill with the intent of building a large mansion there, was forced to dispose of both, along with the greater part of his property and effects, through judicial sale.[75] Archibald Cockburn of Cockpen, who had earlier attempted to convince the Court of Session that he had not officially acquired a third share in Douglas, Heron & Co. just one month prior to the bank's collapse, had to sell his family's Cockpen estate in 1785 to the Earl of Dalhousie and move to Hope Park.[76]

Not even Adam Smith's pupil and patron, the twenty-six-year-old Henry Scott, Duke of Buccleuch, was unaffected. In a letter to Baron Mure of the

Thistle Bank dated 3 August 1772, Scottish physician and writer Dr. John Moore wrote, of the events of June 1772, "I was so much affected with these sad scenes, that for several days I could think on no other subject." Referring to the young Henry, Duke of Buccleuch, he further added: "Conscious that no thing can be more improper, nor more disagreeable, to one of the duke's age and prospects, than the company of a melancholy man, I have struggled to get the better of this, and to banish desponding ideas from my mind; I have appeared gay, with a heart wounded by the misfortunes of my friends." The duke, he observed, was himself "not an unfeeling spectator of the distresses of individuals and the calamity of his country."[77] In 1774, the duke even had to sell his 1,520-acre estate and fifty-six-room manor house at Adderbury to cover his liability in Douglas, Heron & Co.[78] With few buyers able to afford the property's staggering £54,000 price tag, Adderbury was in fact sold to one of the wealthiest sees in the country, that of the Bishop of Winchester.[79]

Buccleuch, furthermore, was one of fifteen partners named in one of eight suits by shareholders against their fellow partners. His two shares made him liable for £4,857 of a £102,000 suit for damages resulting from the annuity transaction.[80] Altogether, the eight suits sought a combined £558,753 from the sixty-one named partners, including also the Duke of Queensberry. Among other charges, £13,768 was sought for the ruinous 5s.-in-the-pound composition settlement with Charles Fergusson & Co., and £22,873 for the equally negligent composition with Fordyce, Malcolm & Co. Claims of mismanagement and irregular debts totaled a staggering £383,611. Suits were additionally brought against Cockburn for unpaid liabilities assigned to his disputed third share, as well as James Craig, a baker in Edinburgh who unsuccessfully attempted to claim that he had sold his single share just a month before the bank stopped payment.[81]

All told, Kerr estimates that £750,000 of property had to be liquidated as a result of the bank's failure.[82] The consequent immense downward pressure on land prices exacerbated the situation. On 12 June 1780, Douglas, Heron & Co. had to inform the Bank of Scotland that they would be late in payments due on £135,000 in loans still outstanding. They explained that, although the company's funds actually exceeded £400,000, the greatest part of which was secured by "good and undoubted mortgages upon estates far beyond that value; yet such are the increasing difficulties of the times in this country, these estates cannot be sold so quickly as we expected."[83] Two years later, with the negotiability and transferability of the bonds authorized by the 1774 act set to expire, Douglas, Heron & Co. again had to solicit the aid of Parliament. "By reason of the great Fall in the Price of Lands," they argued, "in which the greatest Part of the Funds of the Company are invested, and the Difficulty of finding Purchasers for the same, and of recovering the other Debts due to the Partnership, in the present State of Credit and Situation of that Part of the United Kingdom," it was necessary that the negotiability and transferability of the bonds be extended to June 1786.[84] Parliament obliged, with the ensuing act receiving royal assent on 25 March, just three months before the bonds had originally been set to expire.[85]

Agonizing though the process of liquidation may have been, however, it was nonetheless necessary to unfreeze Scottish credit markets. After the Duke of Buccleuch's personal appeal to the directors of the Old and Royal Banks on 15 June 1773 convinced them that sufficient security stood behind Douglas, Heron & Co., and that the firm would shortly be pursuing a bond issue to help wind up its affairs in orderly fashion, the two chartered banks finally agreed to again accept Ayr Bank notes, and even sent £16,800 of their own guinea notes to Douglas, Heron & Co. to expedite mopping up the defunct bank's notes.[86] An initial agreement to accept £40,000 each was expanded to £50,000 in October 1773 and to £65,000 at the end of May 1774, after the bond issue had formally received parliamentary authorization and royal assent. By that time, Bank of Scotland's holdings of Ayr Bank notes had swelled to £62,500.[87]

The Dundee Banking Company, meanwhile, had slashed its own note circulation from £47,330 on 16 March 1772, before the June crisis, to a low of £15,402 by the end of October. Their largest denomination notes, for £5, were withdrawn from circulation with particular intensity. While the Dundee Bank contracted its outstanding £1 notes by 43 percent from January 1772 to January 1773, they reduced their £5 note circulation by a staggering 75 percent over the same period. From January 1773 to January 1774, moreover, while they re-expanded their £1 circulation by 21 percent, they simultaneously further shrunk their £5 note stock by 38 percent. Not until 1775 did the Dundee Bank again begin to cautiously reissue more of its largest denomination note, which, in the absence of the optional clause, was especially dangerous to reserve levels in the event of panic or speculative redemption demands. Overall, after languishing from October 1772 to February 1773 (the last month for which weekly or monthly data are available), the bank's total note circulation seems to have resumed expansion. By the start of 1774, total circulation had increased by 18 percent over the February 1773 figure, and grew a further 29 percent by 1775, consistent with the hypothesis that Scottish credit markets did not seriously begin to thaw until the situation with proprietors of the Ayr Bank was clarified in the latter half of 1773 and first half of 1774.

For the Scottish banking system as a whole, 1773 to 1774 again appears to have been marked by a rapid recovery in the flow of credit. After contracting 21 percent from 1772 to 1773, total banknotes in circulation swelled by 36 percent in 1774, topping their pre-crisis peak. Figure 4.1 plots total advances, cash accounts, bills discounted, and other credits (mainly lending on heritable bonds) from 1768 (the first year from which consistent aggregate time series are possible) to 1776 (the last year before the financial disruptions of the American conflict complicate the picture), normalized to 1768 = 100. Because data are not available for most private banks, the series cover only the Old and Royal Banks, as well as the provincial banking companies in Glasgow, Ayr, Dundee, Perth, and Aberdeen. Thus, Figure 4.1 likely understates the magnitude of lending volatility, particularly between 1771 and 1773, by excluding the Edinburgh private banks. In any case, overall, total advances of credit fell by 7.5 percent in 1772, compared to 1771, and then by a further 5 percent in 1773.

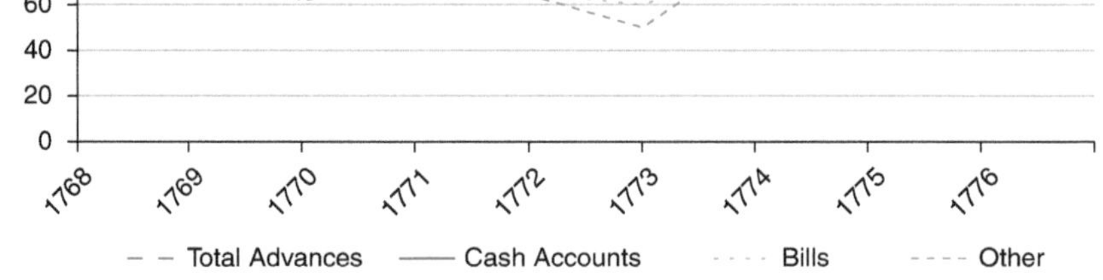

FIGURE 4.1. Total credit advances, 1768–1776. *Data sources:* Balance sheet and cash books, Lloyds Banking Group Archives; Sederunt books, Royal Bank of Scotland Group Archives; Boase, *Banking in Dundee;* Checkland, *Scottish Banking;* Munn, *Scottish Provincial Banking.*

In 1774, credit advances actually grew 10 percent, and by 1776 had surpassed their pre-crisis level.

As we can see from the graph, however, there was considerable variation among asset classes. While the banks tended to keep advances on cash accounts fairly stable, the volume of bills discounted and loans extended on heritable bonds was much more volatile. For the system as a whole, cash accounts actually grew by 3 percent in 1772, before contracting 3 percent in 1773, and expanding again in 1774 by 3 percent. Discounting of bills of exchange, on the other hand, plummeted 38 percent in 1772, and fell a further 9 percent in 1773. In 1774, however, bill discounts recovered sharply, growing 29 percent, and a further 17 percent the following year. By 1776, the volume of bill discounts had already surpassed its pre-crisis level. The pattern was similar with lending on heritable securities, which plunged by 9 percent in 1772 and 22 percent in 1773, before surging 66 percent in 1774, leaping past pre-crisis volumes. The unthawing of credit markets, moreover, seems to have been accompanied by a recovery in economic activity. After bottoming in 1773, a fifth below their pre-crisis peak, Scottish imports grew 7 percent in 1774 and 5.5 percent in 1775. Linen production, having likewise slid by 20 percent, from 1.35 million yards in 1771 to 1.07 million yards in 1773, rebounded by 6 percent in 1774 and again in 1775, and by the end of 1776 had surpassed the pre-crisis peak.

The official winding up of Douglas, Heron & Co., moreover, quickly cleared the ground for several new bank formations in the latter half of 1773 and early 1774. In October 1773, in Ayr itself, Robert, William, and James Hunter and William Wood, all merchants in Ayr, launched the banking firm Hunter & Co. with a starting capital of £10,000. The copartnery contract was highly conservative; no bills exceeding £300 were to be discounted, total bills drawn on any one person or company were not to exceed £1,000, and the bank was not to employ agents for pushing their notes into circulation.[88] In Edinburgh, Sir William Forbes and James Hunter Blair formally separated from the Coutts, forming the new firm of Forbes, Hunter & Co. Also in 1773, Donald Smith, formerly a partner in the failed private bank of Johnston, Smith & Co., used funds recently acquired through marriage to launch a new bank, Donald Smith & Co.[89] Two more banks in Edinburgh, Bertram, Gairdner & Co. and Allan, Alexander & Co., were established by the end of 1776.[90]

Meanwhile, all of the banks that survived the crisis—including the Old, Royal, and Linen Banks; the Arms, Ship, and Thistle; the Dundee, Aberdeen, and Perth Banking Companies; Mansfield, Hunter & Co.; William Cumming and Sons; Campbell, Thomson & Co.; and John Coutts & Co.—were able to resume lending and bill discounting after 1773 because, though all had been counterparties to Douglas, Heron & Co., they were possessed of easily transferable bonds secured by the estates of the Ayr Bank shareholders. These bonds could be pledged as collateral for loans or inter-bank note clearing arrangements, or held to maturity, bearing 5 percent interest per annum.

As noted earlier, given the immensely consequential role played by the question of liability in the aftermath of the June crisis, it is odd that Adam Smith did not elect to address it in his lengthy discussion of the Ayr Bank in *The Wealth of Nations.* Indeed, his only mention of the unlimited joint and several liability of the partners in Douglas, Heron & Co. was to note in passing that the enormous wealth behind the bank likely enabled it to grow so big so fast. He writes:

> The estates of the proprietors of this bank were worth several millions, and by their subscription to the original bond or contract of the bank, were really pledged for answering all its engagements. By means of the great credit which so great a pledge necessarily gave it, it was, notwithstanding its too liberal conduct, enabled to carry on business for more than two years.[91]

Regardless of whether or not Smith had, as Gherity contends, a hand in drafting the November 1763 essay in *The Scots Magazine* criticizing the solidity of the Edinburgh public banks on the grounds of their shareholders' limited liability, it must certainly have been an argument with which he was familiar, given his intimate friendships with the partners in the Arms, Ship, and Thistle.[92] It is therefore doubly puzzling that he should choose to remain silent on what was a salient aspect of Scottish banking.

With Smith having instructed two friends, Joseph Black and James Hutton, to destroy all his unpublished papers before his death, it is possible only to speculate as to his reasons for excluding any discussion of liability.[93] One potential rationale that cannot be ruled out is the quite simple possibility that reiterating the 1763 arguments about the virtues of unlimited liability might have generated considerable awkwardness for a man whose pupil and patron, the Duke of Buccleuch, now owed in excess of £15,000, who was about to be sued for an additional £4,857, and who was in the painful process of liquidating, among other assets, the Adderbury estate where Smith had been a frequent guest. Smith himself was by then receiving a lifetime pension from Buccleuch in the amount of £300 per annum.[94] And the duke, as we have seen, was hardly alone; the editor of Sir William Forbes's memoirs, Robert Chambers, even noted that "for the remainder of their lives, [Douglas, Heron & Co.'s] shareholders were never done with paying; and we have been told that their families, in some instances, did not get their accounts satisfactorily closed till some time after the passing of the Reform Act, at the distance of upwards of sixty years from the calamity!"[95]

It is important to note, though, that depositors and other creditors were made whole by the issue of the 5 percent bonds, which matured, after Parliament granted Douglas, Heron & Co. an extension, in 1786. References to ongoing liquidations and litigation beyond 1786 are to settlement *among the partners themselves,* as wealthier shareholders, who had largely funded the annuity payments and subsequent bond redemptions in the hope of preventing their less wealthy partners from being driven into bankruptcy by forced estate liquidations at fire-sale prices, sought to realize their fellow partners' liabilities. The bank's wealthiest shareholders, in other words, had recognized that their losses would be even greater if they did not deploy their substantial personal wealth as a temporary backstop.

Whatever Smith's rationale, however, the question of allocating liability in banking concerns has featured prominently in more recent finance literature. Stiglitz and Weiss demonstrate that a bank's propensity to overinvest in risky assets is exacerbated by limited liability status.[96] As Hickson and Turner elaborate, ceteris paribus, limited liability violates a fundamental principal of efficient contract design, namely, that with asymmetric information, liability should be assigned to the contract party facing the lowest cost of acquiring information. Second, ceteris paribus, liability should be assigned to the contract party that is least risk-averse.[97] Limited liability may thus be particularly inefficient in banking if knowledge of the true values of a bank's assets and liabilities is asymmetric—owners know more than note holders, depositors, and other creditors—and if bank creditors are more risk-averse than bank owners. Given that, by nature, a bank's liabilities are shorter-term and more liquid than its assets, this latter condition is likely generally satisfied.[98] One of the essential functions of a banking system, after all, is to transfer risk from parties less willing or able to bear it to parties more willing or more able to do so.

There is, furthermore, a time-inconsistency problem involved, as demonstrated by Diamond and Dybvig.[99] Unless the contractual time horizon is infinite or the rate of time discount sufficiently low, a bank will have an incentive to increase the risk profile of its assets and expand its liabilities in the next-to-last time period until the present discounted value of its liabilities is zero.[100] Assuming full rationality, by backward induction, creditors will refuse to hold the bank's liabilities from the first period. As Klein and Goodhart admit, even investment in firm-specific reputational capital may be insufficient to credibly overcome this time-inconsistency problem.[101]

Two possible solutions to the time-inconsistency problem exist. The first is for government to regulate banks so as to limit issuance of liabilities and investment in risky assets. A second solution, however, is the institution of unlimited liability on the part of bank shareholders. Provided the incentives of owners and managers can be contractually aligned, unlimited liability potentially allows banks to offer a credible commitment to depositors and note holders that they will not default. Because of this commitment, we would expect banks with unlimited shareholder liability to pay lower risk premiums on their liabilities, at the cost of higher equity premiums. In a Modigliani-Miller setting, at least, the net effect on the value of the firm could therefore in fact be negligible.

While consistent time-series data is unavailable for liability risk premiums, we can compare returns on equity for public versus private Scottish banks, the former with limited and the latter with unlimited liability. Figure 4.2 plots

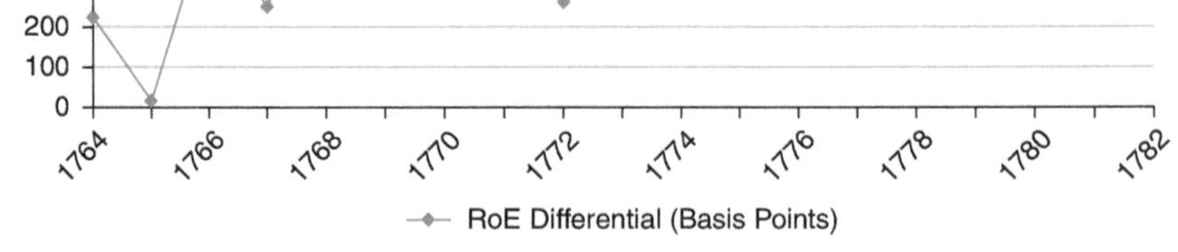

FIGURE 4.2. Excess return on equity, Dundee Banking Co. vs. Bank of Scotland, 1764–1782. *Data source:* Boase, *Banking in Dundee.*

the differential, in basis points, of the return on equity for the Dundee Banking Company relative to the Bank of Scotland. For the period from 1764 to 1782, the average return on subscribed capital for the Dundee Bank was 500 basis points higher than that of the Bank of Scotland. This premium rose especially after 1772, perhaps as the risks of unlimited liability were rendered starker by the collapse of Douglas, Heron & Co. Indeed, while for the nine years through 1772, the average return on equity for the Dundee Bank was approximately 400 basis points higher than the Old Bank's, the average post-1772 excess return was 600 basis points. Note, moreover, that post 1772 the premium does not especially rise until 1775; since Dundee Banking Company balance-sheet data is from February of each year, this means the spike was largely during 1774. A spike in the equity premium during 1774 would be consistent with the Ayr Bank bond issue underscoring the extent and inalienability of the shareholders' unlimited liability, especially as the bank did not formally cease business until August 1773, and in any event trading of bank shares had essentially ground to a halt during the uncertainty of 1772–1773. To be sure, with the Old and Dundee Banks we are hardly comparing apples to apples, but regardless the data are certainly consistent with an equity premium for unlimited liability.

A potential threat to the effectiveness of unlimited liability as a check on overissue and/or overinvestment in risky assets is that shareholder wealth may be diluted, particularly at moments of financial stress. As the value of an unlimited liability share depends upon the expected return, it will be worth less to those whose payout in the event of bankruptcy is greater. Thus, as the probability of bankruptcy increases, there will be a tendency for shares to be transferred from more to less wealthy investors, with the result that the overall wealth backing the firm's shares will decline precisely as the likelihood of failure rises.[102]

As Hickson and Turner document, however, Scottish banks developed contractual arrangements that effectively mitigated the risk of wealth dilution. First and foremost, any share transfer had to be vetted and approved by fellow copartners or, in some cases, directors to whom such responsibility had been delegated. This was to ensure that no current partner might impose negative externalities on his fellow partners by selling his share or shares to a third party of significantly lower wealth.[103] By their original contract of copartnery, Douglas, Heron & Co., for instance, required that share transfers could occur only at the twice-annual general meetings of the partners, and only by a two-thirds majority of those present. As this was later found to be exceedingly inconvenient and stringent, the contract was amended on 5 November 1770. But the transfer restrictions remained strict; transfers had to be unanimously approved by all of the directors.[104] Directors, furthermore, were typically authorized to refuse successors of deceased partners and, in the case of the Aberdeen Banking Company, could even eject, by a two-thirds vote, "Improper" partners whose personal wealth was deemed insufficient. The ousted partner then had three weeks to sell his share to an acceptable buyer.[105]

Crucially, even in the event of an approved transfer, the partner disposing of his share remained indefinitely liable for debts incurred during his ownership. For example, the contract of Douglas, Heron & Co. noted that by an approved sale "the Company hereby bind and oblige themselves to free and relieve the seller of all debts and contractions made *posterior to the actual sale* which are hereby declared to be transferred from the seller to the purchaser, to all intents and purposes whatever."[106] The Aberdeen and Dundee Banking Companies additionally stipulated that any shareholder whose share(s) was claimed by third-party creditors had three months to discharge the debt or else face expulsion from the partnership, lest his share(s) pass to a third party of unknown wealth.[107]

A second standard feature of copartnery agreements was a limitation on the maximum number of shares that could be owned by any one shareholder. This was intended primarily to prevent any one individual from gaining outsized voting power, but also had the effect of keeping shareholder liability more broadly dispersed.[108] Douglas, Heron & Co., for example, restricted shareholders to four shares, with explicit prohibition of ownership on behalf of a third-party individual or entity.[109] An additional contractual safeguard against insider opportunism was the requirement for relatively large boards of directors with frequent rotation. The Aberdeen Banking Company, with 109 partners, had 13 directors with at least 4 replaced annually.[110] Douglas, Heron & Co., with 136 partners at inception, stipulated 9 directors each at its Ayr, Edinburgh, and Dumfries branches, all chosen annually.[111] The 36-partner Dundee Banking Company had 10 directors at its founding.[112] To ensure that interests of owners and managers were properly aligned, candidates for directorship were typically required to own at least two shares.

Contracts furthermore specified strict rules on lending. The Perth United Banking Company, for instance, prohibited loans larger than £1,500. The

Dundee Banking Company mandated that at least three directors had to approve any loan.[113] The contract of Douglas, Heron & Co. stipulated that no cash accounts be granted in excess of £1,000 and further required that any cash account or bill discount be approved by a quorum of five directors.[114]

The problem, in the case of Douglas, Heron & Co., was thus not that such rules did not exist, but rather that they were consistently and brazenly flouted by the management without penalty. On this point, the conclusions of the committee of inquiry stand in direct contradiction to those of Smith. Smith claimed, in *The Wealth of Nations,* that "over and above the accidents to which they are exposed from the unskilfulness of the conductors of this paper money," banks "are liable to several others, from which no prudence or skill of those conductors can guard them."[115] In contrast, the committee of inquiry was "fully satisfied, that if those established rules of conduct had been observed, even with a moderate degree of fidelity, the Company's affairs could not have been plunged into such distress and ruin." The company's demise, it wrote, had been occasioned, not by "mere imprudence, ignorance, or speculative errors," but rather "by an open disregard, not only of the principles of the Copartnery, but of the express and positive rules and regulations laid down for the conduct of the Managers."[116]

Managers at the Ayr and Edinburgh offices, in particular, repeatedly disregarded the rules concerning the granting of cash accounts and discounting bills of exchange. Indeed, throughout 1771 at the Edinburgh office, affairs were generally conducted by just three directors, two short of the required quorum for approving such transactions. Stipulations that no single person be received as a cautioner in more than three cash accounts, and the requirement that total credits to any one borrower were not to exceed £1,000 without approval by all three offices, were similarly serially ignored.[117] Though company bylaws also prohibited more than one director at any office from simultaneously being a current member of any trading company, at Ayr that rule was violated from the start, with most of the directors, and even the cashier, being "deeply connected with, and concerned in" one or more Ayr trading companies, on whom they lavished generous credits.[118]

The flow of information from directors to the proprietors of the company, especially, appears to have been wholly inadequate for the scale and risk of transactions undertaken. Already by May 1770 the company's debts to London had escalated so rapidly that, in private correspondence, several of the directors acknowledged that "the state of the matter should be *fairly stated* to the

Proprietors at their general meeting and further aid required." No such account was subsequently made at the next general meeting, which, in the words of the committee of inquiry, constituted the "only channel of information" through which the extended proprietors were apprised as to the state of their affairs.[119] And, having "no opportunity of being informed about their affairs, from any other quarter than the report of their Directors," nor the possibility of making "any useful investigation at a general meeting," the proprietors were thus largely reduced to a rubber-stamp body.[120]

This abundant lack of managerial accountability is perhaps closely related to the changes observed subsequent to the legislative interventions of 1765 concerning bank size. A primary advantage of unlimited liability regimes is that shareholders under such arrangements, with the entirety of their personal wealth at risk, have a strong incentive to closely supervise and monitor management.[121] Their ability to do so effectively, however, was decreasing in firm size and scope. Douglas, Heron & Co., with 136 partners at founding and 226 by the time of its collapse, and a balance sheet of almost £1.3 million, was quite simply the largest bank in Scotland, eclipsing even the Edinburgh chartered banks. By subscribed capital, they were fully ten times larger than the largest pre-1765 private bank, and double even the size of the Aberdeen Banking Company, founded in 1767.[122] Moreover, Douglas, Heron & Co. was one of the first Scottish banks to engage in branch banking, which, though valuable for diversification, also involved the attendant complexity of overseeing and coordinating bill discounting, extension of cash accounts, and lending on heritable securities at three different offices. As the bank's balance sheet rapidly ballooned, directors at one office were hence frequently called upon to approve transactions at other offices about which they often had little or no direct knowledge. The partners, meanwhile, most of whom had no background whatsoever in banking, were oblivious as to the true cost, on an annualized basis, of the extensive borrowing in the London bills of exchange market to which the bank's directors had soon resorted.[123]

In Douglas, Heron & Co. we thus observe a fundamental tension between the benefits and the risks of scale. On the one hand, increased size not only implied a larger equity base but also permitted greater asset and liability diversification. Partnership contracts restricting the number of shares owned by any one individual ensured that larger banks enjoyed more diffuse ownership, with the risks of corporate insolvency thus spread over a larger and more diverse set of shareholders. This both bolstered creditor confidence, thereby lowering risk premiums on bank liabilities, and attenuated the risk of runs. Indeed, of the sixteen banks that failed in 1772, all but Douglas, Heron & Co. had fewer than six partners, while all three that failed and inflicted losses on creditors had fewer than six partners. For the entire Scottish free-banking period, Acheson, Hickson, and Turner actually find that all of the banks that failed and inflicted losses upon creditors had fewer than seven partners.[124] This strongly suggests that a crucial element in the superior stability of the Scottish financial system, relative to England's, during the free-banking period was the absence of any restrictions analogous to the latter's six-partner limit, which had been instituted to protect the Bank of England's privileged status.

On the other hand, however, Douglas, Heron & Co. seems to have passed the saddle point beyond which the benefits of a larger and broader capital base were outweighed by higher monitoring costs. While minimum share requirements certainly mitigated the risk of moral hazard on the part of elected directors, who were thereby discouraged from taking excessive risks out of confidence in the unlimited liability of fellow partners, the company's two annual general meetings were in any event clearly insufficient for effective oversight of an enterprise with three branches, a £1.3 million balance sheet, and an increasingly complex web of London liabilities.

The necessity of effective oversight, however, was perhaps especially critical when credit markets were tight, and thus the usury ceiling of 5 percent more likely to be binding. Smith, of course, while he had made no mention of usury laws in his *Lectures on Jurisprudence,* had by the time of *The Wealth of Nations* come to support a legal maximum rate of interest. "The legal rate," he argued, "although it ought to be somewhat above, ought not to be much above the lowest market rate." He did not, however, support an interest ceiling on the more commonly heard grounds of protecting borrowers from usurious lenders. Rather, his reasoning was that if the usury ceiling were "fixed so high as eight or ten per cent., the greater part of the money which was to be lent, would be lent to prodigals and projectors, who alone would be willing to give this high interest." But "sober people, who will give for the use of money no more than a part of what they are likely to make by the use of it, would not venture into competition."[125]

Here, however, Smith seems to undermine his own case. If his support for an interest-rate ceiling of 5 percent—which he felt was "perhaps as proper as any"—was to prevent the allocation of capital from being skewed toward "prodigals and projectors," then we must ask why the existence of just such a law evidently failed to restrain the "chimerical projectors" in Scotland whose projects, he claimed, had been the ruin of the bankers engaged in financing them?[126] Smith himself even noted that "this bank [Douglas, Heron & Co.], therefore, had, in little more than the course of two years, advanced to different people upward of eight hundred thousand pounds *at five per cent*"; in other words, at no more than the legal rate.[127]

Available lending data supports Smith's observation that the usury ceiling was in fact partially binding, at least on loans.[128] While bank-level interest-rate data are unfortunately not consistently available for the period under consideration, we can gain some sense of the distribution of interest rates by tallying quoted rates in Scottish newspapers, as shown in Figure 4.3. For the period from 1750 to 1780, we see four large spikes in the share of all listed rates quoted at 5 percent—1756, 1763, 1769, and 1772. The first two years, recall, coincided with severe wartime balance of payments crises. The tightness of 1769 accords with Smith's observation of a great demand for credit in Scotland at that time, which gave rise, in his words, to "great clamor and distress" that the establishment of Douglas, Heron & Co. in that year was "for the express purpose of relieving."[129] Seventeen seventy-two, of course, was then the year of the crisis. For the entire thirty-year period, the average share of interest rates quoted at 5 percent was 32 percent, only rising above 40 percent in

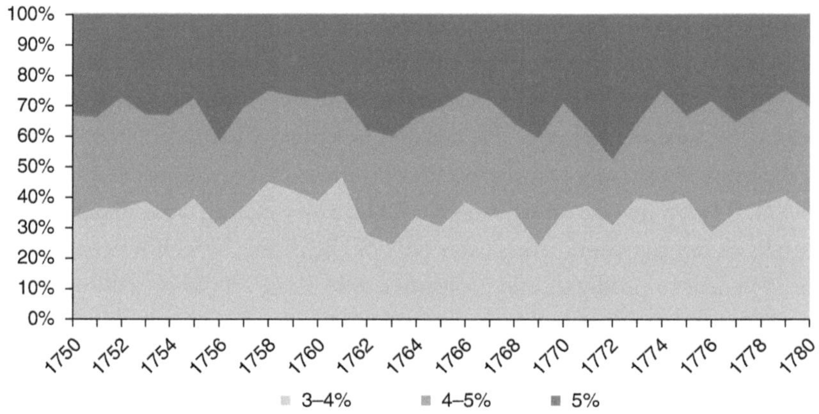

FIGURE 4.3. Quoted Scottish interest rates, 1750–1780. Totals are summed from available years of *The Scots Magazine, Edinburgh Evening Courant, Edinburgh Advertiser, Caledonian Mercury, Aberdeen Journal,* and *Glasgow Journal.*

each of the four years cited above. For the four calendar years of Douglas, Heron & Co.'s life, fully 39 percent of all quoted rates were at the legal maximum, with an average rate of 4.1 percent, implying either a very tight distribution or else a severely truncated distribution, consistent with a binding interest ceiling.

The reason this question is of importance is that in the absence of an effective price mechanism alternative rationing mechanisms are required. In the market for credit, one such mechanism is the practice of insider lending, and it appears to have been rampant at Douglas, Heron & Co. While Lamoreaux has demonstrated that insider lending can mitigate the problem of asymmetric information by clarifying the enterprises with which particular banks were especially involved, in the case of Douglas, Heron & Co. both the nature and the extent of insider lending was wholly unknown to the majority of the company's shareholders.[130] At the time of failure, fully £400,000 of £694,175 in loans at the Ayr, Dumfries, and Edinburgh branches were to the directors themselves and a handful of other partners.[131] Though credit advances made to partners in Scottish banks were by no means uncommon practice, in the instance of Douglas, Heron & Co. such loans, as we have seen, were often extended either without security or on the security of subsequently dishonored bills. And while credits to trading enterprises in which specific partners were involved were allowed under the copartnery agreement, such loans could not be authorized by the interested partners themselves, who, as already noted, were explicitly barred from directorship so long as they were simultaneously commercially involved. More troubling still was the fact that many of the complicit directors acted as cosignatories for one another.[132]

In the conclusion of the committee of inquiry, the extent of insider lending thus "threw such large sums into the hands of a *few* individuals, that the Company-funds became altogether inaccessible to a very great amount, and were entirely withdrawn from the command of the Company." Instead, "had the credits, in conformity to our *social motto,* been more impartially and more generally diffused, *pro bono publico,* the consequences of an excessive credit could not have been so calamitous; the resources would have been more numerous; and our funds more at command."[133] The allocation of credit by insider lending, in other words, severely compromised the dispersion of risk in Douglas, Heron & Co.'s lending portfolio and concentrated the firm's assets in the very "chimerical projectors" that Smith thought a reasonable usury ceiling would exclude, thereby also elevating the firm's overall level of risk.

Of course, banks seek to maximize expected returns while minimizing variance, which means that in the presence of a binding interest-rate ceiling they are unlikely to *willingly* assume additional risk uncompensated by commensurately higher returns. At a well-managed bank, insider lending may in fact even reduce portfolio risk by partially resolving informational asymmetries, which is perhaps why we do not observe insider lending as having constituted a significant problem at other Scottish banks. At a bank as poorly managed and supervised as Douglas, Heron & Co., however, the increased allocation of credit by non-price mechanisms was clearly a poor method for rationing credit and managing risk.

Perhaps more critically, though, in the midst of a liquidity crisis, the usury limit appears to have limited the ability of Scottish banks to attract or retain deposits through higher rates, or to offer adequate compensation for delayed or suspended payment. In both 1763 and 1772, for instance, even the Edinburgh chartered banks raised deposit rates to the legal limit, which suggests that the smaller private banks were likely even more constrained by a binding ceiling.[134] Every optional clause printed before prohibition, meanwhile, bore compensatory interest of 5 percent, the same rate offered as compensation on suspended payments in 1772. In the tight credit environments of 1762–1764 and 1769–1772, this may have constituted inadequate recompense for maturity transformation, a point Sir James Steuart had made earlier in his marginal comments to Ingram's draft memorial. "The value of cash," he wrote there,

> is in proportion to the use that can be made of it. Could cash therefore produce no more any where than five per cent, when lent out or employed, the bank notes bearing five p. cent, would be equally valuable as cash; but if cash sent to London shall produce more than five p. cent., then the Banks of Scotland, on refusing payment for six months, ought, in justice to the holders of these notes, to allow an interest on them equivalent to the profit which they might make on the cash were it payed to them.[135]

The inability to pay market rates on marked notes, before 1765, or suspended notes, in 1772, may therefore have intensified the incentive to be first in line for redemption demands, with consequent effects of contagion.

PERHAPS THE CRUCIAL LESSON to be learned from the crisis of 1772, however, is that the cost of the misbegotten investments of Smith's "chimerical projectors" was ultimately borne primarily by the projectors themselves. Moreover, it was precisely the "bailing in" of these projectors that eventually arrested the crisis and facilitated a recovery in Scottish credit markets. The unlimitedly liable shareholders in Douglas, Heron & Co., once the initially ambiguous extent of their liability was clarified, constituted a highly credible lender of last resort; in particular, the £500,000 bond issue, secured by £3,000,000 in mortgages to the partners' personal estates, allowed the firm to satisfy creditors while the company's assets, and those of its shareholders, were gradually liquidated.

The tendency for financial institutions to overissue liabilities and overinvest in risky assets is the fundamental time-inconsistency problem that lies at the heart of banking. To this problem, Smith, it seems, chose the trivial solution—public regulation of bankers. It is possible that the alternative solution of rendering shareholders unlimitedly liable seemed to him less persuasive in the wake of Douglas, Heron & Co.'s spectacular collapse, or in any event less diplomatic, given the immense financial losses suffered by his own friends and benefactors. But closer inspection of the firm's demise reveals that the principal advantage of unlimited liability—namely, a strong incentive for owners to effectively monitor management—was critically undermined by the bank's size and the insufficient flow of information to shareholders. From this perspective, both the regulations of 1765, which Smith promoted, and the prevailing usury ceiling, which he supported, far from mitigating banking excess, probably exacerbated it.

The interaction effects of usury restrictions with the legislation of 1765 on bank size and insider lending, in particular, illustrates that the regulator's challenge lies, not in conceiving well-intentioned legal restraints on financial activity, but rather in correctly foreseeing the second-, third-, and fourth-order effects of those restraints, and discerning whether the imposition of a binding constraint on one margin might prompt adverse responses along other margins. On this account, history generally, and the history of the Ayr Bank crisis specifically, are perhaps especially valuable subjects of investigation, as they permit a more precise identification of causal links than it is possible to find in contemporary contexts.

5

Upon Daedalian Wings

RECALL THAT, when relating the unfolding crisis of June 1772 to Smith, Hume asked whether "these Events any-wise affect your Theory? Or will it occasion the Revisal of any Chapters?" Hume himself considered the late events as, in any case, "Food for your Speculation."[1] We can really only speculate ourselves as to whether Smith's thinking was, in fact, "any-wise" affected.

Smith's discussions of banks and banking are, in many respects, complicated and not always entirely harmonious. Just six years before the collapse of the Ayr Bank, he had lectured that "The ruin of a bank would not be so dangerous as is commonly imagined." Inviting students to "suppose all the money in Scotland was issued by one bank and that it became bankrupt," he argued that "a very few individuals would be ruined by it, but not many, because the quantity of cash or paper that people have in their hands bears no proportion to their wealth. Neither would the wealth of the whole country be much hurt by it, because the 100 part of the riches of a country does not consist in money."[2]

In the aftermath of the Ayr Bank crisis, it seems, Smith was compelled to modify this statement, stressing the importance of size and competition. "The late multiplication of banking companies," he suggested in *The Wealth of Nations,* "instead of diminishing, increases the security of the public." It not only "obliges all of them to be more circumspect in their conduct," but also "restrains the circulation of each particular company within a narrower circle." By thus "dividing the whole circulation into a greater number of parts," he concluded, "the failure of any one company, an accident which, in the course of things, must sometimes happen, becomes of less consequence to the public."[3]

In this sense, banking was no different from any other branch of trade or division of labor, rendered always more "advantageous to the public" by "freer and more general" competition.

To be sure, his conclusion certainly resonates with the circumstances of June 1772. What made the crisis so disruptive, after all, was not so much the failure of many marginal "beggarly bankers," but the failure of one massive bank in particular. It is thus curious that rather than investigating how one financial institution came to be so large that its ruin was indeed of very considerable "consequence to the public," Smith instead seems to have embarked upon an apparent contradiction. On the one hand, his model of a monetary economy is a self-equilibrating one: any bank attempting to circulate paper "over and above what the circulation can easily absorb and employ" shortly discovers that excess liabilities "return upon it almost as fast as they are issued." At the macro-level, too, he argued that "should the circulating paper at any time exceed" what the circulation of the country could absorb and employ, "as the excess could neither be sent abroad nor be employed in the circulation of the country, it must immediately return upon the banks to be exchanged for gold and silver."[4] But, on the other hand, he then contended that the paper money supplied by Scotland's banks seemed somehow to have exceeded, in the early 1760s and again in the run-up to June 1772, "What the circulation of the country could easily absorb and employ."

How does Smith reconcile this apparent contradiction between the automatic, self-equilibrating nature of his model and the evident disequilibrium of his empirical claims? He squares this circle by indicting the extensive practice of drawing on London, or what he called "raising money by circulation." As elaborated by Checkland, Smith's account summarily proceeds as follows. During the Seven Years' War, "When the high profits of trade afforded a great temptation to overtrading," Scottish traders and "projectors," encountering increasing caution from Scotland's banks, resorted to the expedient of drawing and redrawing bills of exchange on London correspondents. As Smith describes the process,

> The trader A in Edinburgh, we shall suppose, draws a bill upon B in London, payable two months after date. In reality B in London owes nothing to A in Edinburgh; but he agrees to accept of A's bill, upon condition that before the term of payment he shall redraw upon A in Edinburgh for the same sum, together with the interest and a commission, another bill, payable likewise two months after date.

This process, Smith noted, could continue for several years, with "the bill always returning upon A in Edinburgh" as A draws a new bill on B in payment of B's redrawn bill, along with accumulated interest and commission on all former bills.[5]

Scotland's banks were thereby, "Not only without their knowledge or deliberate consent, but for some time, perhaps, without their having the most distant suspicion," drawn into this circle by advancing banknotes upon such "circulating" bills. As Smith observed, "When two people, who are continually drawing and redrawing upon one another, discount their bills always with the same banker," that banker must "immediately discover what they are about." But discovery "is not altogether so easy when they discount their bills sometimes with one banker, and sometimes with another, and when the same two persons do not constantly draw and redraw upon one another but occasionally run the round of a great circle of projectors." Indeed, Smith thought, it may be "as difficult as possible," under such circumstances, for the banker to "distinguish between a real and fictitious bill of exchange," or between "a bill drawn by a real creditor upon a real debtor, and a bill for which there was properly no real creditor but the bank which discounted it."[6] As Scottish banks gradually grew wise to the extent of their exposure to this highly risky trade, they prudently moved to curtail credit, which only "enraged in the highest degree those projectors" demanding more credit.

It was, Smith concluded, "In the midst of this clamor and distress," that a new bank, Douglas, Heron & Co. (though he never mentions the bank by name), was established in Scotland for the express purpose of relieving the distress of the country.[7] While Smith attempted to exculpate the firm's founders (including, presumably the Duke of Buccleuch), by noting that "the *design* was generous; but the *execution* was imprudent," he argued that the bank was to prove itself "more liberal than any other had ever been," making "scarce any distinction between real and circulating bills."[8] Upon such bills, as well as upon the exceedingly generous provision of cash accounts, Douglas, Heron & Co. would thus advance upward of £1.3 million in credit, which, being "over and above what the circulation of the country could easily absorb and employ," meant the company's notes returned quickly upon it, necessitating recourse to the expensive method of the bank itself drawing heavily upon London. At the time of its collapse, on top of a £220,000 note issue, the bank had accordingly been compelled to draw some £600,000 in bills on London correspondents, including, most notably, Alexander Fordyce's firm of Neale,

James, Fordyce and Down.[9] In Smith's estimation, then, "The operations of this bank increased the real distress of the country which it meant to relieve," by in essence enabling "chimerical projectors" to dig themselves ever deeper into debt, such that when the inevitable collapse arrived, "it fell so much heavier upon them and upon their creditors."[10]

While Smith's story certainly accords with the general topology of Scottish financial history from the early 1760s through the crisis of 1772, it does not accord, entirely, with his proposed remedies, nor does it correctly identify the underlying macroeconomic causes of strain on the Scottish financial system. To be sure, his advocacy of the "real bills" doctrine follows logically his indictment of the "ruinous" practice of raising funds by drawing and redrawing financial bills of exchange. Had Douglas, Heron & Co., and every other Scottish bank for that matter, adhered to the principle of discounting only "a real bill of exchange drawn by a real creditor upon a real debtor, and which, as soon as it becomes due, is really paid by that debtor," then they might, perhaps, have avoided allowing themselves to be unwittingly dragged into speculative long-term capital investments.[11] But application of the real bills doctrine is merely an exercise in treating a symptom, the underlying condition being overheated investment demand, and is, in any event, somewhat easier said than done. Meanwhile, Smith's support for a legal usury limit, though intended to exclude "prodigals and projectors" from access to credit, instead intensified the substitution of non-price mechanisms of rationing credit in the form of insider lending. And if the problem was, in fact, "Overtrading by some bold projectors," then his advocacy of bans on small notes and optional clauses in order to prevent the entrance of "beggarly bankers" is largely a non sequitur.

Ultimately, in contrast to Smith, the evidence presented here indicates that the fundamental issue was that Scotland's was a rapidly emerging economy with a fixed exchange rate, large external debt, and a chronic current account deficit balanced by large but often highly volatile capital inflows. In particular, in 1756 and 1762–1763, large capital outflows due to exogenous political events exerted immense pressure on a financial system constrained by a fixed exchange rate. The result was a massive excess supply of Scottish bills, as importers scrambling to acquire bills on London in order to render payment were joined by investors attempting to remit capital for speculation in the East India Company, the Bank of England, and British government securities. Wartime excise tax hikes in 1760 only further intensified the drain of specie and demand for bills on London. As the London exchanges soared 35 percent through 1762, Scottish bills slid from 2 percent under par with London, to 4.5 percent and even 5 percent discount.[12] The Scottish banks, and in particular the chartered banks in Edinburgh, bore the brunt of this imbalance, as interest arbitrageurs were able to sell bills on London at high premiums for Scottish banknotes, which they then immediately dumped on the public banks for redemption in specie. The public banks, without recourse to higher deposit rates owing to a binding usury ceiling, therefore attempted to grind out a real exchange rate depreciation by curtailing credit. But for an economy already short on circulating media owing to speculative remittances of specie, the consequent cash crunch invited numerous small-scale note issuers—Smith's "beggarly bankers"—to plug the gap, which only exacerbated the challenge for the Edinburgh public banks.

Hence, with deposit rates already at the legal maximum, the chartered banks finally capitulated by discriminately imposing capital controls, in the form of highly selective exercise of the optional clause. Temporary capital controls between 1762 and 1764 appear, then, to have allowed for the underlying macro-imbalances to work themselves out without a painful contraction of the money supply and accompanying deflation. After tumbling 30 percent in 1762 and 35 percent in 1763, net exports surged by 90 percent in 1764 as the depreciation of Scottish bills delivered a tremendous fillip to Scottish exporters while at the same time dampening imports.[13] By the end of 1764, total exports were already 7 percent above their pre-crisis peak in 1761.[14] The Scottish financial system was therefore able to weather the shocks of 1756 and 1763 in large part because the application of temporary capital controls allowed time for the current account deficit to sort itself out through nominal adjustments in the bills of exchange market. Meanwhile, financial arbitrage, though wrenching for Scotland's larger banks, nonetheless attenuated the exchange imbalance as speculators rushed to sell bills on London drawing posts.

But, from the perspective of the Bank of Scotland, Royal Bank of Scotland, and several of the larger provincial banking companies, the issuance of notes by Smith's beggarly bankers had complicated their efforts to impose order on a difficult macroeconomic situation through credit contraction and defense of the exchange rate, and had certainly cost them dearly in the short run by intensifying the external drain of reserves. Their application, in 1764, for legislative intervention by Parliament to raise barriers to entry in Scottish banking was thus not purely an exercise in rent seeking—though there were certainly anticompetitive motivations—but also a reasoned attempt to impose centralized control over the highly decentralized Scottish monetary system during a period of highly volatile international capital flows. The end result, however, was that the Bank Act of 1765 did nothing to resolve the fundamental problem that Scotland's rapidly developing economy was vulnerable to large, speculative capital flows, while at the same time it undermined some of the strengths that had previously enabled the Scottish banking system to absorb such volatility. In other words, in the wake of 1765, you still had an unresolved perennial balance of payments problem, but now with the additional problem of bigger, more systemically important financial institutions. Thus, when a major financial shock hit in 1772, the flexibility and resilience that the system had exhibited in 1756 and 1763 were substantially diminished.

Available statistical evidence underscores the point that, especially after the failed Jacobite uprising of 1745, Scotland's economy experienced rapid economic development and growth, accelerated by wartime demand during the Seven Years' War. Figure 5.1 plots the quantity and value of linen goods manufactured in Scotland from 1728 through 1780. After remaining roughly flat from 1730 to 1745, from 1745 until the end of the war in 1763, Scottish linen manufactures surged 124 percent in quantity terms and 146 percent in value terms. In the subsequent eight years leading up to the crisis of 1772, they grew a further 9 percent and 12 percent, respectively. The tobacco reexport trade, similarly, was booming, as shown in Figure 5.2. In the decade preceding the 1772 crisis, Scottish tobacco imports grew a staggering 105 percent, with fully

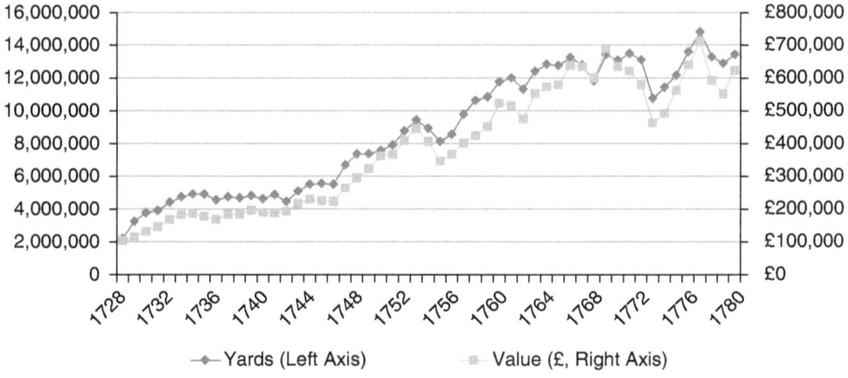

FIGURE 5.1. Quantity and value of linen goods stamped in Scotland, 1728–1780. *Data source:* Warden, *The Linen Trade, Ancient and Modern*, 480.

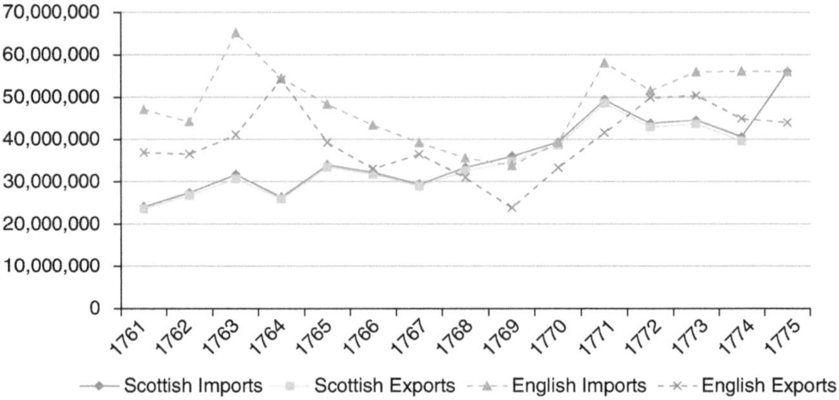

FIGURE 5.2. Tobacco imports and exports (lbs.), 1761–1775. *Data source:* Macpherson, *Annals of Commerce,* 583.

98 percent of all imports sold on for reexport. During the same period, English tobacco imports grew just 23 percent, with only 80 percent of English imports subsequently reexported. From 1755, the first year for which aggregate data are available, through 1771, overall Scottish exports grew 72 percent, and imports 67 percent.[15] The total tonnage of oceangoing vessels passing through Scottish ports rose from 54,407 in 1759 to 109,895 tons in 1771, and for coastal vessels from 150,995 to 257,494.[16]

Supporting this surging international trade required large-scale investment in transport infrastructure. In 1762, a comprehensive survey of the Forth and Clyde was completed, with a capital subscription being opened in 1767 for construction of the Forth and Clyde Canal. This was followed in 1770 by a subscription for the Monkland Canal project linking Glasgow to the coalfields of Coatbridge. Extensive road building in the highlands likewise accelerated after 1745, while the Convention of Royal Burghs was simultaneously overseeing construction of harbors and bridges across the country.[17] The city of Edinburgh drained the North Loch and commissioned a bridge linking the old and planned new towns, with the foundation stone for New Town being laid on 26 October 1767.[18]

Manufacturing and agriculture, too, were booming. In addition to the burgeoning linen industry, sugar refining, rope and sailcloth manufacture, tanning, soap production, and fisheries all experienced rapid growth.[19] Iron manufacturing received a substantial boost in 1759 from the establishment of the Carron Company, with a subscribed capital of £12,000, which had grown to £130,000 on the eve of the crisis. Indeed, by 1771 the Carron Company had become Scotland's largest industrial concern, employing nearly 10,000 workers.[20] During the same time, coal output increased from 900,000 tons in 1755 to 1.3 million tons in 1771.[21]

Agriculture, meanwhile, was experiencing rapid change as landowners rushed to improve their estates on account of growing import demand from England. Smith in fact observed that "the Union opened the market of England to the Highland cattle," such that "their ordinary price is at present about three times greater than at the beginning of the century, and the rents of many Highland estates have been tripled and quadrupled in the same time."[22] Increased integration after the failure of the Jacobite uprising of 1745, coupled with high wartime demand during the 1750s and early 1760s, further lifted rents. Responding to this demand required the purchase not only of additional stock but also fencing, which, in areas where stone was scarce, constituted a major expense. Furthermore, larger herds stimulated the cultivation of new land for growing fodder, which often involved the construction of costly dikes, draining fens, and more intensive use of fertilizer.[23]

The transformation from just a half-century before was staggering. As one early Scottish economic historian put it, at the turn of the eighteenth century, "The different parts of the country were separated from each other by tracts of uninhabited waste, across which it was dangerous to travel, alike from the terrors of robbers as from the inclemency of the seasons." Roads, he recounted, "were present merely as tracks worn deeply into the soil by centuries of traffic, along which strings of packhorses crept from town to town twice or thrice in the year, forming the only general means of conveyance open to the public."[24]

The bottom line, however, is that all this development was highly capital-intensive. Smith himself estimated that "the ordinary profits of stock in the greater part of mercantile projects" in Scotland ran "between six and ten per cent."[25] The sums involved, moreover, vastly exceeded what could be provided by the relatively poor, undercapitalized Scottish economy, which is why subscriptions repeatedly had to enlist considerable English direct investment, while bills drawn on London were continuously relied upon for working capital.[26] Scottish banks were thus crucial links in short-term financing by advancing credit through bill discounts and cash accounts (which they invented), thereby allowing merchants and industrialists to effectively liquidize assets otherwise temporarily frozen in accounts receivable, inventory, or fixed capital, as well as to pay factors. Smith even cited, though he did not necessarily assent to, claims "that the trade of the city of Glasgow doubled in about fifteen years after the first erection of the banks there; and that the trade of Scotland has more than quadrupled since the first erection of the two public banks at Edinburgh."[27] The British Linen Company, the "Linen Bank," founded in 1746, had at first not even been established as a bank, but quickly concentrated on the lucrative trade of providing cash and credit to the numerous factors involved in spinning, weaving, and bleaching the country's burgeoning linen products.

The extent of external financing requirements suggests it should thus not be surprising that Scotland experienced acute balance of payments crises in 1756 and 1763; we are, after all, talking about a small, open economy, with substantial inward capital investment, external debt, and a fixed exchange rate, during a period of extreme international political and economic instability. What should be surprising is that the nascent Scottish financial system was able to absorb such exogenous shocks without disruptive bank failures or general suspensions of payment, and while largely insulating the real economy from the full effects of external reserve drains.

The new problem, after 1765, was thus twofold. First, as demonstrated in Chapter 3, optional clause and small-notes prohibition resulted in fewer and larger banks, and banks that had to withhold much more capital in the form of idle reserves, as the loss of the optional clause had removed a key deterrent to hostile note raids, while at the same time the small-notes ban meant lumpier average redemptions. The consequent credit crunch, which Smith observed had "enraged" the country's projectors, who blamed the "distress of the country" on the "ignorance, pusillanimity, and bad conduct of the banks, which did not give a sufficiently liberal aid to the spirited undertakings," thus generated a vacuum which only a financial institution of adequate scale, such as Douglas, Heron & Co., could fill. Indeed, as shown in Figure 4.3, Scottish interest rates appear to have spiked in 1769, the year Douglas, Heron & Co. was established. In other words, then, the credit environment created by the 1765 legislation begged the establishment of a financial institution sufficiently large enough to operate within the new regulatory framework.

But, second, the regulatory changes of 1765 also increased the likelihood that future financial shocks would be more disruptive. Higher capital costs compelled banks to raise the risk profile of their assets to maintain margins while at the same time increasingly substituting rival bank paper for gold and silver reserves, thereby significantly elevating the level of counterparty risk on their balance sheets, especially given the outsized presence of one counterparty in particular—namely, Douglas, Heron & Co. The scale of Douglas, Heron & Co.'s operations was in fact so large that after earlier rebuffing them, even the Edinburgh chartered banks in 1771 had no choice but to begin accepting Ayr Bank notes.[28] Furthermore, while the only evidence of option ever actually being invoked was against large-scale speculators in bills of exchange during the ongoing balance of payments crisis of 1762–1764, the pattern of payment suspensions in 1772 suggests that prohibition of contingent liability notes substantially raised the probability that portfolio losses would be transmitted to depositors and note holders through disorderly bank runs, closures, and institutional liquidation. In addition, there were considerable adverse interaction effects between size, credit market conditions, and usury laws that the regulatory changes of 1765 activated. Specifically, increased scale seems to have weakened the effectiveness of shareholder oversight at Scotland's largest banks, while the combination of tight credit with a partially binding official interest-rate ceiling—which Smith enthusiastically supported—exacerbated the problem of risky insider lending.

Curiously, however, on one essential feature of Scottish banking that ultimately stabilized the aftershocks of June 1772—the unlimited liability of the shareholders in Douglas, Heron & Co.—Smith was surprisingly mum. But whatever his reasons for silence on this topic, I find that, in the absence of a formal lender of last resort, the unlimited liability of the partners in Douglas, Heron & Co. in effect served that role through the issuance of bonds, backed by mortgages to the proprietors' own personal estates, which allowed the defunct bank to gradually work off its toxic assets and satisfy creditors while the company's assets, and those of its partners, were slowly liquidated. The problem in 1772 was largely that Douglas, Heron & Co. initially sent mixed messages to the public concerning the liability of their partners, such that for some time there was considerable confusion as to whether they were, in fact, unlimitedly liable to the full extent of their personal wealth. Even after that question was clarified in the affirmative, the extent of the firm's debts was such that fully unfreezing Scottish credit markets necessitated the creation of a more liquid market for securities backed by the proprietors' estates, which first required (due to the strictures of the Bubble Act) an act of Parliament expressly authorizing the bankrupt firm to issue tradable bonds. Thereafter, however, the rapid recovery in Scottish credit markets and economic activity challenges the conclusion of Reinhart and Rogoff that deep financial crises, especially those coupled with burst real-estate bubbles, necessarily entail long, slow economic recoveries.[29] Unlimited joint and several liability on the part of Douglas, Heron & Co.'s proprietors mitigated concerns of counterparty risk in the Scottish financial system, and therefore facilitated a rapid recovery in the flow of credit within three years of the crisis.

Concluding his discussion of the Ayr Bank, Smith employs a striking visual metaphor to elucidate his conception of money and banking. Gold and silver money, he explains, are like a highway that, though it "carries to market all the grass and corn of the country, produces itself not a single pile of either." The "judicious operations of banking," he therefore continues, "by providing, if I may be allowed so violent a metaphor, a sort of wagon-way through the air, enable the country to convert, as it were, a great part of its highways into good pastures and corn-fields, and thereby to increase very considerably the annual produce of its land and labour." But the metaphor also includes a warning, as Smith adds that "the commerce and industry of the country, . . . though they may be somewhat augmented, cannot be altogether so secure when they are thus, as it were, suspended upon the Daedalian wings of paper money as when they travel about upon the solid ground of gold and silver."[30]

Rockoff has traced the evolution of the metaphor of the suspended highway in Smith's writings, observing, astutely, that it first appeared in an April 1763 draft of *The Wealth of Nations,* but *without* mention of Daedalian wings.[31] There, Smith writes that "banks enable us, as it were, to plough up our high roads, by affording us a sort of communication through the air by which we do our business equally well." (Figure 5.3 shows an Ayr banknote.) He goes on to argue that, in consequence, "to confine them by monopolies or any other restraints, except such as are necessary to prevent frauds and abuses, must obstruct the progress of public opulence."[32] Similarly, in a lecture he gave on 8 April 1763, Smith again used the metaphor of the elevated highway—again without Daedalian wings. "The high roads," he declares, "may in one sense be said to bear more grass and corn than any other ground of equall bulk, as by facilitating carriage they cause all the other ground to be more improved and encourage cultivation, by which means a greater quantity of corn and grass is producd. But of themselves they produce nothing . . . . Paper money is an expedient of this sort."[33] Three years later, in 1766, he once again repeated the metaphor, noting that money "may be compared to the high roads of a country, which bear neither corn nor grass themselves but circulate all the corn and

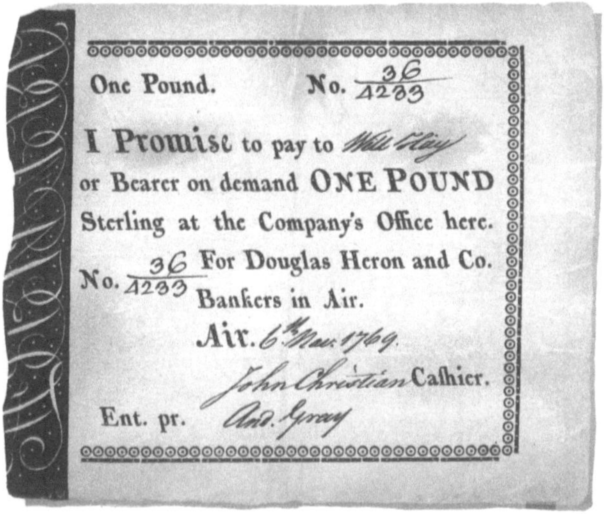

FIGURE 5.3. An Ayr banknote. Graham, *One Pound Note,* 86.

grass in the country. If we could find any way to save the ground taken up by highways, we would increase considerably the quantity of commodities and have more to carry to the market."[34] Still no Daedalus.

The absence of the Daedalian reference in Smith's earlier uses of the suspended highway analogy is, perhaps, revealing. In Ovid's *Metamorphoses,* of course, Daedalus crafts wings held together by wax and thus warns his son, Icarus, not to fly too high lest the sun melt the wax. But Icarus, forgetting his father's counsel, does soar too high, the sun softens the wax, and he falls into the sea and drowns. Rothschild has already noted that Ovid's *Metamorphoses,* of which Smith owned a copy, was a possible source of Smith's "invisible hand" metaphor (Caeneus, at Troy, "Twisted and plied his invisible hand, inflicting wound within wound").[35] It hardly requires a stretch of the imagination to suppose that, in the aftermath of the fall of the "Air Bank," Smith would find the Daedalian reference an appropriate one; paper money, though it may provide an efficient "wagon-way through the air," ought not suspend those roads too high, lest the sun singe the paper wings holding them aloft.

However, so far as I can find, the most compelling candidate for Smith's Daedalian inspiration is none other than Jonathan Swift, who in 1721 had explicitly used the myth of Daedalus to describe the infamous South Sea Bubble. In *The Bubble: A Poem,* Swift wrote:

On *Paper* Wings he takes his Flight,
With *Wax* the *Father* bound them fast;
The *Wax* is melted by the Height,
And down the tow'ring Boy is cast.

A Moralist might here explain
The Rashness of the *Cretan* youth;
Describe his Fall into the Main,
And from a Fable form a Truth.

His *Wings* are his *Paternal Rent,*
He melts his *Wax* at ev'ry Flame;
His Credit sunk, his Money spent,
In Southern Seas *he leaves his Name.*[36]

Smith often expressed great admiration for Swift, particularly for his "plain style," irony, and precision and clarity of expression.[37] The somewhat pejorative sense in which Smith uses the term "projectors" even closely resembles their rather uncomplimentary portrayal in *Gulliver's Travels.*[38] To find a suitably expressive metaphor for the ruin of 1772, it is thus entirely plausible that Smith reached for the work of one of his favorite writers commenting on the foremost financial crisis of his own time.

In any case, though colorful, it is not an altogether instructive metaphor. Certainly, in the trivial sense, it could be said that Scottish projectors, imprudently financed by paper money of the "Air Bank," flew too close to the sun, as it were, and were consequently burned. But it says nothing about why we should care. After all, as Smith himself concluded in the same 1766 lecture in which he again invoked the metaphor of the suspended highways, "The ruin of a bank would not be so dangerous as is commonly imagined." We have seen that the collapse of the prominent banking house of Adam and Thomas Fairholme in 1764 had only minor consequences for the Scottish financial system and wider economy. In *The Wealth of Nations,* Smith cryptically suggests that "over and above the accidents to which they are exposed from the unskilfulness of the conductors of this paper money, they are liable to several others, from which no prudence or skill of those conductors can guard them."[39] But the only example of such extraordinary accidents he then provides is the exceptional instance of "an unsuccessful war . . . in which the enemy got possession of the capital," as happened in Scotland during the Jacobite uprising of

1745; an event that in actuality caused little disruption to Scottish financial markets.

The resort to metaphors of Daedalian wings and unspecified highway accidents was thus, at the end of the day, inadequate, for it left entirely unexplained why overly bold projectors or the disruptions of war did not similarly upend Scottish credit markets and the Scottish economy in 1762–1764, 1756, or, for that matter, 1745. But the explanation was, in fact, right under Smith's nose. In 1764, the "ruin of a bank" did not entail the ruin of the country precisely because no single bank was of such systemic importance that its failure constituted an existential threat to the operation of Scottish credit markets, let alone the wider economy; and Scottish banks, in any event, had at their disposal contractual mechanisms for attenuating such unexpected shocks. The same stabilizing features no longer held, or at least no longer held to the same extent, in the wake of the regulatory regime change of 1765.

As I noted in Chapter 1, an important rationale for studying the Scottish experience of "free banking" is not that it provides a model for current financial reform, nor even that it reveals unambiguous "lessons" for contemporary finance and financial regulation. Rather, it is informative because the relatively unregulated nature of eighteenth-century Scottish banking allows us to more clearly identify, or at the very least think through, the potential implications of particular types of regulatory change and institutional arrangements in financial markets. There are thus, I would argue, five issues to which the Scottish experience of free banking, especially in the context of the financial crisis of 1772 and with contemporary financial crises in mind, should direct our attention.

First and foremost, the collapse of the Ayr Bank invites a more nuanced consideration of the problems of regulatory and intellectual capture. To be sure, the regulatory changes of 1765 in Scotland were the outcome of intense political lobbying by the largest, most established Scottish banks, and were deliberately intended to raise barriers to entry and lower competition in the Scottish banking sector. But the Bank Act of 1765 was not simply an exercise in effective rent seeking; it was also an authentic attempt by Scotland's largest banks to impose order on a highly difficult and poorly understood macroeconomic situation, an effort that, from their perspectives, was complicated by unrestricted entry of smaller banks and notes issuers. In the grip of a postwar balance of payments crisis, there was a strong sentiment among many, including Smith's Glaswegian banking friends, that *something* needed to be done. But with genuine confusion as to the true sources of Scotland's macroeconomic challenges, the impulse to regulate was almost bound to result in misdiagnosis or, in the case of the optional clause, introduction by the country's largest banks of a regulatory red herring that would simultaneously deliver the desired result of raising rivals' costs.

Unfortunately, not only did the resulting legislation misdiagnose the underlying macro-imbalances as instead a problem of unrestrained and unregulated entry, it also failed to anticipate the adverse second- and third-order effects of regulatory intervention, effects that, as we have seen, layered new problems of systemic risk and financial inflexibility onto a still unresolved chronic balance of payments issue. Indeed, each of the major legal restrictions imposed on Scottish banking—the ban on small notes, prohibition of banknote optional clauses, and already existing usury laws—generated both adverse main effects and equally destabilizing interaction effects. Attempts to regulate specific categories of financial activity can therefore generate not simply offsetting changes in bank behavior, but changes that interact in often unpredictable ways with existing institutions, as well as with unanticipated changes in economic circumstances.

On an adjacent front, Steuart and Smith's support for counterproductive regulatory interventions, and the extreme caution with which the latter approached questions relating to the liability of his patron and pupil, the Duke of Buccleuch, suggest that the problem of intellectual capture, too, ought not to be conceived in the simplistic sense of the hired academic gun. Rather, they speak to the reality that ideas are shaped in social contexts and are informed by social interactions. First, as highlighted in Chapter 3, many of Smith's closest friends and acquaintances were not just bankers, but bankers at Glasgow and Edinburgh's largest banks. His perception, therefore, of the challenges confronting the Scottish financial system was not, and could not be, independent of theirs. The consequences ought to further remind us of the risks of rushing to conceive regulation *in the middle of* an ongoing financial crisis and *before* the causes of that crisis are sufficiently understood.

Second, though the Ayr Bank crisis unambiguously warns against the familiar problem of "too big to fail," nor does it offer an unqualified endorsement of the maxim that, in banking, "small is beautiful." As shown in Chapter 4, while larger bank size after 1765 raised monitoring costs and undermined effective shareholder oversight of management, the larger shareholder base of Scottish banks, relative to English private banks constrained by the six-partner rule, allowed for larger equity reserves and greater asset and liability diversification. Of the sixteen banks that failed in 1772, all but Douglas, Heron & Co. had fewer than six partners, while all three that failed and inflicted losses on creditors had fewer than six partners. Particularly in an unlimited liability setting, scale thus offered substantial benefits; but only, as the collapse of Douglas, Heron & Co. illustrates, to a point. It might therefore, perhaps, be the case that "medium is beautiful."

Relatedly, third, Scottish free banking and the financial crisis of 1772 ought to challenge us to think more critically about the allocation of financial liability. Here, unlimited joint and several liability, on the one hand, and complete public socialization of loss in the form of taxpayer-funded bailouts, on the other, might comprise two extremes of a continuum of alternative possible liability regimes. Over and above the simple principles of efficient contract design, the Scottish experience of free banking generally and the failure of the Ayr Bank specifically suggest, in any event, that two additional empirical points are worth keeping in mind. First, in a full-information context, an unlimited liability regime in banking can be a powerful stabilizing force during moments of acute financial stress by "bailing in" shareholders for more than their subscribed capital. Indeed, as a voluntarily contracted, discriminate socialization of loss, unlimited joint and several liability can even in effect achieve the purpose of a traditional lender of last resort; provided, however, that the nature of that liability and the extent of shareholder wealth securing it are known. Second, the incentive effects of unlimited liability may mitigate the probability of such crises arising in the first place. The Scottish banker, in general, was legendary—indeed, parodied—for his conservatism.[40] As the great nineteenth-century English economist William Stanley Jevons put it, humorously, "Englishmen and Americans, and natives of all countries, may well admire the wonderful skill, sagacity, and caution with which Scotch bankers have developed and conducted their system," while those in English banking circles often lamented the "brutality of the Scotch banker."[41] The record of Scottish development in the eighteenth century, moreover, reveals that, perhaps for Modigliani-Miller reasons, such conservatism on the part of the proprietors of Scottish banks does not appear to have imposed any substantial drag on real economic growth.

Fourth, on the topic of economic development, the Scottish experience invites us to consider whether or not "Daedalian wings of paper money" may in fact, even if singed, be an essential component for any "take-off" phase of development. As Janeway has argued, sometimes, on rare occasions, bubbles may be necessary for mobilizing sufficient volumes of capital to allow for nascent technologies and industries to achieve critical scale.[42] The challenge lies in ensuring that when such bubbles burst, the losses are confined to equity markets, and are not allowed to infect credit markets more broadly. At the end of the day, despite Smith's criticism of the "golden dreams" of Scotland's "bold projectors," many of those projects were eventually seen through to fruition, to the complete transformation of the Scottish economy.[43] The Forth and Clyde and Monkland canals were finally completed, in 1790 and 1794, respectively. By the early nineteenth century, the Carron Company was the largest ironworks in Europe. Construction of New Town Edinburgh eventually resumed, while Scottish linen output continued to expand; by the turn of the century, total linen production had increased fivefold from its level at the time of the Forty-Five.[44] For the entire Scottish free-banking period, including even the crisis of 1772, the country's banking system seems to have successfully walked the fine line between accommodating speculative long-term investment while simultaneously insulating the broader credit and payments systems from inevitable failures and adverse shocks.

Fifth, and finally, lest the reader interpret the foregoing as a paean to "free" or unregulated banking, it is worthwhile to consider that the Scottish financial system at various moments during this period bore more than a passing resemblance to contemporary instances of financial repression, defined loosely as the combination of financial restrictions designed to liquidate the overhang of public and private debt, and to ease the burden of servicing those debts.[45] Crucially, in the Scottish case, this resemblance is not simply owing to regulatory intervention by the state. Reinhart and Sbrancia identify five key elements of financial repression:

1. Interest-rate caps.
2. High reserve requirements.
3. State ownership or control of domestic financial institutions combined with barriers to entry.
4. Maintenance of a captive domestic market for government debt, typically by means of specific capital requirements.
5. Capital controls.

In the case of "free banking" Scotland, condition 1 was, as we have seen, imperfectly imposed by a partially binding usury law. Condition 2 was not only indirectly imposed by the legislation of 1765, but also by the intense competition among Scottish banks in launching rival note raids throughout the free banking period, though particularly after prohibition of the optional clause. Condition 5 was effected, at least before 1765, by exercise of the optional clause.

Conditions 3 and 4, unfortunately, lie largely beyond the scope of this study, though together they would constitute an extremely fascinating line for future research. Obviously, the Scottish free banking system was not characterized by state ownership, or by a captive market for government debt, either by capital requirements or any other means. *However,* in several crucial respects, the structure of Scottish banking did render the banks semi-captive buyers of *private* debts, and after 1765, as we have seen, there were at least some prohibitive barriers to entry.[46] As noted in Chapter 4, it was not uncommon—in fact, it was quite typical—for Scottish banks to be established with an explicit mandate for aiding a particular branch of industry or trade, of which at least several partners were often members. Hence, the Linen Bank was engaged in providing credit to Scotland's linen industry, the Glasgow Ship Bank was founded to finance the transatlantic tobacco trade, the Thistle was established largely to channel funds to the agricultural projects of its aristocratic, landowning partners.

At their worst, as in the case of Douglas, Heron & Co., such incestuous arrangements merely resulted in rampant insider lending and highly concentrated, risky loan portfolios. At their best, however, under carefully crafted and enforced partnership agreements, they could align the interests of borrowers and lenders and channel vital credit to enterprises in which the partners had valuable insider knowledge. While banks were certainly not contractually obligated to buy the debts of their proprietors, there were often indirect incentives, such as partnership agreements that authorized directors to grant cash credits to partners amounting to one-half of the value of their equity without having to post additional collateral.[47] Given the immense external capital requirements of the Scottish economy during this period, it would be worthwhile to explore the extent to which the combination of these private measures of proto-financial repression might have aided the Scottish financial system in both keeping capital at home, and easing the cost of servicing debt. Yet the parallel must not be overdrawn; though particular banks may have each focused on a particular segment of Scottish debt markets, there is little evidence that the system as a whole was not even remotely captive to any type of low-yielding private debt, in the way that a repressed financial system is captive to low-yielding government debt.

Above all, however, the study of the "Air Bank" crisis ought to demystify how we think about banking and finance. It is always tempting, in financial history, to reach for the romantic and the histrionic. But doing so not only distracts, it misleads, inviting us to glance at yet another past crisis and offer little more than the poignant yet utterly meaningless conclusion "Well, it happens." When, however, we descend to street, or better yet, till level, we begin to see like the banker, to comprehend the micro- and macro-constraints under which he operates, and to appreciate that his trade is at once more simple and vastly more complex than it appears from a bird's-eye view. More simple because fundamentally the banker always does the same three things—credit intermediation, inter-temporal consumption smoothing, and risk transferal. More complex, however, because the particular institutional context in which he conducts his trade is always shaped, not simply by prudential policy concerns, but also by the binding assertion of Sutton's Law. Why do we regulate, praise, bash, celebrate, and otherwise tinker with banks? Because that is where the money is.

Notes

Bibliography

Acknowledgments

Index

Notes

1. A Very Melancholy Situation

1. David Hume to Adam Smith, 27 June 1772, in *The Correspondence of Adam Smith,* vol. 6, ed. Ernest Mossner and Ian Ross (Oxford: Oxford University Press, 1987), 161–163.

2. "Account of the Stagnation of Public Credit," *The Scots Magazine* 34 (September 1772): 311. Fordyce himself was a colorful character, as well as "a handsome, dashing man, possessed of considerable energy of character, with a great flow of natural eloquence, and much suavity of manner," according to nineteenth-century economic historian Frederick Martin. In one speculation in 1766, also in East India Company stock, he netted a staggering £100,000. Thereafter, he purchased a substantial estate, "with splendid mansion," at Roehampton, "and entered upon a series of fêtes, banquets, and entertainments, which threw those of royalty in the shade." Moreover, "To show his zeal for religion, he built a church adjoining his mansion, supporting it by himself, and 'worshipping' on a sort of velvet throne, surrounded by a glittering posse of tall footmen and bedizened lackeys." He then dropped some £14,000 on an unsuccessful bid for Parliament. See Frederick Martin, *Stories of Banks and Bankers* (London: Macmillan and Co., 1865), 108–110.

3. Huw Bowen, *East India Company: Trade and Domestic Financial Statistics, 1755–1838* [computer file] (Colchester, Essex: UK Data Archive [distributor], September 2007), SN: 5690.

4. Quoted in Martin, *Stories of Banks,* 113.

5. "Account of the Stagnation of Public Credit," 311–312.

6. Charles Boase, *A Century of Banking in Dundee* (Edinburgh: R. Grant & Son, 1867), 88.

7. William Forbes, *Memoirs of a Banking House* (Edinburgh: William and Robert Chambers, 1860), 40–41.

8. Horace Walpole to Horace Mann, 1 July 1772, in *The Letters of Horace Walpole,* vol. 8, *1771–1774,* ed. Paget Toynbee (Oxford: Clarendon Press, 1905), 178–180; Horace Walpole, *Journal of the Reign of King George the Third, from the Year 1771 to 1783,* vol. 1, ed. John Doran (London: Richard Bentley, 1859), 122.

9. Forbes, *Memoirs,* 40–43.

10. "Account of the Stagnation of Public Credit," 313.

11. Directors' Minute Books, Lloyds Banking Group Archive, 15 June 1772.

12. Directors' Minute Books, Royal Bank of Scotland Archive, 15 June 1772.

13. Andrew Kerr, *History of Banking in Scotland* (Glasgow: David Bryce & Son, 1884), 103. There is some confusion as to which Monday was "Black Monday." Sir William Forbes recounts that "it was Monday the——of June—emphatically called the Black Monday—that Fordyce's house stopped payment." Similarly, Frederick Martin places the failure of Neale, James, Fordyce, and Down on 8 June 1772, which he refers to as "Black Monday." However, contemporary sources clearly state that Neale, James, Fordyce, and Down failed on 10 June 1772, a Wednesday, with word arriving in Edinburgh by rider on the afternoon of Friday, 12 June. This would suggest that the Monday immediately following, 15 June, could have been "Black Monday." The *London Chronicle,* however, described Monday, 22 June 1772, as a day of exceptional panic, when "an universal bankruptcy was expected; the stoppage of every banker's house in London was looked for. The whole City was in an uproar; the whole City was in tears." The twenty-second also seems to have witnessed the stoppage of the prominent London banking house of Glyn and Hallifax, so it seems likely that 22 June was in fact "Black Monday," as this was also the day that Douglas, Heron & Co. suspended payment at their head office in Ayr and solicited the aid of the Bank of Scotland and Royal Bank of Scotland for a second time. The Scots Magazine, similarly, reported that "words cannot describe the general consternation of the metropolis on the twenty-second. An universal bankruptcy was expected, and the stoppage of every banker looked for. The whole city was in an uproar, and many of the first families in tears." See Forbes, *Memoirs,* 41; "Account of the Stagnation of Public Credit," 311–312; "The Monthly Chronologer," *The London Magazine, or, Gentleman's Monthly Intelligencer* 42 (June 1772): 292; Martin, *Stories of Banks,* 107–117; John Clapham, *The Bank of England: A History,* vol. 1 (Cambridge: Cambridge University Press, 1968), 247; Wilfred Acres, *The Bank of England from Within: 1694–1900,* vol. 1 (London: Oxford University Press, 1931), 201.

14. Directors' Minute Books, Royal Bank of Scotland Archive, 24 June 1772.

15. "Account of the Stagnation of Public Credit," 313.

16. Richard Saville, *Bank of Scotland: A History, 1695–1995* (Edinburgh: Edinburgh University Press, 1996), 164.

17. "Account of the Stagnation of Public Credit," 313.

18. Ibid., 312–313; Forbes, *Memoirs,* 41–43.

19. "An Account of the Examination of Mr. Alexander Fordyce, Banker in London, before the Commissioners of Bankruptcy," *The Scots Magazine* 34 (September 1772): 473. Similarly, the editor of Sir William Forbes's *Memoirs of a Banking House,* Robert Chambers, remarked that the failure of the Ayr Bank left "an amount of destruction in their wake such as Scotland had not experienced since the wreck of the Darien Expedition."

20. Walpole, *Journal,* 122–123.

21. Adam Smith to William Pulteney, 3 September 1772, in Mossner and Ross, *Correspondence of Adam Smith,* 6:163.

22. Adam Smith, *An Inquiry into the Nature and Causes of the Wealth of Nations,* vol. 1 (1776; reprint, New York: P. F. Collier & Son, 1902), 445–446. Bankruptcy figures from Robert Rait, *The History of the Union Bank of Scotland* (Glasgow: John Smith & Son, 1930), 167, taken from John Buchanan, "Ancient and Modern Scottish Banks" (unpublished manuscript, 1862). Paganelli and Rockoff have both written superb papers that incorporate Smith's reference to "Daedalian Wings of Paper Money" into their titles. As Rockoff notes, however, it is too colorful a metaphor to be passed up.

23. Smith, *Wealth of Nations,* 1:450.

24. Kerr, *Banking in Scotland,* 85. Smith wrote: "That the trade and industry of Scotland . . . have increased very considerably during this period [the decades preceding *The Wealth of Nations*], and that the banks have contributed a good deal to this increase, cannot be doubted. Smith, *Wealth of Nations,* 1:411. See also Richard Hildreth, *The History of Banks* (Boston: Milliard, Gray & Company, 1837); William Graham, *The One Pound Note in the Rise and Progress of Banking in Scotland, and its Adaptability to England* (Edinburgh: James Thin, 1886); Thomas Ashton, *Economic Fluctuations in England and Wales, 1750–1800* (Oxford: Oxford University Press, 1959); Rondo Cameron, *Banking in the Early Stages of Industrialization* (New York: Oxford University Press, 1967); Lawrence White, *Free Banking in Britain: Theory, Experience and Debates, 1800–1845* (Cambridge: Cambridge University Press, 1984).

25. Henry Meulen, *Free Banking: An Outline of a Policy of Individualism* (London: Macmillan, 1934); White, *Free Banking;* George Selgin, *A Theory of Free Banking* (Totawa, NJ: Rowman and Littlefield, 1988); Kevin Dowd, "Option Clauses and the Stability of a Laissez Faire Monetary System," *Journal of Financial Services Research* 1 (December 1988): 319–333; Kevin Dowd, "Option Clauses and Bank Suspension," *Cato Journal* (Winter 1991): 761–774; Kevin Dowd, *Laissez-Faire Banking* (New York: Routledge, 1993); Tyler Cowen and Randall Kroszner, "Scottish Banking before 1845: A Model for Laissez-Faire?," *Journal of Money, Credit and Banking* 21, no. 2 (May 1989): 221–231; Randall Kroszner, "Free Banking: The Scottish Experience as an Example for Emerging Economies," World Bank Policy Research Working Paper 1536 (November 1995); Charles Hickson and John Turner, "Free Banking and the Stability of

Early Joint-Stock Banking," *Cambridge Journal of Economics* 28 (2004): 903–919; Graeme Acheson, Charles Hickson, and John Turner, "Organisational Flexibility and Governance in a Civil-Law Regime: Scottish Partnership Banks during the Industrial Revolution," *Business History* 53, no. 4 (July 2011): 505–529.

26. Sydney Checkland, *Scottish Banking: A History, 1695–1973* (Glasgow: Collins, 1975); Larry Sechrest, "White's Free-Banking Thesis: A Case of Mistaken Identity," *Review of Austrian Economics* 2, no. 1 (1988): 247–257.

27. I argue in Chapter 4 that though shareholders in English banks also faced unlimited liability, the six-partner rule of the 1708 Bank of England Act, designed to protect the Bank of England's privileged position, meant that English banks were often critically undercapitalized, with the result that creditors to English banks were much more likely to endure losses in the event of institutional bankruptcy than their counterparts lending to Scottish banks.

28. David Hume to Adam Smith, October 1772, in Mossner and Ross, *Correspondence of Adam Smith,* 6:164–165; David Hume to Adam Smith, 10 April 1773, in Mossner and Ross, *Correspondence of Adam Smith,* 6:167–168.

29. Ian Simpson Ross, *The Life of Adam Smith* (Oxford: Oxford University Press, 1995), 12, 74–75, 199, 242; Papers of the Montague-Scott Family, Dukes of Buccleuch, National Records of Scotland, GB234/GD224; Kerr, *Banking in Scotland,* 107. For instance, Archibald Crawfurd of Ardmillan, with two shares in Douglas, Heron & Co., totaling £1,000, eventually had to sell his Ardmillan estate to an uncle, Thomas Crawfurd. Dr. John Campbell, of Wellwood, also with two shares of £500 each, was similarly stripped, "Like many other Ayrshire lairds, of nearly all he possessed," leading to the sale of his estate. See James Paterson, *History of the County of Ayr: with a Genealogical Account of the Families of Ayrshire,* vol. 2 (Ayr: John Dick, 1852), 78, 393; "Partners in the Douglas Heron and Company Bank," *The Scots Magazine* 34 (June 1772): 304–305. Other Ayrshire properties that had to be liquidated in the wake of the crisis included the Carcluie estates of John Hamilton; the lands of Cockhill and Mosshill of William Donald; the lands of Cuningpark, Windyhall, and Gairholme of John Christian; and the Bridgehouse estate, owned by the trustees of James Brown. See James Paterson, *History of the County of Ayr: with a Genealogical Account of the Families of Ayrshire,* vol. 1 (Ayr: John Dick, 1847), 205, 211–212.

30. Robert Somers, *The Scotch Banks and System of Issue* (Edinburgh: Adam and Charles Black, 1873), 103; Frank Brady, "So Fast to Ruin," *Ayrshire Collections* 11, no. 2 (1973): 34n; "The Contract of the Douglas Heron & Company Bank," *The Scots Magazine* 34 (June 1772): 304.

31. Forbes, *Memoirs,* 42n.

32. Precipitation and Fall of Messrs. Douglas, Heron and Company, Late Bankers in Air, with the Causes of their Distress and Ruin (Edinburgh, 1778); "Minutes at a Meeting of Defenders, and Doers for Defenders, in Actions of Damages &c. Raised at the Instance of Some of the Partners of Douglas, Heron, and Company: Against

the Directors, &c. of Said Company" (Edinburgh, 19 January 1780), Goldsmiths' Library, University of London.

33. Sydney Checkland, "Adam Smith and the Bankers," in *Essays on Adam Smith,* ed. Andrew Skinner and Thomas Wilson (Oxford: Clarendon, 1975), 504–523; James Gherity, "The Evolution of Adam Smith's Theory of Banking," *History of Political Economy* 26, no. 3 (1994): 423–441; Hugh Rockoff, "Upon Daedalian Wings of Paper Money: Adam Smith and the Crisis of 1772," NBER Working Paper 15594 (December 2009).

34. James Gherity, "An Early Publication by Adam Smith," *History of Political Economy* 25, no. 2 (1993): 241–282.

35. Adam Smith, *An Inquiry into the Nature and Causes of the Wealth of Nations,* (1776; reprint, Petersfield, UK: Harriman House, 2007), 229.

36. Smith, *Wealth of Nations,* 1:421, 432–436.

37. Ibid., 456.

38. Gherity, "Smith's Theory of Banking," 423–441; Gherity, "An Early Publication by Adam Smith," 241–282.

39. Samuel Johnson, *The Letters of Samuel Johnson with Mrs. Thrale's Genuine Letters to Him,* vol. 1, ed. Robert Chapman (Oxford: Clarendon Press, 1952), 279.

40. *Churbaierisches Intelligenzblatt* 14 (18 July 1772): 223.

41. "Engeland," *Gazette van Gend* 56 (29 June 1772).

42. Stock prices from John Castaing's Course of Exchange, European State Finance Database.

43. "De Londres, le 4 Juillet 1772," *Gazette de France* 57 (17 July 1772): 263–264. Reports of Douglas, Heron & Co.'s distress appeared in the Dutch press at least as early as 26 June. See "Engeland," *Gazette van Gend* 56 (2 July 1772).

44. "Grande-Bretagne," *Journal Politique ou Gazette des Gazettes* 2 (July 1772): 66.

45. "Engeland," *Gazette van Gend* 56 (13 July 1772).

46. David Macpherson, *Annals of Commerce, Manufactures, Fishers, and Navigation,* vol. 3 (London: Nichols and Son, 1805), 534. Also reported in "Hollande," *Journal Politique ou Gazette des Gazettes* 2 (March 1773): 6.

47. *De Koopman* 4, no. 53 (1773): 427.

48. *De Koopman* 4, no. 38 (1773): 301.

49. Clapham, *Bank of England,* 248. For more on the 1772–1773 crisis in the Netherlands, see Charles Wilson, "The Economic Decline of the Netherlands," *Economic History Review* 9, no. 2 (May 1939): 111–127.

50. "Hollande," *Journal Politique ou Gazette des Gazettes* 2 (February 1773): 71.

51. Ibid. See also "Hollande," *Journal Historique et Politique des Principaux Evénements des différents Cours de l'Europe* 2 (22 January 1773): 64.

52. *De Koopman* 4, no. 44 (1773): 207–208, 299, 302, 306, 318, 325, 352, 355–356, 358, 364, 424. See also Wilson, "Economic Decline of the Netherlands," 125. In Scotland, meanwhile, the directors of the Bank of Scotland resolved in October 1772 to

cease discounting foreign bills presented by Jewish traders, whom they accused of remitting specie to Holland to "profit from the exchange." See "Angleterre," *Le Clef du Cabinet des Princes de l'Europe, ou Recuéil Historique & Politique sur les Matières du Temps* (October 1772): 310–311.

53. Geert Rouwenhorst, "The Origins of Mutual Funds," Yale International Center for Finance Working Paper 04-48 (12 December 2004), 1–2, 5–10.

54. "Allemagne," *Journal Historique et Politique des Principaux Evénements des différents Cours de l'Europe* 4 (10 February 1773): 35.

55. William Cobbett and Thomas Hansard, eds., *The Parliamentary History of England from the Earliest Period to the Year 1803*, vol. 17, *A. D. 1771–1774* (London: T. C. Hansard, 1813), 1115.

56. Ernst Baasch, *Holländische Wirtschaftsgeschichte* (Jena: G. Fischer, 1927), 239–240.

57. J. H. Soltow, "Scottish Traders in Virginia, 1750–1775," *Economic History Review* 12, no. 1 (1959): 83–98; Richard Sheridan, "The British Credit Crisis of 1772 and the American Colonies," *Journal of Economic History* 10, no. 2 (June 1960): 161–186; Lawrence Gipson, "Virginia Planter Debts before the American Revolution," *The Virginia Magazine of History and Biography* 69, no. 3 (July 1961): 259–277; Thomas Devine, "Glasgow Merchants and the Collapse of the Tobacco Trade 1775–1783," *Scottish Historical Review* 52, no. 153 (April 1973): 50–74; Thomas Devine, "Sources of Capital for the Glasgow Tobacco Trade, c. 1740–1780," *Business History* 16 (1974): 113–129; Thomas Devine, "The Colonial Trades and Industrial Investment in Scotland, c. 1700–1815," *Economic History Review* 29, no. 1 (February 1976): 1–13; Thomas Devine, "An Eighteenth-Century Business Elite: Glasgow-West India Merchants, c. 1750–1815," *Scottish Historical Review* 57, no. 163 (April 1978): 40–67.

58. Tobacco accounted for approximately 80 percent of Scottish imports. See Macpherson, *Annals of Commerce*, 3:518–519; Jacob Price, "The Rise of Glasgow in the Chesapeake Tobacco Trade, 1707–1775," *William and Mary Quarterly* 11, no. 2 (1954): 179.

59. Sheridan, "British Credit Crisis of 1772 and the American Colonies," 166, 169, 180, 183; Devine, "Glasgow Merchants," 59; Devine, "Sources of Capital for the Glasgow Tobacco Trade," 117.

60. Sheridan, "British Credit Crisis of 1772 and the American Colonies," 183.

61. Devine, "Sources of Capital for the Glasgow Tobacco Trade," 117.

62. Thomas Moore, "To the Lord Viscount Forbes," in *The Works of Thomas Moore, Comprehending all his Melodies, Ballads, etc.*, vol. 2 (Paris: A. and W. Galignani, 1823), 153.

63. Price, "The Rise of Glasgow," 196–197. By 1775, the Caledonian Mercury reported that the debts owed to Glasgow by the tobacco regions of the Chesapeake had doubled to £1,000,000. See *Caledonian Mercury* (1 February 1775). Cited in Devine, "Glasgow Merchants," 59.

64. Sheridan, "British Credit Crisis of 1772 and the American Colonies," 181.

65. Ibid., 168–169.

66. Price, "The Rise of Glasgow," 197.

67. Soltow, "Traders in Virginia," 95.

68. Alexander McCaul to Thomas Jefferson, 8 July 1772, in *The Papers of Thomas Jefferson,* vol. 1, *1760–1776,* ed. Julian Boyd (Princeton, NJ: Princeton University Press, 1950), 92–93.

69. John Norton to John H. Norton, 6 August 1772, in *John Norton & Sons, Merchants of London and Virginia,* ed. Francis Mason (Richmond, VA: Dietz Press, 1937), 266, quoted in Sheridan, "British Credit Crisis of 1772 and the American Colonies," 178.

70. William Wiatt to Francis Wiatt, 26 June 1773, in *William and Mary College Quarterly* 12 (1903–1904): 113–114, quoted in Sheridan, "British Credit Crisis of 1772 and the American Colonies," 178.

71. Benjamin Franklin to Richard Bache, 7 October 1772, in *The Writings of Benjamin Franklin,* vol. 5, ed. Albert Smyth (London: Macmillan, 1907), 441–442.

72. Norton to Norton, 6 August 1772, in Mason, *John Norton & Sons,* 266, quoted in Sheridan, "British Credit Crisis of 1772 and the American Colonies," 178.

73. William Allason to John Backhouse, 15 July 1773, in "The Letters of William Allason, Merchant of Falmouth, Virginia," *Richmond College Historical Papers* 2, no. 1 (1917): 150. Quoted in Sheridan, "British Credit Crisis of 1772 and the American Colonies," 175.

74. W. Cunninghame to J. Robinson, 1 July 1772, quoted in Devine, "Glasgow Merchants," 59; Soltow, "Scottish Traders," 90; Sheridan, "British Credit Crisis of 1772 and the American Colonies," 169.

75. To Thomas Jefferson from Perkins, Buchanan & Brown, 2 October 1769, in Boyd, *Papers of Thomas Jefferson,* 1:33–34; Katharine Kellock, "London Merchants and the pre-1776 American Debts," *Guildhall Studies in London History* 1, no. 3 (October 1974): 139.

76. Gregory Clark, "The Price History of English Agriculture, 1209–1914," *Research in Economic History* 22 (2004): 41–124.

77. Sheridan, "British Credit Crisis of 1772 and the American Colonies," 178.

78. Bruce Ragsdale, *A Planters' Republic: The Search for Economic Independence in Revolutionary Virginia* (Madison, WI: Madison House Publishers, 1996), 179.

79. "Meeting at Annapolis, Maryland. The suffering of Boston, the common cause of America. A stoppage of Trade with Great Britain will preserve North America and her Liberties. Gentlemen of the Law in the Province should bring no suit for the recovery of a debt due to an Inhabitant of Great Britain, until the Boston Port Act be repealed. The Inhabitants of Annapolis will, and the Province ought, immediately to break off all Trade with the Colony or Province which shall refuse to adopt similar Resolutions with a majority of the Colonies. Committee appointed to unite with

others of the Province, to effect an Association to secure American Liberty," 25 May 1774, American Archives, series 4, vol. 1, p. 0352.

80. John Scharf, *History of Maryland, 1765–1812* (Baltimore: J. B. Piet, 1879), 150–154.

81. Devine, "Glasgow Merchants," 61.

82. James Parker to Charles Steuart, 7 June 1774, Charles Steuart Papers, National Library of Scotland. Quoted in Ragsdale, *A Planters' Republic,* 201.

83. Ragsdale, *A Planters' Republic,* 212.

84. Herbert Sloan, *Principle and Interest: Thomas Jefferson and the Problem of Debt* (New York: Oxford University Press, 1995), 18–19.

85. James Madison to William Bradford, 1 July 1774, in *The Papers of James Madison,* vol. 1, *16 March 1751–16 December 1779,* ed. William Hutchinson and William Rachal (Chicago: University of Chicago Press, 1962), 114–117.

86. Landon Carter, *The Diary of Landon Carter of Sabine Hall, 1752–1778,* vol. 5, ed. Jack Greene (Charlottesville: University of Virginia Press, 1987), 821. Mentioned in Ragsdale, *A Planters' Republic,* 185. For more on Anglo-Virginia hostility to Scottish traders, see Albert Tillson, *Accommodating Revolutions: Virginia's Northern Neck in an Era of Transformations, 1760–1810* (Charlottesville: University of Virginia Press, 2010), 168–171.

87. Devine, "Glasgow Merchants," 62.

88. Macpherson, *Annals of Commerce,* 3:539.

89. Court Minutes, Bank of England Archive, 8 October 1772; "Foreign and Domestic Intelligence," *The Oxford Magazine* 8 (1772): 156.

90. "Grande-Bretagne," *Journal Politique ou Gazette des Gazettes* 2 (July 1772): 88–98; *Mercurio Histórico y Político* (1772): 125–128. Within five years, Colebrooke himself was in fact bankrupted; see Lucy Sutherland, "Colebrooke, George (1729–1809), of Gatton, Surr.," in *The History of Parliament: The House of Commons, 1754–1790,* ed. Lewis Namier and John Brooke (London: Secker & Warburg, 1964), 235–237.

91. "East India Company: Trade and Domestic Financial Statistics, 1755–1838," United Kingdom Data Archive, Study Number 5690; Alfred Thomas Story, *The Building of the British Empire: 1689–1895* (London: G. P. Putnam's Sons, 1898), 157; Macpherson, *Annals of Commerce,* 3:529.

92. "An Act to allow a Drawback of the Duties of Customs on the Exportation of Tea to any of his Majesty's Colonies or Plantations in America; to increase the Deposit on Bohea Tea to be sold at the East-India Company's Sales; and to empower the Commissioners of the Treasury to grant Licenses to the East-India Company to export Tea Duty-free," 13 Geo. 3 c. 44; Macpherson, *Annals of Commerce,* 3:538.

93. "An Act for establishing certain Regulations for the better Management of the Affairs of the East-India Company, as well in India as in Europe," 13 Geo. 3 c. 63; Macpherson, *Annals of Commerce,* 3:541–543; Clapham, *Bank of England,* 250.

94. Macpherson, *Annals of Commerce,* 3:545–546.

95. "Deaths," *The London Magazine, or, Gentleman's Monthly Intelligencer* 42 (April 1773): 205.

96. Walpole to Mann, 1 July 1772, in Toynbee, *Letters,* 178–180; Walpole, *Journal,* 122.

97. "Grande-Bretagne," *Journal Politique* 2 (July 1772), 66.

98. Court Minutes, Bank of England Archive, 18 June, 2 July 1772; "Considerations on the Present State of Credit," *The Scots Magazine* 34 (September 1772): 315.

99. "Considerations on the Present State of Credit," 315–317; Court Minutes, Bank of England Archive, 2 July 1772; Mr. Glover to Earl Temple, 12 July 1772, in *The Grenville papers: being the Correspondence of Richard Grenville, Earl Temple, K.G., and the Right Hon: George Grenville, their Friends and Contemporaries,* vol. 4, ed. William James Smith (London: John Murray, 1853), 539–543.

100. Court Minutes, Bank of England Archive, 30 July 1772; Clapham, *Bank of England,* 246.

101. Court Minutes, Bank of England Archive, 9, 23 July 1772; Clapham, *Bank of England,* 249; Edith Lady Haden-Guest, "Herries, Sir Robert (1730–1815), of Richmond, Surr.," in Namier and Brooke, *History of Parliament,* 615–616.

102. Saville, *Bank of Scotland,* 165.

103. George Stigler, "The Theory of Economic Regulation," *Bell Journal of Economics* 2, no. 1 (Spring 1971): 3–21.

104. Simon Johnson, "The Quiet Coup," *The Atlantic* (May 2009); Simon Johnson, *13 Bankers: The Wall Street Takeover and the Next Financial Meltdown* (New York: Random House, 2010).

105. Andrew Haldane and Robert May, "Systemic Risk in Banking Ecosystems," *Nature* 469 (20 January 2011): 351–355.

106. Cameron, *Banking in the Early Stages of Industrialization;* Randall Kroszner, "Free Banking: The Scottish Experience as an Example for Emerging Economies," World Bank Policy Research Working Paper 1536 (November 1995).

107. For discussion of the formal, informal, and absent institutions governing Scottish banking in the run-up to the Ayr Bank crisis, see Tom Kärrlander, "Douglas Heron and Company, Bankers in Air (Ayr Bank): A Bank Crash in Scotland in 1772," Stockholm University Department of Economic History Working Paper 16 (2005).

108. This point is made with particular persuasiveness by Selgin. See George Selgin, *Bank Deregulation and Monetary Order* (London: Routledge, 1996), 5–7, 214.

109. Carmen Reinhart and Kenneth Rogoff, *This Time Is Different: Eight Centuries of Financial Folly* (Princeton, NJ: Princeton University Press, 2009).

110. Graeme Acheson, Charles Hickson, and John Turner, "Organisational Flexibility and Governance in a Civil-Law Regime: Scottish Partnership Banks during the Industrial Revolution," *Business History* 53, no. 4 (July 2011): 512.

111. Nassim Nicholas Taleb, *Antifragile: Things That Gain from Disorder* (New York: Random House, 2012); Lawrence White, "Antifragile Banking and Monetary Systems," Cato Institute 30th Annual Monetary Conference, 15 November 2012, mimeo.

112. Selgin, *Bank Deregulation,* 230.

113. Printed in "Poetical Essays," *The Scots Magazine* 34 (October 1772): 561. Author uncredited.

2. Beggarly Bankers

1. Adam Smith, *An Inquiry into the Nature and Causes of the Wealth of Nations,* vol. 1 (1776; reprint, New York: P. F. Collier & Son, 1902), 450.

2. For studies of the evolution of Smith's thought on banking and bank regulation, and particularly on the influence of 1760–1765 in Scotland on his views, see Sydney Checkland, "Adam Smith and the Bankers," in *Essays on Adam Smith,* ed. Andrew Skinner and Thomas Wilson (Oxford: Clarendon, 1975), 504–523; James Gherity, "The Evolution of Adam Smith's Theory of Banking," *History of Political Economy* 26, no. 3 (1994): 423–441; Edwin West, "Adam Smith's Support for Money and Banking Regulation: A Case of Inconsistency," *Journal of Money, Credit and Banking* 29, no. 1 (February 1997): 127–134; Mathieu Carlson, "Adam Smith's Support for Money and Banking Regulation: A Case of Inconsistency?," *History of Economics Review* 29 (Winter 1999): 1–15.

3. Andrew Kerr, *History of Banking in Scotland* (Glasgow: David Bryce & Son, 1884); William Graham, *The One Pound Note in the Rise and Progress of Banking in Scotland, and its Adaptability to England* (Edinburgh: James Thin, 1886); Henry Hamilton, "Scotland's Balance of Payments Problem in 1762," *Economic History Review* 5, no. 3 (1953): 344–357.

4. Kerr, *Banking in Scotland,* 85–86.

5. Graham, *One Pound Note,* 65–66.

6. Murray Rothbard, "The Myth of Free Banking in Scotland," *Review of Austrian Economics* 2 (1988): 232.

7. Charles Munn, *The Scottish Provincial Banking Companies, 1747–1864* (Edinburgh: John Donald Publishers), 18.

8. Parth Shah, "The Option Clause in Free-Banking Theory and History: A Reappraisal," *Review of Austrian Economics* 10, no. 2 (1997): 24.

9. Henry Meulen, *Free Banking: An Outline of a Policy of Individualism* (London: Macmillan, 1934); Lawrence White, *Free Banking in Britain: Theory, Experience and Debates, 1800–1845* (Cambridge: Cambridge University Press, 1984); George Selgin, *A Theory of Free Banking* (Totawa, NJ: Rowman and Littlefield, 1988); Kevin Dowd, "Option Clauses and the Stability of a Laissez Faire Monetary System," *Journal of Financial Services Research* 1 (December 1988): 319–333; Kevin Dowd, "Option Clauses and Bank Suspension," *Cato Journal* (Winter 1991): 761–774; Kevin Dowd, *Laissez-Faire Banking* (New York: Routledge, 1993); Tyler Cowen and Randall Kroszner,

"Scottish Banking before 1845: A Model for Laissez-Faire?," *Journal of Money, Credit and Banking* 21, no. 2 (May 1989): 221–231; Randall Kroszner, "Free Banking: The Scottish Experience as an Example for Emerging Economies," World Bank Policy Research Working Paper 1536 (November 1995).

10. Cowen and Kroszner, "Scottish Banking," 224–225; Douglas Diamond and Philip Dybvig, "Bank Runs, Deposit Insurance, and Liquidity," *Journal of Political Economy* 91 (June 1983): 401–419.

11. George Selgin and Lawrence White, "The Option Clause in Scottish Banking," *Journal of Money, Credit and Banking* 29, no. 2 (May 1997): 270–273.

12. Quoted in Meulen, *Free Banking,* 131.

13. Directors' Minutes, Lloyd's Banking Group Archives, 6 November 1730; ibid., 12 December 1732.

14. *The Scots Magazine* 18 (July 1756): 365. Gherity erroneously suggests that Arms and Ship notes bore the clause from 1752. See James Gherity, "The Option Clause in Scottish Banking, 1730–65: A Reappraisal," *Journal of Money, Credit and Banking* 27, no. 3 (August 1995): 716.

15. Often referred to as the "aristocratic bank" owing to the fact that several of its founding partners were prominent Scottish landowners. "On the Present State of the Paper-Money of Scotland," *The Scots Magazine* 27 (February 1765): 83n; Robert Rait, *The History of the Union Bank of Scotland* (Glasgow: John Smith & Son, 1930), 121; Neil Munro, *The History of the Royal Bank of Scotland* (Glasgow: Grimsay Press, 1928), 60.

16. Directors' Minutes, Lloyds Banking Group Archives, 27 March 1728. Checkland notes that the Old Bank also paid interest on outstanding notes on the other two occasions before 1730 when they had to suspend payment, in 1704 and 1715. Both suspensions were the results of exogenous political shocks (internal specie drain owing to Marlborough's 1704 Danube campaign and the Jacobite rising of 1715), and the bank resumed payment five months and eight months later, respectively. See Sydney Checkland, *Scottish Banking: A History, 1695–1973* (Glasgow: Collins, 1975), 38, 47.

17. "An Exact State or Abbreviate of the Affairs of the Bank of Scotland, as they Stand Ballanced to the 27th March 1728, the Day upon which they were Obliged to Stop Payments, through Deficiency of Cash: and how the Same Stands this 18th June the Said Year," 18 June 1728, Goldsmiths' Library, University of London.

18. Charles Malcolm, *The Bank of Scotland, 1695–1945* (Edinburgh: R. & R. Clark, 1948), 48–50.

19. "Memorial above Referred to—with Notes by Sir James Stuart of Coltness," 4 February 1763, in *Selections from the Mure Family Papers Preserved at Caldwell,* pt. 2, vol. 1, ed. William Mure (Paisley: Alexander Gardner, 1883), 208.

20. Selgin and White, "The Option Clause," 272.

21. Directors' Minutes, Lloyds Banking Group Archives, 1 April 1762. *The Scots Magazine* issue for that month noted the Old Bank's exercise of option, writing that "the benefit of this option has on this occasion (and we believe it is the first time)

been taken in some instances, by marking notes presented for payment." See also "Affairs in Ireland and Scotland," *The Scots Magazine* 24 (April 1762): 225.

22. National Library of Scotland, MS 17591, Fletcher of Saltoun Papers; Charles Boase, *A Century of Banking in Dundee* (Edinburgh: R. Grant & Son, 1867), 35.

23. Rait, *Union Bank,* 27–28; Graham, *One Pound Note,* 41–42; Kerr, *Banking in Scotland,* 72–73. It is unclear when exactly the Aberdeen Company began printing notes. An advertisement in the *Aberdeen Journal* dated 5 January 1748, however, reports that "on the 29th of last month, were amissing, Three Promissory Notes of the Aberdeen Company's—one for £10, and Two for Twenty Shillings each; and of the Bank of Scotland, Two for Twenty Shillings each.—Whoever brings them to the Publisher of this Paper shall have Two Guineas Reward, and no questions asked." This suggests that the Aberdeen Company began circulating notes as early as 1747. See "Advertisement," *Aberdeen Journal* (5 January 1748).

24. Directors' Minutes, Lloyds Banking Group Archives, 19 July 1751.

25. According to James Fleming, "The Ruin and Bankruptcy of the principal Undertakers . . . ensued very soon thereafter." See James Fleming, *Scottish Banking: A Historical Sketch* (Edinburgh: W. Blackwood, 1877), 50. The failure was not without controversy. *The Scots Magazine* of July 1753 reports that "a gentleman possessed of notes of a private banking company at Aberdeen, having asked payment, and been refused, took a protest. But the clerks of session, upon being offered the protest to be registered, that summary diligence might pass, as is competent on bills, demurred, and reported the case to the court. The Lords unanimously refused to register the protest, because such notes are not of the nature of bills. So the creditor has no legal way of operating payment but by an ordinary action." See "Manufactures, Fisheries, Aberdeen Bank-notes, &c.," *The Scots Magazine* 15 (July 1753): 361. Essentially, excepting those issued by the Bank of Scotland, the Court of Session ruled that banknotes were merely promissory notes rather than bills. According to statutes passed in 1681 and 1696, foreign and inland bills were subject to summary diligence, but promissory notes fell under no such statute. See Rait, *Union Bank,* 28.

26. "Mess. Alexander Livingston, William Mowat, William Bremner, and John Dingwell, the banking company of Aberdeen, have given public notice, that they have resolved to put an end to their partnership, and to issue no more notes." "Queensferry Advertisement, Eymouth Harbour, &c.," *The Scots Magazine* 16 (January 1754): 49.

27. The Ship Bank owed its name to the image of a ship in full sail that appeared upon its notes. Buchanan, *Banking in Glasgow,* 14. The Arms Bank similarly owed its name to the fact that its notes featured the coat of arms of Glasgow. James Douglas, *Scottish Banknotes* (London: Stanley Gibbons, 1975), 138.

28. Munn, *Scottish Provincial Banking,* 12.

29. Directors' Minutes, Royal Bank of Scotland Archives, 27 July 1751.

30. Ledgers, Lloyds Banking Group Archives, June 1751–January 1752.

31. Royal Bank of Scotland, "A List of the Names of the Proprietors of the Royal Bank of Scotland," 13 February 1760, Goldsmiths' Library, University of London.

32. Douglas, *Scottish Banknotes,* 194. Also mentioned by Munro, *Royal Bank,* 123.

33. "A Process Relating to the Glasgow Banks," *The Scots Magazine* 18 (June 1756): 303–306.

34. Directors' Minutes, Lloyds Banking Group Archive, 18 October 1756.

35. National Library of Scotland, MS 17592, Fletcher of Saltoun Papers, 2 October 1756.

36. Directors' Minutes, Lloyds Banking Group Archive, 18 October 1756.

37. Ibid., 3 February 1757.

38. William Forbes, *Memoirs of a Banking House* (Edinburgh: William and Robert Chambers, 1860), 5. Forbes further recounts that after leaving the copartnery of Coutts & Co., Trotter unsuccessfully attempted to establish himself as an accountant.

39. "Information for Archibald Trotter, Merchant in Glasgow, Pursuer, against Andrew Cochran, John Murdoch, and Company, Bankers in Glasgow, Defenders" (Glasgow, 5 February 1760), National Library of Scotland. Note that, at the time in Scotland, silver was then legal tender to an unlimited amount.

40. Forbes, *Memoirs,* 5n–6n.

41. "A Run on the Glasgow Banks," *The Scots Magazine* 18 (May 1756): 249. According to the magazine, Trotter was informed that he could return for payment between the hours of three and five o'clock but failed to do so.

42. Graham, *One Pound Note,* 45. Less than a month before, on 16 October 1758, Trotter had attempted to redeem £600 in Arms notes. Nine days later, he had received just £475 of this sum.

43. "Banks, Child-murder, Divorce, &c." *The Scots Magazine* 18 (July 1756): 365; "On the Present State of the Paper-Money of Scotland," *The Scots Magazine* 27 (February 1765): 83n.

44. "Memorial," in Mure, *Selections,* pt. 2, 1:211.

45. Ibid., 212. This unpublished, draft memorial, sent by Archibald Ingram, Lord Provost of Glasgow and founding partner of the Arms Bank, to the Lord Privy Seal, James Stuart-Mackenzie, is the only evidence I can find of option ever being invoked by private banks. Referring to arbitrageurs endeavoring to remit specie to London via high-volume note redemptions, the memorial notes: "With regard to those who were quite obstinate, one of the Banks at Edinburgh fairly executed its threats, taking advantage of the Optional Clause, by marking its notes on the back, as presented on such a day, in order to be paid with interest six months after demand, and two of the Companies at Glasgow have lately, in some instances, followed their example."

46. "A Run on the Glasgow Banks," *The Scots Magazine* 18 (May 1756): 250.

47. "Memorial," in Mure, *Selections,* pt. 2, 1:211.

48. For Scottish trade statistics from 1760 to 1780, see David Macpherson, *Annals of Commerce, Manufactures, Fishers, and Navigation,* vol. 3 (London: Nichols and Son,

1805), 339, 351, 364–365, 384–385, 409–410, 434–435, 455–456, 475–476, 486–487, 494–495, 508, 518–519, 532–533, 549–550, 564, 585, 599, 614, 632, 651, 673.

49. The harvest failure is reflected in malt duties, which fell from £26,443 in 1754–1755 to £15,656 in 1756–1757, before rebounding to £24,069 in 1758–1759 and £37,073 in 1759–1760. Excise duties on beer and ale dropped from £37,233 in 1754–1755 to £33,170 in 1756–1757, recovering to £42,704 by 1759–1760. Total duties excluding malt, in contrast, only fell from £73,447 in 1754–1755 to £71,109 in 1756–1757, recovering to £80,595 by 1759–1760. Hamilton, "Scotland's Balance of Payments," 348.

50. A writer to *The Scots Magazine* in 1764 describes the process thus: "The person here has an agent in London, who is worth nothing, that will accept any bills he shall draw upon him; and the gentleman here, I shall suppose, draws upon him for 1000 l. at 30 days date; which bill he sells to a banker, who gives him 3 *per cent.* for it, and pays him in bank-notes, the bill and exchange 1030 l. The gentleman comes immediately to the bank; demands cash for his 1000 l.; goes directly to the waggon with it; they carry it in 20 days to London for twelve shillings *per cent.* which is 6 l.; his correspondent receives it, and with it retires his friend's draught for said sum. The transaction is finished, and these two pocket 24 l. by this bargain; which they may renew every day, nay, every hour of the day, if they can find people to purchase their bills." "Cause and Cure of our Scarcity of Specie," *The Scots Magazine* 26 (February 1764): 91–92.

51. Hamilton, "Scotland's Balance of Payments," 344–357.

52. Stock prices from John Castaing's *Course of Exchange,* European State Finance Database.

53. Macpherson, *Annals of Commerce,* 3:339, 351, 364–365, 384–385, 409–410, 434–435, 455–456, 475–476, 486–487, 494–495, 508, 518–519, 532–533, 549–550, 564, 585, 599, 614, 632, 651, 673.

54. *Caledonian Mercury* (May 1764), quoted in Boase, *Banking in Dundee,* 52–53. Kerr also discusses the practice of drawing fictitious bills on London to export specie. See Kerr, *Banking in Scotland,* 88–89. The figure of £500,000 is confirmed by Sir James Steuart, see James Steuart, *Principles of Political Economy,* vol. 2 (London: A. Millar and T. Cadell, 1767), 188.

55. "Cause and Cure of Our Scarcity of Specie," *The Scots Magazine* 26 (February 1764): 89–92.

56. "Remarks on the Considerations Relating to the Banks," *The Scots Magazine* 24 (March 1762): 131.

57. "Regulations Proposed for Banking," *The Scots Magazine* 24 (March 1762): 135.

58. Quoted in Meulen, *Free Banking,* 131.

59. Christopher Crabtree, "To the Publisher of the Edinburgh Advertiser," *The Edinburgh Advertiser* 3, no. 112 (25 January 1765): 57. Crabtree also recounts that "this practice of getting money from the banks, to answer their credit at London, was the introduction to a worse, that of sending away the cash, and drawing for it again once

every three weeks; so that a person might turn his money, by this method, at least sixteen times in the year, which, at three percent is 48 l. gained by exchange, for each 100 l. employed in this kind of traffic, yearly.

60. "Copies of the Instrument of Protest, Archibald Trotter Merchant in Glasgow, against Andrew Cochran, John Murdoch and Company; of Two Letters from Mr Trotter to those Gentlemen; and of a Summons Raised at his Instance against them," January 1759, Harvard University Law Library.

61. Ibid.; "Information for Archibald Trotter, Merchant in Glasgow, Pursuer, against Andrew Cochran, John Murdoch, and Company, Bankers in Glasgow, Defenders," 5 February 1760, National Library of Scotland.

62. Directors' Minutes, Lloyd's Banking Group Archives, 2 February 1764.

63. Ibid., 30 December 1762; John Clapham, *The Bank of England: A History,* vol. 1 (Cambridge: Cambridge University Press, 1968), 238.

64. Directors' Minutes, Lloyd's Banking Group Archives, 13 March 1764.

65. Ibid., 21 March 1764; Out Letter Book, Lloyd's Banking Group Archives, 6 July 1764; Report from the Select Committee on Banks of Issue, vol. 5 (1841), 303.

66. Richard Saville, *Bank of Scotland: A History, 1695–1995* (Edinburgh: Edinburgh University Press, 1996), 143.

67. "Affairs in Scotland," *The Scots Magazine* 26 (April 1764): 229.

68. Douglas, *Scottish Banknotes,* 54–55.

69. Ibid., 24–27, 117, 138–139, 147–148, 153, 194, 210–211, 216; "Of the Roads and Paper-Currency in Scotland," *The Scots Magazine* 25 (October 1763): 580. Douglas's catalog documents optional clauses on 5s. and 10s. notes issued by the Dundee Banking Company in 1763, but this is contradicted by company records presented by Boase (see Boase, *Banking in Dundee,* 51) and also by note reprints in *The Scots Magazine* (see "Affairs in Scotland," *The Scots Magazine* 26 [September 1764]: 518).

70. "Affairs in Scotland," *The Scots Magazine* 26 (September 1764): 518. Mentioned in Boase, *Banking in Dundee,* 56. Smiton's notes, it should be mentioned, were not intended for circulation beyond his coffeehouse, and therefore were redeemable "on demand, in money or drink, two shillings and sixpence sterling."

71. *The Scots Magazine* 23 (August 1761): 442.

72. John Home Stevenson, ed., *The Scottish Antiquary or Northern Notes & Queries* (Edinburgh: George P. Johnston, 1886), 34.

73. Ibid., 69.

74. Graham, *One Pound Note,* 63; Kerr, *Banking in Scotland,* 87; Douglas, *Scottish Banknotes,* 189. Though it must be admitted that guinea notes, because of their odd value (21s.) were also issued as a tactic for conserving specie.

75. Rockoff, "Upon Daedalian Wings," 10.

76. Three, if we include the Dundee Banking Company, but, as noted above, Douglas's record of 5s. and 10s. notes issued by that company with option in 1763 is contradicted by company records presented by Boase and by Dundee note reprints in

The Scots Magazine. See Douglas, *Scottish Banknotes,* 116; Boase, *Banking in Dundee,* 51; "Affairs in Scotland," *The Scots Magazine* 26 (September 1764): 518. It should also be noted that Douglas did not have specimens of the notes issued by the six banking companies that in 1766 merged to form the Perth United Company. Rait writes that these companies "traded in a very small way, availing themselves of the optional clause and issuing notes for trivial sums," so it is possible that several of them issued notes under £1 with option, though the surviving specimens of one—Blacklaws, Wedderspoon & Co.—at least, did not include option. See Rait, *Union Bank,* 130.

77. Smith, *Wealth of Nations,* 1:448.

78. Ibid., 1:451.

79. Ibid., 1:448–449.

80. Graham, *One Pound Note,* 60.

81. Kerr, *Scottish Banking,* 84.

82. Munro, *Royal Bank,* 108–130.

83. To be fair, both Shah and White use the phrase "small note mania" in quotation marks, and White quotes Boase ridiculing the claims of a "mania." Checkland, *Scottish Banking,* 108–111; Munn, *Scottish Provincial Banking,* 18–19; Shah, "Option Clause," 13; Lawrence White, "Free Banking in Scotland before 1844," in Kevin Dowd, ed., *The Experience of Free Banking* (London: Routledge, 1992), 164.

84. Rait, *Union Bank,* 34–35; Saville, *Bank of Scotland,* 142–148.

85. Rockoff, "Upon Daedalian Wings," 10–11.

86. Ibid.

87. Boase, *Banking in Dundee,* 56. Also reprinted in "Affairs in Scotland," *The Scots Magazine* 26 (January 1764): 518.

88. Mitchell and Wyllie both placed advertisements for payment of their notes in *The Aberdeen Journal* in 1763. See Gavin Tourreff, ed., *Antiquarian Gleanings from Aberdeenshire Records* (Aberdeen: George and Robert King, 1859), 255, 266.

89. "Affairs in Scotland," *The Scots Magazine* 26 (December 1764): 518, 574; Boase, *Banking in Dundee,* 65, 554; Kerr, *Banking in Scotland,* 87.

90. *The Aberdeen Journal* (1763), in Tourreff, *Antiquarian Gleanings,* 266.

91. Boase, *Banking in Dundee,* 65.

92. "Affairs in Scotland," *The Scots Magazine* 26 (September 1764): 518. Mentioned in Boase, *Banking in Dundee,* 56; Stevenson, *Scottish Antiquary,* 70.

93. Printed in *The Scots Magazine.* The editor, however, adds in a footnote that the true number could have been twice that. "Of Abolishing or Regulating Private Banking," *The Scots Magazine* 26 (November 1764): 595.

94. Douglas, *Scottish Banknotes,* 147–148, 189.

95. "Aberdeen Resolution Concerning Paper-Currency," *The Scots Magazine* 26 (December 1764): 635; "Kellar and Company's Advertisements," *The Scots Magazine* 26 (December 1764): 636. Keller's case is in fact a bit murky. *The Scots Magazine* in February 1765 reported rumors that Keller, having been issued a court summons, had absconded. Quoting a letter to the *Edinburgh Courant,* they described Keller as " 'an

obscure person of no fortune, who settled some years ago [in Glasgow], as a French schoolmaster, afterwards turned merchant; failed, and compounded with his creditors; set up in business again; and, within these few months, thought proper to issue notes of 5s. 10s. and 20s. to a considerable extent, in name of himself and company. No body knew his partners; and, it is believed, he had none; and now he is said to have fled the country." See "An Explanation of & Co. in Notes, Called For," *The Scots Magazine* 27 (February 1765): 82; "Prosecution Against J. Baillie for Forging Bank-Notes," *The Scots Magazine* 27 (February 1765): 95–96. Yet there is evidence that a George Keller & Co. was still conducting business after 1765, as the 1770 edition of *The Universal Accountant and Complete Merchant* records an invoice for the company from 11 July 1769. Keller himself could therefore plausibly have been the victim in 1764–1765 of a charlatan printing additional notes in his name. See William Gordon, *The Universal Accountant and Complete Merchant,* vol. 2 (Glasgow: Alexander Donaldson, 1770), 328. An additional curiosity is that Keller, listed as a wine merchant in Glasgow, appears to have in 1765 subscribed to two copies of *The American Negotiator.* See J. Wright, *The American Negotiator: Or, The Various Currencies of the British Colonies* (London: J. Smith, 1765), 48. Regardless, however, of whether or not Keller was a mountebank, the fact that his is the only publicized instance of note fraud (aside from forgeries), and that his case received so much media attention from Aberdeen to Glasgow to Edinburgh, is perhaps revealing in and of itself as to the rarity of such cases.

96. John Buchanan, *Banking in Glasgow during the Olden Time* (Glasgow: David Robertson, 1862), 7n.

97. "Affairs in Scotland," *The Scots Magazine* 26 (September 1764): 518. The note is signed "P. Williamson." Peter Williamson was a famous Aberdonian, kidnapped and enslaved in his youth, who later wrote a history of his adventures. In addition to operating an Edinburgh coffeehouse, he also started the first penny post in Edinburgh. Whether his "Ready Money Bank" was intended as a pure gag or as a humorous but genuine form of credit for his clients is therefore unclear. See Peter Williamson, *French and Indian Cruelty Exemplified, in the Life, and Various Vicissitudes of Fortune, of Peter Williamson, who was Carried off from Aberdeen in his Infancy, and Sold for a Slave in Pennsylvania* (Edinburgh: J. Stewart, 1792), Bodleian Library, University of Oxford.

98. Rait, *Union Bank,* 34; Stevenson, *Scottish Antiquary,* 71–73; Boase, *Banking in Dundee,* 57. *The Scots Magazine* issue for October 1764 takes the Mason Barrowman Company note signed by Johnston and Dunbar as genuine; see "Affairs in Scotland," *The Scots Magazine* 26 (October 1764): 574. Graham and Kerr likewise seem to take one of the Mason Barrowman Company notes seriously; see Graham, *One Pound Note,* 61; Kerr, *Banking in Scotland,* 87.

99. Buchanan, *Banking in Glasgow,* 7n–8n; Boase, *Banking in Dundee,* 61.

100. Buchanan, *Banking in Glasgow,* 62; Boase, *Banking in Dundee,* 61.

101. Stevenson, *Scottish Antiquary,* 71–72.

102. Forbes, *Memoirs,* 9.

103. *The Scots Magazine* 26 (April 1764): 229n. More likely, they ceased note issuance under pressure from the public banks.

104. *The Scots Magazine* 23 (August 1761): 442.

105. Cited in Boase, *Banking in Dundee,* 61, 64.

106. Buchanan, *Banking in Glasgow,* 5.

107. *Edinburgh Evening Courant* (July 1730) quoted in Buchanan, *Banking in Glasgow,* 6–7.

108. *The Glasgow Journal* (May 1767), quoted in Buchanan, *Banking in Glasgow,* 8. David Watson's firm eventually became the private banking house of his sons, James and Robert Watson & Co.

109. John M'Ure, *The History of Glasgow* (Glasgow: Hutchison & Brookman, 1830), 227–229. Cited by Buchanan, *Banking in Glasgow,* 6.

110. "Of Abolishing or Regulating Private Banking," *The Scots Magazine* 26 (November 1764): 596.

111. Kerr, *Banking in Scotland,* 85.

112. Hamilton, "Scotland's Balance of Payments," 355.

113. Smith, *Wealth of Nations,* 1:451.

114. Quoted in Boase, *Banking in Dundee,* 45.

115. Directors' Minutes, Lloyds Banking Group Archive, 17 January 1763.

116. Royal Bank of Scotland, "A List of the Names of the Proprietors of the Royal Bank of Scotland," 13 February 1760, Goldsmiths' Library, University of London; "A List of the Names of the Adventurers in the Bank of Scotland," 6 February 1765, Goldsmiths' Library, University of London; Charter of the British Linen Company, 1746, Goldsmiths' Library, University of London.

117. Directors' Minutes, Lloyds Banking Group Archive, 28 January 1765.

118. The resolution, furthermore, was not to take effect until 15 May the following year. The gentlemen of Banff agreed to publish the resolution "in the Aberdeen and Edinburgh newspapers and to be read in every Parish Church within the County the 24th day of March and two following Sundays."

119. Directors' Minutes, Lloyds Banking Group Archive, 25 March 1765.

120. Quoted in Boase, *Banking in Dundee,* 45–46.

121. Ibid.

122. "On Our Banks and Paper-Currency," *The Scots Magazine* 26 (February 1764): 89; emphasis in original.

123. Munn, *Scottish Provincial Banking,* 19.

124. Boase, *Banking in Dundee,* 2.

125. Ibid.

126. "On Our Banks and Paper-Currency," *The Scots Magazine* 26 (February 1764): 89.

127. "On the Banks and Currency in Scotland," *Caledonian Mercury* (1764), reprinted in *The Scots Magazine* 26 (October 1764): 528.

128. The excess supply of Scottish bills relative to bills on London, a result of the postwar trade deficit, meant that London-based merchants could buy Scottish bills well below par and ship them to agents in Edinburgh to purchase Scottish goods for importation into England.

129. For Scottish trade statistics from 1760 to1780, see David Macpherson, *Annals of Commerce,* 3:339, 351, 364–365, 384–385, 409–410, 434–435, 455–456, 475–476, 486–487, 494–495, 508, 518–519, 532–533, 549–550, 564, 585, 599, 614, 632, 651, 673.

3. Procuring an Act

1. Adam Smith, *An Inquiry into the Nature and Causes of the Wealth of Nations,* vol. 1 (1776; reprint, New York: P. F. Collier & Son, 1902), 446.

2. Andrew Kerr, *History of Banking in Scotland* (Glasgow: David Bryce & Son, 1884); Robert Rait, *History of the Union Bank of Scotland* (Glasgow: J. Smith & Son, 1930); Charles Munn, *The Scottish Provincial Banking Companies, 1747–1864* (Edinburgh: John Donald Publishers), 18–20; Kevin Dowd, *Laissez-Faire Banking* (New York: Routledge, 1993); James Gherity, "The Option Clause in Scottish Banking, 1730–65: A Reappraisal," *Journal of Money, Credit and Banking* 27, no. 3 (August 1995), 713–726; Randall Kroszner, "Free Banking: The Scottish Experience as an Example for Emerging Economies," World Bank Policy Research Working Paper 1536 (November 1995); Richard Saville, *Bank of Scotland: A History, 1695–1995* (Edinburgh: Edinburgh University Press, 1996), 148.

3. Lloyd's Banking Group Archives, Directors' Minute Books, 6 January 1764. For listings of the directors of the three chartered banks, see John Chapman, *The Universal Scots Almanack* (Edinburgh: Walter Ruddiman, John Richardson and Co., 1767).

4. Lloyd's Banking Group Archives, Directors' Minute Books, 30 December 1763; Lloyd's Banking Group Archives, Directors' Minute Books, 6, 9 January 1764.

5. Ibid.

6. Lloyd's Banking Group Archives, Directors' Minute Books, 6 January 1764. The delegates were additionally instructed to remain neutral so far as the British Linen Company, which also held a royal charter, was concerned. Lord Milton, Deputy Governor of the Royal Bank, was also a major shareholder, founder, and former Deputy Governor of the British Linen Company.

7. Ibid.

8. Ibid.

9. Ibid.

10. Neil Munro, *The History of the Royal Bank of Scotland* (Glasgow: Grimsay Press, 1928), 128. Also quoted in Munn, *Scottish Provincial Banking,* 20.

11. Provost Ingram to Lord Privy Seal, 2 January 1764, in *Selections from the Mure Family Papers Preserved at Caldwell,* pt. 2, vol. 1, ed. William Mure (Paisley: Alexander Gardner, 1883), 208.

12. Ibid., 1:209.

13. Ibid., 1:209–220.

14. Mure suggests the probable author was Ingram himself or John Glassford. See Mure, *Selections,* pt. 2, 1:220n.

15. "Thoughts Concerning Banks, and the Paper Currency of Scotland. With Notes by Sir James Stuart of Coltness," in Mure, *Selections,* pt. 2, 1:227. Regarding resolutions by prominent merchants, most notably in Aberdeen, to receive only notes issued by the two public banks, the memorial's authors made sure to highlight the ambiguity as to "whether these resolutions have resulted wholly from a persuasion of this being the best remedy to the disease, or have partly been owing to the influence of the two Banks at Edinburgh."

16. Ibid., 1:230.

17. Ibid., 1:223.

18. Quoted in Charles Boase, *A Century of Banking in Dundee* (Edinburgh: R. Grant & Son, 1867), 45–46. Furthermore, Sir James and his fellow Renfrewshire Commissioners resolved "That, therefore, as an effectual remedy for the evils so justly complained of, the meeting resolve to apply to Parliament for a law to abolish these optional clauses, and to oblige all Banks or branches in Scotland to make ready and punctual payment, on demand, of the Notes issued by them, in good and lawful money of Great Britain: and recommend to the Presses to transmit a copy of these resolutions to Patrick Crawfurd, Esq., their representative, and to the members of either House of Parliament who have interests in this county, and to request them to promote a law for these purposes." The meeting ordered these resolutions to be published in the Edinburgh and Glasgow newspapers.

19. Several days before the meeting between the partners of the Thistle and Ship, Glassford and Mure evidently met with political economist Sir James Steuart of Coltness, who had earlier offered detailed notes and comments on the memorial.

20. John Glassford to Baron William Mure, 8 January 1765, in *Selections from the Mure Family Papers Preserved at Caldwell,* pt. 2, vol. 2, ed. William Mure (Paisley: Alexander Gardner, 1883), 3.

21. Glassford to Mure, 8 January 1765 in Mure, *Selections,* pt. 2, 2:5.

22. Ibid. It is perhaps telling that the Thistle was the only one of the big three Glasgow banks fully committed to banning optional clauses, as it was the only bank against which option was ever possibly invoked by another bank, when in February 1764 the Old and Royal Banks resolved to mark notes in the event of a rumored note raid by the Thistle (see Chapter 2). Directors' Minute Books, Lloyds Banking Group Archives, 2 February 1764.

23. Sydney Checkland, *Scottish Banking: A History, 1695–1973* (Glasgow: Collins, 1975), 104–106; Tyler Cowen and Randall Kroszner, "Scottish Banking before 1845: A Model for Laissez-Faire?," *Journal of Money, Credit and Banking* 21, no. 2 (May 1989): 224–225.

24. *The Scots Magazine* 27 (January 1765): 41.

25. See Royal Bank of Scotland, "A List of the Names of the Proprietors of the Royal Bank of Scotland," 13 February 1760, Goldsmiths' Library, University of London. Sir Gilbert refers to ambassadors from "the Bank," so it is unclear to which bank he is referring. Given, however, that the Bank of Scotland and Royal Bank of Scotland were typically referred to as the "Old Bank" and "New Bank" respectively, it seems sensible that by "the Bank" Sir Gilbert is here referring to the bank in which Baron Mure was partner. Charles Boase, *A Century of Banking in Dundee* (Edinburgh: R. Grant & Son, 1867), 59.

26. Sir Gilbert Elliot to Baron William Mure, 22 February 1764, in Mure, *Selections,* pt. 2, 1:239–240.

27. Lloyd's Banking Group Archives, Directors' Minute Books, 19 January 1764.

28. Lord Privy Seal to Baron Mure, 2 February 1764, in Mure, *Selections,* pt. 2, 1:232–233.

29. See Munn, *Scottish Provincial Banking,* 19–20.

30. "Memoranda from Lord Privy Seal," in Mure, *Selections,* pt. 2, 1:234–235. Accompanying the declaration they included a memorial—presumably a revised draft of that sent by Lord Provost Ingram to the Lord Privy Seal—expounding their reasons for dropping the optional clause.

31. John Campbell, 4th Duke of Argyll and formerly M.P. for Dunbartonshire, was also a member of the Privy Council but had left the House of Commons upon inheriting his peerage. See *The London Gazette,* 2 January 1762, p. 1; Romney R. Sedgwick, "Campbell, John (c. 1693–1770), of Mamore, Dunbarton, and Coombe Bank, Kent," in *The History of Parliament: The House of Commons, 1754–1790,* ed. Lewis Namier and John Brooke (London: Secker & Warburg, 1964), 186–187.

32. James Gherity, "An Early Publication by Adam Smith," *History of Political Economy* 25, no. 2 (Summer 1993): 246–247. See also James Gherity, "The Evolution of Adam Smith's Theory of Banking," *History of Political Economy* 26, no. 3 (Fall 1994): 436–437; Sydney Checkland, "Adam Smith and the Bankers," in *Essays on Adam Smith,* ed. Andrew Skinner and Thomas Wilson (Oxford: Clarendon, 1975), 509. Gherity (1993) further notes that, given Smith's close friendships with several of the partners of the Thistle and Arms and the fact that they often met at several of the Glasgow clubs to which they all belonged, it would be odd for the partners to have sought the counsel of Sir James Steuart—who had only recently returned from almost two decades in exile and whose only connection to the bankers was through his cousin, Baron Mure—but not Smith. Here, Gherity cites David Murray, *Early Burgh Organization in Scotland* (Glasgow: Maclehose, Jackson, 1924), 353n, 443–450; Charles Fay, *Adam Smith and the Scotland of His Day* (Cambridge: Cambridge University Press, 1956), 34; John Bell, "Adam Smith, Clubman," *Scottish Journal of Political Economy* 7 (June 1960): 109–110; John Rae, *Life of Adam Smith* (New York: Augustus M. Kelley, 1965), 91, 94, 258–259.

33. Lord Privy Seal to Baron Mure, 2 February 1764 in Mure, *Selections,* pt. 2, 1:232.

34. Checkland, *Scottish Banking,*120; Gherity, "The Evolution of Adam Smith's Theory of Banking," 437. Further evidence cited by Gherity for Smith's presence in London in late January 1764 is a letter from Glasgow to Smith by Joseph Black, dated 23 January 1764, in which Black mentions that Smith's mother had been pleased to receive a letter from him, apparently in London, several days earlier. Since Smith did not arrive in Paris until 13 February 1764, his presence in London just before then is highly probable. See Gherity, "An Early Publication by Adam Smith," 245–247; Joseph Black to Adam Smith, 23 January 1764, in *The Correspondence of Adam Smith,* vol. 6, ed. Ernest Mossner and Ian Ross (Oxford: Oxford University Press, 1987), 98.

35. Emphasis in original.

36. Lloyd's Banking Group Archives, Directors' Minute Books, 26 January 1764.

37. Ibid. 3 and 4 Anne c. 9 (1704); 7 Anne c. 25 (1708).

38. Lloyd's Banking Group Archives, Directors' Minute Books, 2 February 1764.

39. Ibid.

40. Charter of the British Linen Company, 1746, Goldsmiths' Library, University of London. It is somewhat unclear whether Sir Gilbert was referring to Alexander Montgomerie, 10th Earl of Eglinton, or his younger brother, Archibald Montgomerie, M.P. for Ayrshire and future 11th Earl of Eglinton (following his brother's murder in October 1769). Three pieces of evidence, however, suggest the former. First, the meeting also included Patrick Murray, 5th Lord Elibank, who sat in the Lords but not the Commons. Second, the October 1769 issue of *The Scots Magazine,* reporting on the 10th Earl of Eglinton's death, noted that "to him chiefly we are indebted for the act respecting the Scottish banks." Third, Sir William Fraser, the prominent nineteenth-century Scottish historian who was invited by the 13th Earl of Eglinton to compile the family's papers, remarked on the 10th Earl of Eglinton's zeal for Scottish bank regulation, writing that "it was in a great measure owing to his prudent and patriotic exertions that the optional clause of the Scottish Bank Act . . . was abolished shortly before his election as one of the representative peers." See "Affairs in Scotland," *The Scots Magazine* 31 (October 1769): 556–558; William Fraser, ed., *Memorials of the Montgomeries, Earls of Eglinton* (Edinburgh, 1859), 120; Edith Lady Haden-Guest, "Montgomerie, Hon. Archibald (1726–96), of Minnoch, Ayr," in Namier and Brooke, *History of Parliament,* 157–158.

41. Quoted in William Graham, *The One Pound Note in the Rise and Progress of Banking in Scotland, and its Adaptability to England* (Edinburgh: James Thin, 1886), 65–66.

42. James Douglas, *Scottish Banknotes* (London: Stanley Gibbons, 1975), 54–55.

43. James Boswell, *James Boswell's London Journal, 1762–1763,* 2nd ed., ed. Frederick Albert Pottle (New Haven, CT: Yale University Press, 2004), 51n, 123.

44. Munn notes that this latter acceptance was a major concession by the public banks, for it essentially meant recognizing the private banks as banks and eliminated one of their main arguments for the superior security of chartered banknotes. Munn, *Scottish Provincial Banking,* 20.

45. Lloyd's Banking Group Archives, Directors' Minute Books, 13 March 1764.

46. Edith Lady Haden-Guest, "Miller, Thomas (1717–89), of Glenlee, Kirkcudbright Stewartry and Barskimming, Ayr," in Namier and Brooke, *History of Parliament,* 139–140; Edith Lady Haden-Guest, "Gilmour, Sir Alexander, 3rd Bt. (c.1737–92), of Craigmillar, Edinburgh," in Namier and Brooke, *History of Parliament,* 502; "A List of the Names of the Adventurers in the Bank of Scotland," 7 February 1760. See also House of Commons, 19 March 1764, *Journals of the House of Commons,* vol. 29 (1764), 963.

47. Munn, *Scottish Provincial Banking,* 21.

48. John Glassford to Adam Smith, 5 November 1764, in Mossner and Ross, *Correspondence of Adam Smith,* 6:104–105.

49. Lloyd's Banking Group Archives, Directors' Minute Books, 19 November 1764.

50. Boase, *Banking in Dundee,* 59.

51. Munn, *Scottish Provincial Banking,* 21.

52. House of Commons, 18 February 1765, *Journals of the House of Commons,* vol. 30 (1765), 156.

53. Archibald Campbell, 3rd Duke of Argyll and 1st Earl of Ilay, had been one of the key promoters and investors in the British Linen Company and served as the bank's first governor. Upon his death, his titles, the Argyll estate, and all Scottish property passed to his cousin, John Campbell, who became 4th Duke of Argyll. See James Balfour Paul, *The Scots Peerage: Founded on Wood's Edition of Sir Robert Douglas's Peerage of Scotland; Containing an Historical and Genealogical Account of the Nobility of that Kingdom,* vol. 1 (Edinburgh: David Douglas, 1904), 380; Charles Malcolm, *The History of the British Linen Bank* (Edinburgh: T. & A. Constable, 1950); Charter of the British Linen Company, 1746, Goldsmiths' Library, University of London.

On 24 May 1765, two days after the Lords approved the Bank Act, Lord Frederick accepted the Office of Keeper of His Majesty's Privy Seal of Scotland and was sworn in on 29 May, replacing Stuart-Mackenzie. See House of Lords, 24 May 1765, *Journals of the House of Lords,* vol. 31 (1765), 433; *The London Gazette,* 1 June 1765, p. 1.

54. Charter of the British Linen Company, 1746, Goldsmiths' Library, University of London.

55. Dempster was in fact later arrested (though eventually acquitted) on the charge of bribery. He was alleged to have attempted to bribe several town councilors to secure their votes in the annual election of magistrates and councilors. *The Scots Magazine* 30 (August 1768): 407–409.

The final member of the drafting team was Sir Alexander Gilmour, M.P. for Edinburghshire. See House of Commons, 18 February 1765, *Journals of the House of*

Commons, vol. 30 (1765), 156; House of Commons, 10 May 1765, *Journals of the House of Commons,* vol. 30 (1765), 415; Charter of the British Linen Company, 1746, Goldsmiths' Library, University of London; Royal Bank of Scotland, "A List of the Names of the Proprietors of the Royal Bank of Scotland," 13 February 1760, Goldsmiths' Library, University of London; Bank of Scotland, "A List of the Names of the Adventurers in the Bank of Scotland," 6 February 1765, Goldsmiths' Library, University of London; "Bank of Scotland Family Tree," Lloyds Banking Group Archives; Edna Healey, *Coutts & Co., 1692–1992: The Portrait of a Private Bank* (Sevenoaks: Hodder & Stoughton, 1992); Edith Lady Haden-Guest, "Campbell, Lord Frederick (1729–1816), of Ardencaple, Dunbarton, and Coombe Bank, Kent," in Namier and Brooke, *History of Parliament,* 182–183; Edith Lady Haden-Guest, "Coutts, James (1733–78), of Hampton, Mdx. and Whitsome Hill, Berwicks," in Namier and Brooke, *History of Parliament,* 263–264; Edith Lady Haden-Guest, "Dempster, George (1732–1818), of Dunnichen, Forfar," in Namier and Brooke, *History of Parliament,* 313–316; Edith Lady Haden-Guest, "Edmonstone, Archibald (1717–1807), of Duntreath, Stirling," in Namier and Brooke, *History of Parliament,* 380–382; Edith Lady Haden-Guest, "Elliot, Gilbert (1722–77), of Minto, Roxburgh," in Namier and Brooke, *History of Parliament,* 390–394; Edith Lady Haden-Guest, "Miller, Thomas (1717–89), of Glenlee, Kirkcudbright Stewartry and Barskimming, Ayr," in Namier and Brooke, *History of Parliament,* 139–140; Edith Lady Haden-Guest, "Oswald, James (1715–69), of Dunnikier, Fife," in Namier and Brooke, *History of Parliament,* 237–240; Edith Lady Haden-Guest, "Stuart Mackenzie, Hon. James (1719–1800), of Rosehaugh, Ross and Belmont, Angus," in Namier and Brooke, *History of Parliament,* 503–507; James Oswald to William Mure, 25 December 1746, in Mure, *Selections,* pt. 2, 1:80–83. Evidently Sir Gilbert Elliot was also on sufficiently familiar terms with Baron Mure to address him as "Willy"; see Gilbert Elliot to Baron Mure, June 1742 in Mure, *Selections,* pt. 2, 1:28–29.

56. House of Commons, 7 March 1765, *Journals of the House of Commons,* vol. 30 (1765), 231; House of Commons, 1 April 1765, *Journals of the House of Commons,* vol. 30 (1765), 316.

57. House of Lords, 2 April 1765, *Journals of the House of Lords,* vol. 31 (1765), 115–116; House of Lords, 15 April 1765, *Journals of the House of Lords,* vol. 31 (1765), 126.

58. House of Lords, 23 April 1765, *Journals of the House of Lords,* vol. 31 (1765), 150.

59. House of Lords, 15 April 1765, *Journals of the House of Lords,* vol. 31 (1765), 126; House of Lords, 19 April 1765, *Journals of the House of Lords,* vol. 31 (1765), 142; House of Lords, 23 April 1765, *Journals of the House of Lords,* vol. 31 (1765), 150; Royal Bank of Scotland, "A List of the Names of the Proprietors of the Royal Bank of Scotland," 13 February 1760, Goldsmiths' Library, University of London; Bank of Scotland, "A List of the Names of the Adventurers in the Bank of Scotland," 6 February 1765, Goldsmiths' Library, University of London.

60. House of Lords, 8 May 1765, *Journals of the House of Lords,* vol. 31 (1765), 185–186.

61. House of Commons, 10, 13, 15 May 1765, *Journals of the House of Commons,* vol. 30 (1765), 413, 421, 426; House of Lords, 15, 16, 17, 20 May 1765, *Journals of the House of Lords,* vol. 31 (1765), 205–206, 209–210.

62. Boase, *Banking in Dundee,* 59–60.

63. Ibid., 61–62; Graham, *One Pound Note,* 63–64. Indeed, it appears that before the final passage of the act, interests sympathetic to banking-sector consolidation in Perth were already pitching their case to the Scottish public. In an advertisement placed in the 19 April 1765 issue of *The Edinburgh Advertiser,* an anonymous writer suggested that "the legislature will certainly attend to the interest of this country, if they pass into a law the bill now depending for regulating the paper currency" and "to suppress all the little circulators of notes" who, he argued, "it is the duty of the rich banks, and of every man who wishes well to his country, to distress." Concluding, the writer urged that the banking companies of "such a trading town as Perth" should join together "to carry on a banking trade, which will yield double their present profit, with credit and honour." A.B., "To the Publishers of the *Edinburgh Advertiser,*" *The Edinburgh Advertiser* 3, no. 136 (19 April 1765): 253.

64. John Buchanan, *Banking in Glasgow during the Olden Time* (Glasgow: David Robertson, 1862), 8n. Kerr reports that the acquisitions occurred on 29 October and 1 January, respectively. Kerr, *Banking in Scotland,* 100.

65. Douglas, *Scottish Banknotes,* 147. Evidence is that George Keller & Co. carried on the trading side of their business after 1765, as the 1770 edition of *The Universal Accountant and Complete Merchant* records an invoice for the company from 11 July 1769. See William Gordon, *The Universal Accountant and Complete Merchant,* vol. 2 (Glasgow: Alexander Donaldson, 1770), 328.

66. Boase, *Banking in Dundee,* 65.

67. On 12 June 1763, Wyllie placed the following signed advertisement in *The Aberdeen Journal:* "Bank Office, Exchange Coffee-House, Aberdeen. Advertisement by Alexander Wyllie, Vintner. Whereas, a considerable number of 5s. Notes, accepted by me, dated the 10th of June 1763, were issued at this office, which are probably dispersed in different parts of the country, a great part of which have not as yet been presented for payment. This is, therefore, intimating to all persons who may be possessed of such Notes that they will be punctually paid at the Exchange Coffee-House here, on or before the 5th day of August next. The holders of such Notes as are not presented before that time must blame themselves if they do not receive payment. (Signed) Alex. Wyllie. Aberdeen, 12th June 1765. N.B.—All the Notes that are presented will be paid in silver, as the persons concerned in this Bank do not pretend to impose upon the public by offering other Notes in exchange." Gavin Tourreff, ed., *Antiquarian Gleanings from Aberdeenshire Records* (Aberdeen: George and Robert King, 1859), 255.

68. Boase, *Banking in Dundee,* 65, 554; Kerr, *Banking in Scotland,* 87.

69. "Affairs in Scotland," *The Scots Magazine* 31 (June 1769): 333. Mentioned in Munn, *Scottish Provincial Banking,* 24.

70. Graham, *One Pound Note,* 88.

71. Cowen and Kroszner, "Scottish Banking," 224–225.

72. Graham, *One Pound Note,* 69; Boase, *Banking in Dundee,* 65; Buchanan, *Banking in Glasgow,* 14–15; Kerr, *Banking in Scotland,* 90–91. Graham reports that the Ship Bank's hours had previously been "from 10 till 12 forenoon, and from 3 till 5 o'clock afternoon, except on Saturdays, when the bank was open only from 9 till 11." Boase likewise writes that before the 1765 act, the Edinburgh banks "opened from between nine and ten till noon, and from between two and three till four P.M." Kerr notes that "a minor effect of this Act was an alteration of the hours during which the banks were open for business. Formerly they were open forenoon and afternoon, with an interval for refreshment: (we read of the worthy citizens going for their 'meridian' when the 'grill-bells' rang at half-past eleven from St. Giles, just as in the afternoon they took their 'four hours' penny,' i.e. a penny glass of ale). This arrangement was changed to a continuous period from nine to three o'clock; these being the hours during which notes not paid on demand might be protested."

73. Rait, *Union Bank,* 28; Kerr, *Banking in Scotland,* 74. Rait reports that "in the prevailing scarcity of specie" the Aberdeen Company "must have had difficulty in meeting any sudden demand, and it is probable that, like the Bank of Scotland in 1704 and 1728, it maintained an inadequate cash reserve. It gave up business voluntarily in 1753 and does not seem to have defaulted." Though failures were rare, exit was not uncommon, occurring typically on the partner's death in single-partner firms.

The failure of the banking house of Adam and Thomas Fairholme is described by William Forbes. Adam Fairholme had gone to London toward the end of the Seven Years' War to speculate in government securities, and though he at one point had an unrealized profit of some £70,000, "By his continuing his operations, they lost their imaginary profits; and being tempted like losing gamesters to enter still more deeply into the Alley, the whole affair ended most unhappily." With losses mounting, in March 1764 he declared himself bankrupt, with the inevitable consequence that the banking house in Edinburgh was forced to stop payment the same month and declare bankruptcy. However, Forbes recounts that "as the misfortune of the Messrs Fairholme was known to have been occasioned by their speculations in the Alley, it produced no injurious effect on the credit of the other established banking-houses in Edinburgh. Nevertheless, the situation of money transactions there was extremely unpleasant. The rate of exchange for bills on London was as high as three, four, and even five per cent against Scotland. This of necessity occasioned demands on the banks at Edinburgh for specie, which they were unable or unwilling to answer; and for that reason they avoided advancing money for the accommodation of the trade of the country, lest their notes, as would have infallibly happened, should instantly return on them for specie." Forbes, *Memoirs of a Banking House,* 20.

74. William Hogg and Sons failed on 16 August, and Ebenezer McCulloch & Co. failed sometime in December. See David Rae, "Answers for William Scot, Writer in Edinburgh, and one of the Depute-Clerks to the Bills, to the Petition of Alexander Farquharson, Accountant in Edinburgh, Trustee for the Creditors of Mess. William Hogg and Son" (Edinburgh, 24 October, 1770); Forbes, *Memoirs of a Banking House,* 24; Saville, *Bank of Scotland,* 157.

75. "Affairs in Scotland," *The Scots Magazine* 33 (June 1771), 326. Buchanan and Kerr report that Alexander Johnston, Hugh Lawson & Co. and McAdam & Co. were acquired for £18,000 and £7,350, respectively. Buchanan, *Banking in Glasgow,* 8n; Kerr, *Banking in Scotland,* 99–100.

76. Graham, *One Pound Note,* 58–59; James Grant, *Old and New Edinburgh,* vol. 3 (London: Cassell, Petter, Galpin & Co., 1883), 235.

77. For descriptions of the cash account and bills of exchange, see Munn, *Scottish Provincial Banking,* 115–126, 286.

78. Lloyd's Banking Group Archives, Directors' Minute Books, 17, 23 December 1765. The issue was again discussed a week later, with directors affirming their earlier decision.

79. Although the August 1768 issue of *The Scots Magazine* reports that both banks did, in fact, issue guinea notes in 1768. "Affairs in Scotland," *The Scots Magazine* 30 (August 1768): 446.

80. Douglas, *Scottish Banknotes.*

81. Forbes, *Memoirs of a Banking House,* 85n; Boase, *Banking in Dundee,* 2.

82. "Affairs in England," *The Scots Magazine* 36 (July 1774), 389.

83. *The Scots Magazine* 34 (July 1772), 395.

84. Boase, *Banking in Dundee,* 89, 97; although the bank ultimately wound up, in 1774, with its creditors paid in full.

85. Ibid., 87; Kerr, *Banking in Scotland,* 102, 105; Saville, *Bank of Scotland,* 180–181.

86. Forbes, *Memoirs,* 9n.

87. Directors' Minutes, Lloyds Banking Group Archives, 27 March 1728; Munro, *Royal Bank of Scotland,* 59; Saville, *Bank of Scotland,* 103.

88. "Account of the Stagnation of Public Credit," *The Scots Magazine* 34 (June 1772): 313.

89. Quoted in Graham, *One Pound Note,* 89–90. The Ayr office had been closed since 22 June. Kerr, *Banking in Scotland,* 103.

90. "Scotland," *The Scots Magazine* 34 (September 1772): 515.

91. "Affairs in Scotland," *The Scots Magazine* 34 (September 1772): 515.

92. Directors' Minute Books, Lloyd's Banking Group Archives, March 1764. Sir William Forbes reports that at the time of the Fairholme's failure: "The situation of money transactions there was extremely unpleasant. The rate of exchange for bills on London was as high as three, four, and even five per cent. against Scotland. This of necessity occasioned demands on the banks at Edinburgh for specie, which they were

unable or unwilling to answer; and for that reason they avoided advancing money for the accommodation of the trade of the country, lest their notes, as would have infallibly happened, should instantly return on them for specie. In London the character and credit of Scottish paper was at the lowest ebb, and the Bank of England was extremely shy of discounting bills drawn on London from Edinburgh." See Forbes, *Memoirs,* 20–21.

93. Ibid., 1, 2 April 1762.

94. Saville, *Bank of Scotland,* 142; Checkland, *Scottish Banking,* 110. Evidently the Edinburgh private banks of William Alexander & Sons, Adam & Thomas Fairholme, and William Cumming & Sons, none of whom issued their own notes, were key in supplying the Glasgow banks with Edinburgh notes. Directors' Minutes, Lloyds Banking Group Archive, 10 February 1762. Also in Edinburgh, the firm of Mansfield, Hunter & Co. issued its own notes in 1761–1762. See *The Scots Magazine* 26 (April 1764): 229n. More likely, they ceased note issuance under pressure from the public banks.

95. Ledger Books, Lloyds Banking Group Archive.

96. Saville, *Bank of Scotland,* 934, 939; Checkland, *Scottish Banking,* 237, 735, 737.

97. Boase, *Banking in Dundee,* 87.

98. Ilay Campbell, "Unto the Right Honourable the Lords of Council and Session, The Petition of Doctor Robert Herriot" (9 July 1766), British Library.

99. "The Late Bankruptcies Accounted For," *The Scots Magazine* 25 (August 1763): 459. See also Isabel Schnabel and Hyun Song Shin, "Liquidity and Contagion: The Crisis of 1763," *Journal of the European Economic Association* 2, no. 6 (December 2004): 929–968.

100. Further, under pressure from the public banks, the leading "Merchants and Dealers in Bills of Exchange" drew up a memorial pledging themselves to "discountenance and prevent all Artificial Demands of Specie on the Publick Banks." Manuscripts, Lloyds Banking Group Archives, 13 March 1764. See Checkland, *Scottish Banking,* 110–111.

101. *De Koopman* 4, no. 53 (1773): 412–413; Ernst Baasch, *Holländische Wirtschaftsgeschichte* (Jena: G. Fischer, 1927), 237–239; *Real-Zeitung, das ist Auszug der Neuesten Weltgeschichte: Mit Erläuterungen* 73 (14 September 1763): 566.

102. "Foreign Affairs," *London Magazine: or, Gentleman's Monthly Intelligencer* 32 (September 1763): 506–507; "The Late Bankruptcies Accounted For," *The Scots Magazine* 25 (August 1763): 458–460.

103. Saville, *Bank of Scotland,* 122–124.

104. Forbes, *Memoirs,* 41–44.

105. Saville, *Bank of Scotland,* 164; Checkland, *Scottish Banking,* 232; Letter Book, Lloyds Banking Group Archives, 23 July 1772; Minutes, Royal Bank of Scotland Group Archives, 15 July 1772.

106. Smith, *Wealth of Nations,* 1:380.

107. Boase, *Banking in Dundee,* 60.

108. "A Supply of Safe Currency Proposed," *The Scots Magazine* 26 (December 1764): 637–638.

109. "Cause and Cure of our Scarcity of Specie," *The Scots Magazine* 26 (February 1764): 89.

110. "A Remedy for the Present Scarcity of Silver," *The Scots Magazine* 26 (June 1764): 300.

111. "Regulations Proposed for Banking," *The Scots Magazine* 24 (March 1762): 135.

112. *The Annual Register, or a View of the History, Politicks, and Literature, for the Year 1765* (London: J. Dodsley, 1766), 90–91.

113. Checkland, *Scottish Banking,* 123; Munn, *Scottish Provincial Banking,* 29.

114. "Affairs in Scotland," *The Scots Magazine* 31 (December 1769): 669.

4. Prodigals and Projectors

1. "Thoughts Concerning Banks, and the Paper Currency of Scotland. With Notes by Sir James Steuart of Coltness," in *Selections from the Mure Family Papers Preserved at Caldwell,* pt. 2, vol. 1, ed. William Mure (Paisley: Alexander Gardner, 1883), 230–231.

2. James Gherity, "An Early Publication by Adam Smith," *History of Political Economy* 25, no. 2 (1993): 241–282.

3. "Thoughts Concerning Banks, and the Paper-Currency of Scotland," *The Scots Magazine* 25 (November 1763): 537; emphasis in original.

4. Ibid.

5. *The Edinburgh Advertiser* 3, no. 139 (30 April 1765): 279; emphasis in original. The list consisted of eight landed gentry, thirty-seven merchants in Dundee, and fifteen professionals.

6. *The Edinburgh Advertiser* 3, no. 145 (17 May 1765): 279.

7. "Thoughts," in Mure, *Selections,* pt. 2, 1:230n.

8. Charles Boase, *A Century of Banking in Dundee* (Edinburgh: R. Grant & Son, 1867), 89, 97. Though the bank ultimately wound itself up in 1774, with creditors paid in full.

9. "Affairs in Scotland," *The Scots Magazine* 34 (July 1772): 395.

10. Court Minutes, Bank of England Archive, 9, 23 July 1772; "Affairs in Scotland," *The Scots Magazine* 34 (July 1772): 395; William Forbes, *Memoirs of a Banking House* (Edinburgh: William and Robert Chambers, 1860), 27–28; John Clapham, *The Bank of England: A History,* vol. 1 (Cambridge: Cambridge University Press, 1968), 249.

11. The loan was in fact supposed to be for just £20,000 in promissory notes, but Douglas, Heron & Co. mistakenly sent an additional £10,000 in company bills, without any additional security from William Alexander and Sons. *The Precipitation*

and Fall of Mess. Douglas, Heron, and Company, Late Bankers in Air, with the Causes of their Distress and Ruin, Investigated and Considered, by a Committee of Inquiry Appointed by the Proprietors (Edinburgh, 1778), Appendix nos. 9, 10, pp. 108, 124, 127.

12. "Affairs in Scotland," *The Scots Magazine* 34 (July 1772): 395.

13. "Partners in the Douglas Heron and Company Bank," *The Scots Magazine* 34 (June 1772): 304–305.

14. Miscellaneous Papers, Lloyds Banking Group Archive, 21 April 1772.

15. "Affairs in Scotland," *The Scots Magazine* 34 (September 1772): 515.

16. Ibid. Saville incorrectly comments that creditors to Johnstone & Smith were paid 15s. in the pound. The wording of the trustee's advertisement, however, indicates that 15s. in the pound was a composition settlement, on account of the fact that some "poor people" could likely "ill afford to wait the future dividends of the estate." That subscribers were willing to offer 15s. in the pound on their own capital, until the estate could be settled, strongly suggests they expected at least that amount in final distribution. See Richard Saville, *Bank of Scotland: A History, 1695–1995* (Edinburgh: Edinburgh University Press, 1996), 181.

17. *Precipitation and Fall of Mess. Douglas, Heron, and Company,* Appendix no. 10, p. 123.

18. Ibid., 125.

19. "Matthew Boulton, Esq. and Others, Creditors of Samuel Garbet, late of Birmingham, and of Prestonpans, in Scotland, Merchant, a Bankrupt; Messrs. Mansfield, Ramsay, & Co. of Edinburgh, Bankers; Messrs. Douglas, Heron & Co., late Bankers in Ayr; and Walter Hogg, Trustee for the Creditors of Samuel Garbet & Co. of Carron Wharf," 18 April 1787, in *Reports of Cases Decided in The House of Loards, Upon Appeal from Scotland from 1753 to 1813,* vol. 3, ed. John Craigie, John Stewart, and Thomas Paton (Edinburgh: T. & T. Clark, 1853), 70–75; John Norris, "The Struggle for Carron: Samuel Garbett and Charles Gascoigne," *The Scottish Historical Review* 37, no. 124 (October 1958): 136–145; Charles Munn, *The Scottish Provincial Banking Companies, 1747–1864* (Edinburgh: John Donald Publishers, 1981), 35, 38n.

20. *Scots Revised Reports: Morison's Dictionary of Decisions* (Edinburgh: William Green and Sons, 1908), 210–211; Norris, "The Struggle for Carron," 140.

21. Both firms maintained London and Edinburgh operations, with Fordyce, Malcolm & Co., operating under the name Fordyce, Grant & Co. in London. Both had been heavily involved with Alexander Fordyce (a distant relative of John Fordyce, partner in Fordyce, Malcolm & Co.), who at the time of his failure owed approximately £64,000 to Fordyce, Malcolm & Co. and £40,000 to Charles Fergusson & Co. "Messrs. Douglas, Heron, and Company, Bankers in Air, Appellants; The Honourable John Grant, Esq.; One of the Barons of His Majesty's Court of Exchequer in Scotland, Respondent; The Respondent's Case," Heard at the Bar of the House of Lords (28 May 1774), British Library; Frank Brady, "So Fast to Ruin," *Ayrshire Collections* 11, no. 2 (1973): 29.

22. Another major creditor to Fordyce, Malcolm & Co. was the Duke of Gordon, who was married to the sister of John Fordyce's wife. The duke was said to have lost £16,000 through the bank's failure. See Brady, "So Fast to Ruin," 40.

23. "Minutes of the Meeting of the Creditors of Mess. Fordyce, Malcolm, and Company, Merchants in Edinburgh," *The Scots Magazine* 34 (August 1772): 424–427.

24. *Precipitation and Fall of Mess. Douglas, Heron, and Company,* 146–148.

25. Ibid., 123–128, Appendix no. 10, pp. 116–123; emphasis in original.

26. Ibid., 127–128. At the time of its failure, Charles Fergusson & Co. was indebted to Douglas, Heron & Co. in the amount of £13,000, while Fordyce, Malcolm & Co. owed the bank £22,373. See *Precipitation and Fall of Mess. Douglas, Heron, and Company,* 123; "Letter to the Partners of Mess. Douglas, Heron, and Company, in Answer to a Letter Addressed to Them, of 12th March 1779, under the Signature of John Fordyce" (18 June 1779), British Library.

27. "Letter to the Partners of Mess. Douglas, Heron, and Company, in Answer to a Letter Addressed to Them, of 12th March 1779, under the Signature of John Fordyce" (18 June 1779), British Library.

28. *Precipitation and Fall of Mess. Douglas, Heron, and Company,* 136.

29. "A List of Sequestrations of Personal Estates, by the Court of Session, on the Act 12 Geo. III. Cap. 72," *The Scots Magazine* 34 (July 1772): 400.

30. Ibid.

31. "Minutes of a Meeting of Creditors on the Bankrupt-Act," *The Scots Magazine* 34 (August 1772): 424–427.

32. Checkland, *Scottish Banking,* 133.

33. Act 12 Geo. III. Cap. 72.

34. Discussed in Checkland, *Scottish Banking,* 132.

35. "On Scottish Bankruptcies," *The Scots Magazine* 32 (January 1770): 21–22. The letter is dated 27 January 1770, in Edinburgh.

36. Act 12 Geo. III. Cap. 72. The paper nominated by the court was the *Edinburgh Evening Courant.* See "An Abstract of the Scots Bankrupt Act," *The Scots Magazine* 34 (June 1772): 281–288.

37. "Directions to the Creditors of Scottish Insolvents," *The Scots Magazine* 34 (July 1772): 362–363.

38. *Precipitation and Fall of Mess. Douglas, Heron, and Company,* 64.

39. Ibid., 115.

40. Ibid., 114.

41. Ibid., 115–120.

42. Ibid., 114, 120.

43. "Affairs in Scotland," *The Scots Magazine* 34 (July 1772): 395; Kerr cites the figure of £356,715, but this is contradicted by Somers, as well as by Douglas, Heron & Co.'s petition to Parliament in 1774, which refers to the sum of "£450,000, and upwards." See Andrew Kerr, *History of Banking in Scotland* (Glasgow: David Bryce & Son, 1884),

103–104; Robert Somers, *The Scotch Banks and System of Issue* (Edinburgh: Adam and Charles Black, 1873), 103; House of Commons, 25 February 1774, *Journals of the House of Commons,* vol. 34 (1804), 494.

44. David Hume to Adam Smith, October 1772, in Ernest Mossner and Ian Ross, *The Correspondence of Adam Smith,* vol. 6 (Oxford: Oxford University Press, 1987), 164–165.

45. Neil Munro, *The History of the Royal Bank of Scotland* (Glasgow: Grimsay Press, 1928), 138; Munn, *Scottish Provincial Banking,* 36; Larry Sechrest, "White's Free-Banking Thesis: A Case of Mistaken Identity," *The Review of Austrian Economics* 2, no. 1 (1988): 252; Tyler Cowen and Randall Kroszner, "Scottish Banking before 1845: A Model for Laissez-Faire?," *Journal of Money, Credit and Banking* 21, no. 2 (May 1989): 227–228; Saville, *Bank of Scotland,* 164–165, 186; Hugh Rockoff, "Upon Daedalian Wings of Paper Money: Adam Smith and the Crisis of 1772," NBER Working Paper 15594 (December 2009): 20; Tom Kärrlander, "Douglas Heron and Company, Bankers in Air (Ayr Bank): A Bank Crash in Scotland in 1772," Stockholm University Department of Economic History Working Paper 16 (2005). Rothbard also implies that the Bank of England was effectively a lender of last resort in late-eighteenth-century Scotland. See Murray Rothbard, "The Myth of Free Banking in Scotland," *Review of Austrian Economics* 2 (1988): 230–233.

46. Directors' Minute Books, Royal Bank of Scotland Archive, 15 June 1772; Court Minutes, Bank of England Archive, 2 July 1772; *The Glasgow Journal* (23 July 1772).

47. David Hume to Adam Smith, October 1772, in Mossner and Ross, *Correspondence of Adam Smith,* 6:164–165.

48. Kerr, *Banking in Scotland,* 111; Munn, *Scottish Provincial Banking,* 36; Saville, *Bank of Scotland,* 164.

49. The Duke of Buccleuch had written to the two public banks on 15 July 1772. The secretary to the joint board of directors reported that the duke's letter intimated that their directors had for some time been negotiating a loan of money in England sufficient to pay off their debts in London in order to enable them to wind up their affairs and to give up business as a banking company. "That they believe and are assured by a gentleman of very great credit in London that he can soon raise as much money upon a plan proposed by him as will answer this purpose provided they are able to command their circulation in Scotland without increasing their debt in London that their notes in the circle in Scotland do not amount to £120,000 in all and that many of them are daily coming in to their different offices in payment of their own debts but that still it will accelerate their business in London very much if the two banks will agree to take their notes in payments, and that Henry Dundas and Ilay Campbell, two of their extraordinary directors will meet with the directors of the banks, and treat further about, and settle the terms on which they proposed may be agreed to, and the security to be given for repayment of the principal and interest on the notes to be so received." Directors' Minutes, Lloyds

Banking Group Archive, 3 July 1773; Miscellaneous Papers, Lloyds Banking Group Archives, 21 October 1773.

50. Ledger Books, Lloyds Banking Group Archive, 1773–1774. Before the crisis broke, the directors of the Bank of Scotland had in fact sought clarification as to whether such bills, signed by Hogg as cashier, would be binding upon all the partners. See Miscellaneous Papers, Lloyds Banking Group Archive, April 1772.

51. "Affairs in Scotland," *The Scots Magazine* 35 (August 1773): 443.

52. Ibid., 668.

53. Richard Glover, "A Speech Introductory to the Proposals Laid Before the Annuitants of Mess. Douglas, Heron and Co. at the King's-Arms Tavern, Cornhill, on the Ninth of February, 1774," in Richard Glover, *The Substance of the Evidence: Delivered to a Committee of the Honourable House of Commons by the Merchants and Traders of London, Concerned in the Trade to Germany and Holland, as Summed Up by Mr. Glover. To which is Annexed, His Speech, Introductory to the Proposals Laid Before the Annuitants of Mess. Douglas, Heron and Co.* (London: J. Wilkie, 1774), 67–72; "Affairs in England and Scotland," *The Scots Magazine* 36 (February 1774): 106.

54. House of Commons, 25 February 1774, *Journals of the House of Commons,* vol. 34 (1804), 493–495.

55. While transferable stock was permitted under Scottish partnership law, the fact that many of Douglas, Heron & Co.'s creditors were English complicated the situation.

56. House of Commons, 25 February 1774, *Journals of the House of Commons,* vol. 34 (1804), 495.

57. House of Commons, 28 March 1774, *Journals of the House of Commons,* vol. 34 (1804), 600–601; "Proceedings in Parliament. Air Bank," *The Scots Magazine* 36 (April 1774): 196–199.

58. East India Company, "A List of the Names of all the Proprietors of East India Stock; Distinguishing the Principal Stock each Proprietor now Holds, and the Time when Such Proprietors became Possessed thereof," 9 March 1773, Goldsmiths' Library, University of London; John Brook, "Cornwall, Charles Wolfran (1735–89), of Barton Priors, nr. Winchester, Hants.," in *The History of Parliament: The House of Commons, 1754–1790,* ed. Lewis Namier and John Brooke (London: Secker & Warburg, 1964), 255; Mary Drummond, "Fuller, Richard (c. 1713–82), of Dorking, Surr.," in Namier and Brooke, *History of Parliament,* 477; Lewis Namier, "Henley Ongley, Robert (c. 1721–85), of Old Warden, Beds.," in Namier and Brooke, *History of Parliament,* 606; "Proceedings in Parliament. Air Bank," *The Scots Magazine* 36 (April 1774): 196–199.

59. Edith Lady Haden-Guest, "Dempster, George (1732–1818), of Dunnichen, Forfar.," in Namier and Brooke, *History of Parliament,* 313–314; Edith Lady Haden-Guest, "Dundas, Sir Lawrence, 1st Bt. (c.1710–81), of Kerse, Stirling and Aske, nr. Richmond, Yorks.," in Namier and Brooke, *History of Parliament,* 357; John Brooke,

"Fox, Hon. Charles James (1749–1806), of Wimbledon, Surr.," in Namier and Brooke, *History of Parliament,* 455; Edith Lady Haden-Guest, "Montgomery, James (1721–1803), of The Whim and Stanhope, Peebles.," in Namier and Brooke, *History of Parliament,* 159; John Brooke, "Seymour Conway, Francis, Visct. Beauchamp (1743–1822).," in Namier and Brooke, *History of Parliament,* 424; John Brooke, "Wedderburn, Alexander (1733–1805).," in Namier and Brooke, *History of Parliament,* 496.

60. House of Commons, 28, 30, 31 March 1774, *Journals of the House of Commons,* vol. 34 (1804), 601, 612, 614–615; House of Lords, *Journals of the House of Lords,* vol. 34 (1774), 104.

61. Miscellaneous Papers, Lloyds Banking Group Archives, 24 May 1780.

62. Ibid., 28 June, 8, 11, 28 July 1774; emphasis in original.

63. Ibid., 12 May 1780.

64. Ibid.

65. Robert Rait, *The History of the Union Bank of Scotland* (Glasgow: John Smith & Son, 1930), 167. Somers reports that there were 225 partners (Somers, *Scotch Banks,* 103). At the February 1774 meeting with annuitants regarding the proposed bond issue, however, the number of partners was cited as 241; "Affairs in England and Scotland," *The Scots Magazine* 36 (February 1774): 106.

66. Somers, *Scotch Banks,* 103; "Proceedings in Parliament. Air Bank," *The Scots Magazine* 36 (April 1774): 196.

67. Frank Brady, "So Fast to Ruin," *Ayrshire Collections* 11, no. 2 (1973): 34n; Edith Lady Haden-Guest, "Fergusson, Sir Adam, 3rd Bt. (1733–1813), of Kilkerran, Ayr," in Namier and Brooke, *History of Parliament,* 419.

68. William Maxwell, *The Decisions of the Court of Session,* vol. 17 (Edinburgh: Bell & Bradfute), 14605, 14668.

69. James Paterson, *History of the County of Ayr: with a Genealogical Account of the Families of Ayrshire,* vol. 1 (Ayr: John Dick, 1847), 205, 211–212; James Paterson, *History of the County of Ayr: with a Genealogical Account of the Families of Ayrshire,* vol. 2 (Ayr: John Dick, 1852), 78, 393; John Ward, "Ayrshire Landed Estates in the Nineteenth Century," *Ayrshire Archaeological and Natural History Collections* 8 (1969): 93–145; Sir John Whitefoord was forced to sell Ballochmyle in 1786, "Having been ruined by his connection with the Douglas and Heron Bank." He was evidently also close to the McAdams, permitting a financially strained James McAdam, formerly of Waterhead and cousin of John McAdam of Craigengillan, and subsequently his daughters, to rent Whitefoord Castle from 1770. See David McClure, "James McAdam and the Loss of Waterhead," *Ayrshire Notes* 33 (Spring 2007): 13–14; Paterson, *History of the County of Ayr,* 2:473.

70. George Robertson, *A Genealogical Account of the Principal Families of Ayrshire,* vol. 1 (Irvine, Ayrshire: Cunninghame Press, 1823), 225.

71. James Paterson, *History of the Counties of Ayr and Wigton,* vol. 1, pt. 2 (Edinburgh: James Stillie, 1863), 612.

72. McClure, "James McAdam," 7–17.

73. Quoted in McClure, "James McAdam," 15; emphasis in original. McAdam here refers to Ralph Nickleby, the principal antagonist in the Charles Dickens novel *The Life and Adventures of Nicholas Nickleby.* Ralph Nickleby is the main character's avaricious, scheming uncle.

74. Paterson, *History of the County of Ayr,* 1:310; Paterson, *Counties of Ayr and Wigton,* vol. 1, pt. 2, 704; McClure, "James McAdam," 15; William MacKenzie; *The History of Galloway: From the Earliest Period to the Present Time,* vol. 2 (Kirkcubright: John Nicholson, 1841), 476.

75. Paterson, *History of the County of Ayr,* 1:205n; Paterson, *History of the Counties of Ayr and Wigton,* vol. 1, pt. 1 (Edinburgh: James Stillie, 1863), 153n. A property reported to have changed hands "at the instance of the Douglas and Heron Banking Company and their creditors" was an estate at Bridgehouse, which in 1763 had been transferred from Andrew Cochrane, Lord Provost of Glasgow, to the trustees of James Brown. It was sold in 1785 to Hugh Hamilton of Pinmore. See Paterson, *History of the County of Ayr,* 1:212.

76. "Answers for Archibald Cockburn, Esq; of Cockpen, to the Petition of certain Partners of Douglas, Heron, and Company," 22 April 1780, Goldsmiths' Library, University of London; *Notes and Queries: A Medium of Inter-Communication for Literary Men, Artists, Antiquaries, Genealogists, Etc.,* vol. 8 (London: Bell & Daldy, 1859), 123; Angus Stewart, ed., *The Minute Book of the Faculty of Advocates,* vol. 46 (Edinburgh: Stair Society, 1999), xxxix.

77. John Moore to Baron Mure, 3 August 1772 in William Mure, ed., *Selections from the Mure Family Papers Preserved at Caldwell,* pt. 2, vol. 2 (Paisley: Alexander Gardner, 1883), 202.

78. Ian Simpson Ross, *The Life of Adam Smith* (Oxford: Oxford University Press, 1995), 12, 74–75, 199, 242.

79. Henry Gepp, *Adderbury* (Banbury: Banbury Guardian Office, 1924), 62–64; Nicholas Allen, *Adderbury: A Thousand Years of History* (Chichester: Phillimore & Co., 1995), 92; Brian Bonnyman, "Agricultural Improvement in the Scottish Enlightenment: The Third Duke of Buccleuch, William Keir and the Buccleuch Estates, 1751–1812" (Ph.D. diss., University of Edinburgh, 2004), 47n.

80. "Minutes at a Meeting of Defenders, and Doers for Defenders, in Actions of Damages &c. Raised at the Instance of Some of the Partners of Douglas, Heron, and Company: Against the Directors, &c. of Said Company," Edinburgh, 19 January 1780, Goldsmiths' Library, University of London.

81. Ibid. "Answers for Mess. Douglas, Heron, and Company, and George Home of Branxton, Esq; Factor and Manager for the said Company, and Others, to the Petition of James Craig Baker in Edinburgh," 1 February 1781, Goldsmiths' Library, University of London; "An Appeal from Scotland. James Craig, Baker in Edinburgh, Appellant. Messrs. Douglas, Heron, and Company, late Bankers in Air, and George

Home of Branxton, Esq. Factor and Manager for the Said Company, and Others," 14 May 1781, Goldsmiths' Library, University of London.

82. Kerr, *Banking in Scotland,* 107.

83. Miscellaneous Papers, Lloyds Banking Group Archive, 12 June 1780.

84. Act 14 Geo. III Cap. 11 in *The Statutes at Large, from the Twentieth Year of the Reign of King George the Third to the Twenty-fifth Year of King George the Third, Inclusive,* vol. 14 (London: Charles Eyre, 1786), 156.

85. House of Commons, 25 March 1782, *Journals of the House of Commons,* vol. 38 (1803), 908.

86. Munro, *Royal Bank,* 137.

87. Miscellaneous Papers, Lloyds Banking Group Archive, 21 October 1773, 21 April 1774, 23 May 1774.

88. Rait, *Union Bank,* 172–176. Citing Hunter & Co.'s ledger books, Rait demonstrates that the partners assiduously adhered to the rules established by the contract of copartnery.

89. This lends further evidence to claims that Douglas, Heron & Co.'s composition settlement with Johnstone, Smith & Co. was hastily and imprudently agreed to. William Forbes, *Memoirs of a Banking House* (Edinburgh: William and Robert Chambers, 1860), 45; Ralph Richardson, *Coutts & Co., Bankers* (London: Elliot Stock, 1902), 97; Savile, *Bank of Scotland,* 183n.

90. Ibid., 181.

91. Adam Smith, *An Inquiry into the Nature and Causes of the Wealth of Nations,* vol. 1 (1776; reprint, New York: P. F. Collier & Son, 1902), 436.

92. Gherity, "An Early Publication," 241–282; "Thoughts Concerning Banks," *Scots Magazine* 25 (November 1763): 537; Sydney Checkland, "Adam Smith and the Bankers," in *Essays on Adam Smith,* ed. Andrew Skinner and Thomas Wilson (Oxford: Clarendon, 1975), 504–523; James Gherity, "The Evolution of Adam Smith's Theory of Banking," *History of Political Economy* 26, no. 3 (1994): 423–441.

93. John Rae, *Life of Adam Smith* (London: Macmillan, 1895), 434.

94. Ibid., 165.

95. Forbes, *Memoirs,* 42n.

96. Joseph Stiglitz and Andrew Weiss, "Credit Rationing in Markets with Imperfect Information," *American Economic Review* 71, no. 3 (June 1981): 393–410.

97. Charles Hickson and John Turner, "Free Banking and the Stability of Early Joint-Stock Banking," *Cambridge Journal of Economics* 28 (2004): 905.

98. Ibid.

99. Douglas Diamond and Philip Dybvig, "Bank Runs, Deposit Insurance, and Liquidity," *Journal of Political Economy* 91, no. 3 (June 1983): 401–419.

100. Hickson and Turner, "Free Banking," 908.

101. Benjamin Klein, "The Competitive Supply of Money," *Journal of Money, Credit and Banking* 6, no. 4 (November 1974): 421–453; Charles Goodhart, *The Evolution of*

Central Banks (Cambridge, MA: MIT Press, 1988), 60–64. Discussed in Hickson and Turner, "Free Banking," 907–908.

102. Hickson and Turner, "Free Banking," 908–909.

103. Graeme Acheson, Charles Hickson, and John Turner, "Organisational Flexibility and Governance in a Civil-Law Regime: Scottish Partnership Banks during the Industrial Revolution," *Business History* 53, no. 4 (2011): 514.

104. "Contract of Copartnery," in *The Precipitation and Fall of Mess. Douglas, Heron, and Company, Late Bankers in Air, with the Causes of their Distress and Ruin, Investigated and Considered, by a Committee of Inquiry Appointed by the Proprietors* (Edinburgh, 1778), Appendix no. 1, 8, 13; "Unto the Right Honourable Lords of Council and Session, the Petition of the Partners of Mess. Douglas, Heron, and Company, Late Bankers in Air," 3 March 1780, Goldsmiths' Library, University of London.

105. Acheson, Hickson, and Turner, "Organisational Flexibility," 514.

106. "Contract of Copartnery," in *Precipitation and Fall,* Appendix no. 1, 13.

107. Acheson, Hickson, and Turner, "Organisational Flexibility," 513–514.

108. Ibid., 519.

109. "Contract of Copartnery," in *Precipitation and Fall,* Appendix no. 1, 2.

110. Acheson, Hickson, and Turner, "Organisational Flexibility," 518.

111. "Contract of Copartnery," in *Precipitation and Fall,* Appendix no. 1, 6–7.

112. Boase, *Banking in Dundee,* xxvii.

113. Acheson, Hickson, and Turner, "Organisational Flexibility," 518–519.

114. *Precipitation and Fall,* 40–41.

115. Smith, *Wealth of Nations,* 1:446.

116. *Precipitation and Fall,* 20.

117. Ibid., 31, 72.

118. Ibid., 21. Several of the companies concerned were Oliphant & Co., Whiteside & Co., Maclure and Maccree, Campbell & Co., Montgomery & Co., and Campbell Crawford & Co.

119. *Precipitation and Fall,* 29; emphasis in original.

120. Ibid. 32–33.

121. Hickson and Turner provide evidence of this. See Charles Hickson and John Turner, "Trading in the Shares of Unlimited Liability Banks in Nineteenth Century Ireland: The Bagehot Hypothesis," *Journal of Economic History* 63, no. 4 (2003): 931–958.

122. Balance sheet and cash books, Lloyds Banking Group Archives; Sederunt books, Royal Bank of Scotland Group Archives; Boase, *Banking in Dundee;* Checkland, *Scottish Banking;* Munn, *Scottish Provincial Banking.*

123. *Precipitation and Fall,* 29–31.

124. Acheson, Hickson, and Turner, "Organisational Flexibility," 512.

125. Adam Smith, *An Inquiry into the Nature and Causes of the Wealth of Nations,* (1776; reprint, Petersfield, UK: Harriman House, 2007), 229.

126. Ibid. Also Smith, *Wealth of Nations,* 1:437–438, 440.

127. Ibid., 1:437; emphasis added.

128. While bills could not be discounted at more than 5 percent, commission as well as drawing and redrawing fees could be and regularly were charged, bringing the effective rate above 5 percent. As Smith noted, "In Scotland, though the legal rate of interest is the same as in England, the market rate is rather higher. People of the best credit there seldom borrow under five per cent. Even private bankers in Edinburgh give four per cent upon their promissory notes, of which payment either in whole or in part may be demanded at pleasure." Simply dividing income on the interest account by total credits for the Dundee Banking Company reveals an implied rate above 5 percent for many years, including 1771 and 1772. See Smith, *Wealth of Nations,* 1:154; Boase, *Banking in Dundee.* A case in 1768 settled the question of whether commission and redrawing fees could be levied on bill discounts without violating usury laws, see "Creditors of George Pitcairne against Samuel Foggo," in *Decisions of the Lords of Council and Session, From 1766 to 1791,* vol. 1 (Edinburgh: William Tait, 1826), 259–261.

129. Smith, *Wealth of Nations,* 1:435.

130. Naomi Lamoreaux, *Insider Lending: Banks, Personal Connections, and Economic Development in Industrial New England* (Cambridge: Cambridge University Press, 1996), 79–80.

131. Somers, *Scotch Banks,* 103.

132. *Precipitation and Fall,* 21–22.

133. Ibid., 22–23; emphasis in original.

134. Saville, *Bank of Scotland,* 143, 154.

135. "Memorial above Referred to—with Notes by Sir James Stuart of Coltness," 4 February 1763, in Mure, *Selections,* pt. 2, 1:212.

5. Upon Daedalian Wings

1. David Hume to Adam Smith, 27 June 1772, in *The Correspondence of Adam Smith,* vol. 6, ed. Ernest Mossner and Ian Ross (Oxford: Oxford University Press, 1987), 161–163.

2. Adam Smith, *Lectures on Jurisprudence,* ed. Ronald Meek, David Raphael, and Peter Stein (Oxford: Clarendon Press, 1978), 505.

3. Adam Smith, *An Inquiry into the Nature and Causes of the Wealth of Nations,* vol. 1 (1776; reprint, New York: P. F. Collier & Son, 1902), 456.

4. Ibid., 416, 418.

5. Ibid., 428–430. See also Sydney Checkland, "Adam Smith and the Bankers," in *Essays on Adam Smith,* ed. Andrew Skinner and Thomas Wilson (Oxford: Clarendon, 1975), 517–518.

6. Ibid. 433–434.

7. Ibid., 434–435.

8. Ibid., 435; emphasis added.

9. Robert Somers, *The Scotch Banks and System of Issue* (Edinburgh: Adam and Charles Black, 1873), 103. Somers's figures correspond almost perfectly with the numbers cited by Smith, who noted that the bank had advanced £800,000, of which £200,000 consisted of banknotes. See Smith, *Wealth of Nations,* 1:436–437.

10. Smith, *Wealth of Nations,* 1:437–438.

11. Though, even here, economists since Thornton have demonstrated that price-money-price feedback loops mean the real bills doctrine can in fact be highly pro-cyclical. As Friedman and Schwartz conclude, "The real bills criterion sets no effective limit to the quantity of money." While Smith's version of the real bills doctrine is partially exempted from this criticism, owing to his assertion that the price level is anchored by the stock of gold and note reflux, Friedman and Schwartz point out that even under a gold standard there remains "much leeway in shorter-run movements." See Milton Friedman and Anna Schwartz, *A Monetary History of the United States, 1867–1960* (Princeton, NJ: Princeton University Press, 1963), 191; David Laidler, "Adam Smith as a Monetary Economist," *Canadian Journal of Economics* 14, no. 2 (May 1981): 196–197; Thomas Humphrey, "The Real Bills Doctrine," *Federal Reserve Bank of Richmond Economic Review* (September/October 1982): 3–13.

12. Stock prices from John Castaing's *Course of Exchange,* European State Finance Database. Bill exchange rates from Henry Hamilton, "Scotland's Balance of Payments Problem in 1762," *Economic History Review* 5, no. 3 (1953): 350.

13. The excess supply of Scottish bills relative to bills on London meant that London-based merchants could buy Scottish bills well below par and ship them to agents in Edinburgh to purchase Scottish goods for importation into England.

14. For Scottish trade statistics from 1760 to1780, see David Macpherson, *Annals of Commerce, Manufactures, Fishers, and Navigation,* vol. 3 (London: Nichols and Son, 1805), 339, 351, 364–365, 384–385, 409–410, 434–435, 455–456, 475–476, 486–487, 494–495, 508, 518–519, 532–533, 549–550, 564, 585, 599, 614, 632, 651, 673.

15. Henry Hamilton, "The Failure of the Ayr Bank, 1772," *Economic History Review* 8, no. 3 (1956): 405.

16. Ibid.

17. Ibid., 405–406.

18. Ibid., 406.

19. Andrew Kerr, *History of Banking in Scotland* (Glasgow: David Bryce & Son, 1884), 69; John Buchanan, *Banking in Glasgow during the Olden Time* (Glasgow: David Robertson, 1862), 6.

20. Hamilton, "Failure of the Ayr Bank," 415.

21. Sidney Pollard, "A New Estimate of British Coal Production, 1750–1850," *Economic History Review* 33, no. 2 (May 1980): 229.

22. Smith, *Wealth of Nations,* 1:233.

23. David Turnock, *The Historical Geography of Scotland since 1707: Geographical Aspects of Modernisation* (Cambridge: Cambridge University Press, 2005), 66–81.

24. William Graham, *The One Pound Note in the Rise and Progress of Banking in Scotland, and its Adaptability to England* (Edinburgh: James Thin, 1886), 169.

25. Smith, *Wealth of Nations,* 1:431.

26. Hamilton, "Failure of the Ayr Bank," 406; "An Inquiry into the Late Mercantile Distresses in Scotland and England; with a Few Thoughts on the Causes of the Difficulties that now Prevail amongst the Greatest Part of the Inhabitants of the Whole Island" (London: T. Evans, 1772), Goldsmiths' Library, University of London.

27. Smith, *Wealth of Nations,* 1:411.

28. Miscellaneous Papers, Lloyds Banking Group Archives, 18 November 1769, 31 July 1771.

29. Carmen Reinhart and Kenneth Rogoff, *This Time Is Different: Eight Centuries of Financial Folly* (Princeton, NJ: Princeton University Press, 2009).

30. Smith, *Wealth of Nations,* 1:445–446.

31. Hugh Rockoff, "Upon Daedalian Wings of Paper Money: Adam Smith and the Crisis of 1772," NBER Working Paper 15594 (December 2009).

32. Smith, *Lectures on Jurisprudence,* 576.

33. Ibid., 378.

34. Ibid., 503.

35. Emma Rothschild, *Economic Sentiments: Adam Smith, Condorcet, and the Enlightenment* (Cambridge, MA: Harvard University Press, 2001), 119.

36. Jonathan Swift, *The Bubble: A Poem* (London: Benjamin Tooke, 1721).

37. John Rae, *The Life of Adam Smith* (London: Macmillan, 1895), 367; Adam Smith, *Lectures on Rhetoric and Belles Lettres,* vol. 1, ed. Hugh Blair (London: T. Cadell and W. Davies, 1812), 234; Rothschild, *Economic Sentiments,* 130.

38. Amartya Sen, "Introduction," in Adam Smith, *The Theory of Moral Sentiments,* ed. Ryan Hanley (London: Penguin, 2010); Jonathan Swift, *Gulliver's Travels,* vol. 1 (London: Jones & Company, 1826), 37, 43.

39. Smith, *Wealth of Nations,* 1:446.

40. Henry Meulen, *Free Banking: An Outline of a Policy of Individualism* (London: Macmillan, 1934), 137.

41. Ibid.; William Jevons, *Money and the Mechanism of Exchange* (New York: D. Appleton and Company, 1877), 319.

42. William Janeway, *Doing Capitalism in the Innovation Economy: Markets, Speculation and the State* (Cambridge: Cambridge University Press, 2012).

43. Hamilton, "Ayr Bank," 416–417.

44. Warden, *Linen Trade,* 480.

45. Carmen M. Reinhart and Belen Sbrancia, "The Liquidation of Government Debt," NBER Working Paper 16893 (March 2011).

46. It is an open question whether the privileged limited liability status of the chartered banks constituted an additional barrier to entry. See Jack Carr and Frank Mathewson, "Unlimited Liability as a Barrier to Entry," *Journal of Political Economy* 96, no. 4 (August 1988): 766–784; Jack Carr, Sherry Glied, Frank Mathewson, "Unlimited Liability and Free Banking in Scotland: A Note," *Journal of Economic History* 49, no. 4 (December 1989): 974–978.

47. Graeme Acheson, Charles Hickson, and John Turner, "Organisational Flexibility and Governance in a Civil-Law Regime: Scottish Partnership Banks during the Industrial Revolution," *Business History* 53, no. 4 (July 2011): 507.

Bibliography

Archives

Bank of England. Court of Directors' Minutes. Bank of England Archive. London, United Kingdom.

British Museum, "The Macaroni Provider." London, United Kingdom.

Lloyd's Banking Group. Directors' Minutes. Lloyd's Banking Group Archive. Edinburgh, United Kingdom.

———. Ledgers. Lloyd's Banking Group Archives. Edinburgh, United Kingdom.

———. Letter Books. Lloyd's Banking Group Archives. Edinburgh, United Kingdom.

———. Manuscripts. Lloyd's Banking Group Archives. Edinburgh, United Kingdom.

———. Miscellaneous Papers. Lloyd's Banking Group Archives. Edinburgh, United Kingdom.

Papers of the Montague-Scott Family, Dukes of Buccleuch. National Records of Scotland. GB234/GD224.

Royal Bank of Scotland. Minutes. Royal Bank of Scotland Group Archive. Edinburgh, United Kingdom.

———. Sederunt Books. Royal Bank of Scotland Group Archive. Edinburgh, United Kingdom.

Manuscripts and Other Primary Sources

"Answers for Archibald Cockburn, Esq; of Cockpen, to the Petition of certain Partners of Douglas, Heron, and Company." 22 April 1780. Goldsmiths' Library. University of London. London, United Kingdom.

"Answers for Mess. Douglas, Heron, and Company, and George Home of Branxton, Esq.; Factor and Manager for the said Company, and Others, to the Petition of James Craig Baker in Edinburgh." 1 February 1781. Goldsmiths' Library. University of London. London, United Kingdom.

"An Appeal from Scotland. James Craig, Baker in Edinburgh, Appellant. Messrs. Douglas, Heron, and Company, late Bankers in Air, and George Home of Branxton, Esq. Factor and Manager for the Said Company, and Others." 14 May 1781. Goldsmiths' Library. University of London. London, United Kingdom.

Bank of Scotland. "A List of the Names of the Adventurers in the Bank of Scotland." 6 February 1765. Goldsmiths' Library. University of London. London, United Kingdom.

British Linen Company. *Charter of the British Linen Company.* Edinburgh: R. Fleming and Company, 1746. Goldsmiths' Library. University of London. London, United Kingdom.

Campbell, Ilay. "Unto the Right Honourable the Lords of Council and Session, The Petition of Doctor Robert Herriot." 9 July 1766. British Library. London, United Kingdom.

Copies of the Instrument of Protest, Archibald Trotter Merchant in Glasgow, against Andrew Cochran, John Murdoch and Company; of Two Letters from Mr Trotter to those Gentlemen; and of a Summons Raised at his Instance against them. N.p., 1759. Harvard University Law Library. Cambridge, Massachusetts, United States.

East India Company. "A List of the Names of all the Proprietors of East India Stock; Distinguishing the Principal Stock each Proprietor now Holds, and the Time when Such Proprietors became Possessed thereof." 9 March 1773. Goldsmiths' Library. University of London. London, United Kingdom.

Eskgrove, Lord David Rae. "Answers for William Scot, Writer in Edinburgh, and one of the Depute-Clerks to the Bills, to the Petition of Alexander Farquharson, Accountant in Edinburgh, Trustee for the Creditors of Mess. William Hogg and Son." Edinburgh: n.p., 24 October 1770.

"An Exact State or Abbreviate of the Affairs of the Bank of Scotland, as they Stand Ballanced to the 27th March 1728, the Day upon which they were Obliged to Stop Payments, through Deficiency of Cash: and how the Same Stands this 18th June the Said Year." Goldsmiths' Library. University of London. London, United Kingdom.

Fletcher of Saltoun. Papers. MS 17591–17592. National Library of Scotland. Edinburgh, London, United Kingdom.

"Information for Archibald Trotter, Merchant in Glasgow, Pursuer, against Andrew Cochran, John Murdoch, and Company, Bankers in Glasgow, Defenders." 5 February 1760. National Library of Scotland. Edinburgh, United Kingdom.

An Inquiry into the Late Mercantile Distresses in Scotland and England; with a Few Thoughts on the Causes of the Difficulties that now Prevail amongst the Greatest Part of the Inhabitants of the Whole Island. London: T. Evans, 1772. Goldsmiths' Library. University of London. London, United Kingdom.

"Letter to the Partners of Mess. Douglas, Heron, and Company, in Answer to a Letter Addressed to Them, of 12th March 1779, under the Signature of John Fordyce." 18 June 1779. British Library. London, United Kingdom.

"Meeting at Annapolis, Maryland. The suffering of Boston, the common cause of America. A stoppage of Trade with Great Britain will preserve North America and her Liberties. Gentlemen of the Law in the Province should bring no suit for the recovery of a debt due to an Inhabitant of Great Britain, until the Boston Port Act be repealed. The Inhabitants of Annapolis will, and the Province ought, immediately to break off all Trade with the Colony or Province which shall refuse to adopt similar Resolutions with a majority of the Colonies. Committee appointed to unite with others of the Province, to effect an Association to secure American Liberty." 25 May 1774. *American Archives,* ser. 4, vol. 1.

"Messrs. Douglas, Heron, and Company, Bankers in Air, Appellants; The Honourable John Grant, Esq.; One of the Barons of His Majesty's Court of Exchequer in Scotland, Respondent; The Respondent's Case." Heard at the Bar of the House of Lords, 28 May 1774. British Library. London, United Kingdom.

"Minutes at a Meeting of Defenders, and Doers for Defenders, in Actions of Damages &c. Raised at the Instance of Some of the Partners of Douglas, Heron, and Company: Against the Directors, &c. of Said Company." Edinburgh, 19 January 1780. Goldsmiths' Library. University of London. London, United Kingdom.

Royal Bank of Scotland. "A List of the Names of the Proprietors of the Royal Bank of Scotland." 13 February 1760. Goldsmiths' Library, University of London. London, United Kingdom.

Thomas Jefferson from Perkins, Buchanan & Brown. 2 October 1769. In *The Papers of Thomas Jefferson,* vol. 1, *1760–1776,* edited by Julian Boyd. Princeton, NJ: Princeton University Press, 1950.

"Unto the Right Honourable Lords of Council and Session, the Petition of the Partners of Mess. Douglas, Heron, and Company, Late Bankers in Air." 3 March 1780. Goldsmiths' Library. University of London. London, United Kingdom.

Official Records

Cobbett, William, and Thomas Hansard, eds. *The Parliamentary History of England from the Earliest Period to the Year 1803.* Vol. 17, *A. D. 1771–1774.* London: T. C. Hansard, 1813.

"Creditors of George Pitcairne against Samuel Foggo." In *Decisions of the Lords of Council and Session, From 1766 to 1791, 259–261,* vol. 1. Edinburgh: William Tait, 1826.

Douglas, Heron, and Company. *The Precipitation and Fall of Mess. Douglas, Heron, and Company, Late Bankers in Air, with the Causes of their Distress and Ruin, Investigated and Considered, by a Committee of Inquiry Appointed by the Proprietors.* Edinburgh, 1778.

Glover, Richard. "A Speech Introductory to the Proposals Laid Before the Annuitants of Mess. Douglas, Heron and Co. at the King's-Arms Tavern, Cornhill, on the Ninth of February, 1774." In *The Substance of the Evidence: Delivered to a Committee of the Honourable House of Commons by the Merchants and Traders of London, Concerned in the Trade to Germany and Holland, as Summed Up by Mr. Glover. To which is Annexed, His Speech, Introductory to the Proposals Laid Before the Annuitants of Mess. Douglas, Heron and Co.,* edited by Richard Glover, 67–72. London: J. Wilkie, 1774.

Glover, Richard, to Earl Temple, 12 July 1772. In *The Grenville papers: being the Correspondence of Richard Grenville, Earl Temple, K.G., and the Right Hon: George Grenville, their Friends and Contemporaries,* vol. 4, edited by William James Smith. London: John Murray, 1853.

Great Britain House of Commons. *Journals of the House of Commons.* Vol. 29. 1764.

———. *Journals of the House of Commons.* Vol. 30. 1765.

———. *Journals of the House of Commons.* Vol. 34. 1773.

———. *Journals of the House of Commons.* Vol. 38. 1781.

———. *Report from the Select Committee on Banks of Issue.* Vol. 5. 1841.

Great Britain House of Lords. *Journals of the House of Lords.* Vol. 31. 1765.

———. *Journals of the House of Lords.* Vol. 34. 1774.

"Matthew Boulton, Esq. and Others, Creditors of Samuel Garbet, late of Birmingham, and of Prestonpans, in Scotland, Merchant, a Bankrupt; Messrs. Mansfield, Ramsay, & Co. of Edinburgh, Bankers; Messrs. Douglas, Heron & Co., late Bankers in Ayr; and Walter Hogg, Trustee for the Creditors of Samuel Garbet & Co. of Carron Wharf." In *Reports of Cases Decided in The House of Loards, Upon Appeal from Scotland from 1753 to 1813,* vol. 3, edited by John Craigie, John Stewart, and Thomas Paton, 70–75. Edinburgh: T. & T. Clark, 1853.

Morison, William Maxwell. *The Decisions of the Court of Session.* Vol. 17. Edinburgh: Bell & Bradfute, 1811.

Namier, Lewis, and John Brooke, eds. *The History of Parliament: The House of Commons, 1754–1790.* London: Secker & Warburg, 1964.

Scots Revised Reports: Morison's Dictionary of Decisions. Edinburgh: William Green and Sons, 1908.

Stewart, Angus, ed. *The Minute Book of the Faculty of Advocates*. Vol. 46. Edinburgh: Stair Society, 1999.

Periodicals

A.B. "To the Publishers of the Edinburgh Advertiser." *The Edinburgh Advertiser* 3, no. 136 (19 April 1765).
"Aberdeen Resolution Concerning Paper-Currency." *The Scots Magazine* 26 (December 1764).
"An Abstract of the Scots Bankrupt Act." *The Scots Magazine* 34 (June 1772).
"An Account of the Examination of Mr. Alexander Fordyce, Banker in London, before the Commissioners of Bankruptcy." *The Scots Magazine* 34 (September 1772).
"Account of the Stagnation of Public Credit." *The Scots Magazine* 34 (June 1772).
"Account of the Stagnation of Public Credit." *The Scots Magazine* 34 (September 1772).
"Affairs in England." *The Scots Magazine* 36 (July 1774).
"Affairs in Ireland and Scotland." *The Scots Magazine* 24 (April 1762).
"Affairs in Scotland." *The Scots Magazine* 26 (January 1764).
"Affairs in Scotland." *The Scots Magazine* 26 (April 1764).
"Affairs in Scotland." *The Scots Magazine* 26 (September 1764).
"Affairs in Scotland." *The Scots Magazine* 26 (October 1764).
"Affairs in Scotland." *The Scots Magazine* 26 (December 1764).
"Affairs in Scotland." *The Scots Magazine* 30 (August 1768).
"Affairs in Scotland." *The Scots Magazine* 31 (June 1769).
"Affairs in Scotland." *The Scots Magazine* 31 (October 1769).
"Affairs in Scotland." *The Scots Magazine* 31 (December 1769).
"Affairs in Scotland." *The Scots Magazine* 33 (June 1771).
"Affairs in Scotland." *The Scots Magazine* 34 (July 1772).
"Affairs in Scotland." *The Scots Magazine* 34 (September 1772).
"Affairs in Scotland." *The Scots Magazine* 35 (August 1773).
"Affairs in Scotland." *The Scots Magazine* 36 (February 1774).
"Allemagne." *Journal Historique et Politique des Principaux Événements des différentes Cours de l'Europe*, February 10, 1773.
"Angleterre." *Le Clef du Cabinet des Princes de l'Europe, ou Recuéil Historique & Politique sur les Matières du Temps* (October 1772).
The Annual Register, or a View of the History, Politicks, and Literature, for the Year 1765. London: J. Dodsley, 1766.
"Banks, Child-murder, Divorce, &c." *The Scots Magazine* 18 (July 1756).
"Cause and Cure of our Scarcity of Specie." *The Scots Magazine* 26 (February 1764).

Churbaierisches Intelligenzblatt, 18 July 1772.
"Considerations on the Present State of Credit." *The Scots Magazine* 34 (September 1772).
"The Contract of the Douglas Heron & Company Bank." *The Scots Magazine* 34 (June 1772).
Crabtree, Christopher. "To the Publisher of the Edinburgh Advertiser." *The Edinburgh Advertiser* 3, no. 112 (25 January 1765): 57.
"Criminal Letters against Mr. Dempster." *The Scots Magazine* 30 (August 1768).
"Deaths." *London Magazine, or, Gentleman's Monthly Intelligencer* 42 (April 1773).
"De Londres, le 4 Juillet 1772." *Gazette de France* 57 (17 July 1772).
"Directions to the Creditors of Scottish Insolvents." *The Scots Magazine* 34 (July 1772).
"An Explanation of the words and & Co. in Notes, Called For." *The Scots Magazine* 27 (February 1765).
"Foreign Affairs." *London Magazine, or, Gentleman's Monthly Intelligencer* 32 (September 1763).
"Foreign and Domestic Intelligence." *The Oxford Magazine* 8 (1772): 156.
"Hollande." *Journal Historique et Politique des Principaux Evènements des diffèrentes Cours de l'Europe* 2 (22 January 1773).
"Hollande." *Journal Politique ou Gazette des Gazettes.* Grande-Bretagne, July 1772.
"Hollande." *Journal Politique ou Gazette des Gazettes.* Grande-Bretagne, February 1773.
"Hollande." *Journal Politique ou Gazette des Gazettes.* Grande-Bretagne, March 1773.
"Kellar and Company's Advertisements." *The Scots Magazine* 26 (December 1764).
"The Late Bankruptcies Accounted For." *The Scots Magazine* 25 (August 1763).
"A List of Sequestrations of Personal Estates, by the Court of Session, on the Act 12 Geo. III. Cap. 72." *The Scots Magazine,* July 1772.
"Manufactures, Fisheries, Aberdeen Bank-notes, &c." *The Scots Magazine* 15 (July 1753).
"Minutes of a Meeting of Creditors on the Bankrupt-Act." *The Scots Magazine* 34 (August 1772).
"Minutes of the Meeting of the Creditors of Mess. Fordyce, Malcolm, and Company, Merchants in Edinburgh." *The Scots Magazine* 34 (August 1772).
"The Monthly Chronologer." *London Magazine, or, Gentleman's Monthly Intelligencer* 42 (June 1772).
"Of Abolishing or Regulating Private Banking." *The Scots Magazine* 26 (November 1764).
"Of the Roads and Paper-Currency in Scotland." *The Scots Magazine* 25 (October 1763).
"On Our Banks and Paper-Currency." *The Scots Magazine* 26 (February 1764).

"On Scottish Bankruptcies." *The Scots Magazine* 32 (January 1770).
"On the Banks and Currency in Scotland." *Caledonian Mercury* (1764). Reprinted in *The Scots Magazine* 26 (October 1764).
"On the Present State of the Paper-Money of Scotland." *The Scots Magazine* 27 (February 1765).
"Partners in the Douglas Heron and Company Bank." *The Scots Magazine* 34 (June 1772).
"Poetical Essays." *The Scots Magazine* 34 (October 1772).
"Proceedings in Parliament. Air Bank." *The Scots Magazine* 36 (April 1774).
"A Process Relating to the Glasgow Banks." *The Scots Magazine* 18 (June 1756).
"Prosecution Against J. Baillie for Forging Bank-Notes." *The Scots Magazine* 27 (February 1765).
"Queensferry Advertisement, Eymouth Harbour, &c." *The Scots Magazine* 16 (January 1754).
"Regulations Proposed for Banking." *The Scots Magazine* 24 (March 1762).
"Remarks on the Considerations Relating to the Banks." *The Scots Magazine* 24 (March 1762).
"A Remedy for the Present Scarcity of Silver." *The Scots Magazine,* 26 (June 1764).
"A Run on the Glasgow Banks." *The Scots Magazine* 18 (May 1756).
"A Supply of Safe Currency Proposed." *The Scots Magazine* 26 (December 1764).
"Thoughts Concerning Banks, and the Paper-Currency of Scotland." *The Scots Magazine* 25 (November 1763).

Other Printed Materials before 1800

Boswell, James. *James Boswell's London Journal, 1762–1763.* 2nd ed. Edited by Frederick Albert Pottle. New Haven, CT: Yale University Press, 2004.
Carter, Landon. *The Diary of Landon Carter of Sabine Hall, 1752–1778.* Vol. 5. Edited by Jack Greene. Charlottesville: University of Virginia Press, 1987.
Chapman, John. *The Universal Scots Almanack.* Edinburgh: Walter Ruddiman, John Richardson and Co., 1767.
Franklin, Benjamin. Benjamin Franklin to Richard Bache, October 7, 1772. In *The Writings of Benjamin Franklin,* vol. 5, edited by Albert Smyth. London: Macmillan, 1907.
Gordon, William. *The Universal Accountant and Complete Merchant.* Vol. 2. Glasgow: Alexander Donaldson, 1770.
Johnson, Samuel. *The Letters of Samuel Johnson with Mrs. Thrale's Genuine Letters to Him.* Vol. 1. Edited by Robert Chapman. Oxford: Clarendon Press, 1952.
Madison, James. James Madison to William Bradford, 1 July 1774. In *The Papers of James Madison,* vol. 1, *16 March 1751–16 December 1779,* edited by William Hutchinson and William Rachal. Chicago: University of Chicago Press, 1962.

McCaul, Alexander. Alexander McCaul to Thomas Jefferson, July 8, 1772. In *The Papers of Thomas Jefferson,* vol. 1, edited by Julian Boyd,. Princeton, NJ: Princeton University Press, 1950.

Mossner, Ernest, and Ian Ross, eds. *The Correspondence of Adam Smith.* Vol. 6. Oxford: Oxford University Press, 1987.

Norton, John. John Norton to John H. Norton, August 6, 1772. In *John Norton & Sons, Merchants of London and Virginia,* edited by Francis Mason. Richmond, VA: Dietz Press, 1937. Quoted in Richard Sheridan, "British Credit Crisis of 1772 and the American Colonies." *Journal of Economic History* 10, no. 2 (June 1960): 178.

Smith, Adam. *An Inquiry into the Nature and Causes of the Wealth of Nations.* 1776; reprint, Petersfield, UK: Harriman House, 2007.

———. *An Inquiry into the Nature and Causes of the Wealth of Nations.* Vol. 1. 1776; reprint, New York: P. F. Collier & Son, 1902.

———. *Lectures on Jurisprudence.* Edited by Ronald Meek, David Raphael, and Peter Stein. Oxford: Clarendon Press, 1978.

———. *Lectures on Rhetoric and Belles Lettres.* Vol. 1. Edited by Hugh Blair. London: T. Cadell and W. Davies, 1812.

Swift, Jonathan. *The Bubble: A Poem.* London: Benjamin Tooke, 1721.

———. *Gulliver's Travels.* Vol. 1. London: Jones & Company, 1826.

Walpole, Horace. Horace Walpole to Horace Mann, July 1, 1772. In *The Letters of Horace Walpole,* vol. 8, *1771–1774,* edited by Paget Toynbee. Oxford: Clarendon Press, 1905.

———. *Journal of the Reign of King George the Third, from the Year 1771 to 1783.* Vol. 1. Edited by John Doran. London: Richard Bentley, 1859.

Wiatt, William. William Wiatt to Francis Wiatt, June 26, 1773. In *William and Mary College Quarterly* 12 (1903–1904): 113–114. Quoted in Richard Sheridan, "British Credit Crisis of 1772 and the American Colonies." *Journal of Economic History* 10, no. 2 (June 1960): 178.

Williamson, Peter. *French and Indian Cruelty Exemplified, in the Life, and Various Vicissitudes of Fortune, of Peter Williamson, who was Carried off from Aberdeen in his Infancy, and Sold for a Slave in Pennsylvania.* Edinburgh: J. Stewart, 1792.

Wright, J. *The American Negotiator: Or, The Various Currencies of the British Colonies.* London: J. Smith, 1765.

Other Printed Materials before 1900

Boase, Charles. *A Century of Banking in Dundee.* Edinburgh: R. Grant & Son, 1867.

Buchanan, John. "Ancient and Modern Scottish Banks." Unpublished manuscript, 1862. Quoted in Robert Rait, *The History of the Union Bank of Scotland.* Glasgow: John Smith & Son, 1930.

———. *Banking in Glasgow during the Olden Time.* Glasgow: David Robertson, 1862.

Chalmers, George. *An Estimate of the Comparative Strength of Great Britain and of the Losses of Her Trade from Every War since the Revolution.* London: John Stockdale, 1804.

Fleming, James. *Scottish Banking: A Historical Sketch.* Edinburgh: W. Blackwood, 1877.

Forbes, William. *Memoirs of a Banking House.* Edinburgh: William and Robert Chambers, 1860.

Fraser, William, ed. *Memorials of the Montgomeries, Earls of Eglinton.* Edinburgh: William Fraser, 1859.

Gepp, Henry. *Adderbury.* Banbury: Banbury Guardian Office, 1924.

Graham, William. *The One Pound Note in the Rise and Progress of Banking in Scotland, and its Adaptability to England.* Edinburgh: James Thin, 1886.

Grant, James. *Old and New Edinburgh.* Vol. 3. London: Cassell, Petter, Galpin & Co., 1883.

Jevons, William. *Money and the Mechanism of Exchange.* New York: D. Appleton and Company, 1877.

Kerr, Andrew. *History of Banking in Scotland.* Glasgow: David Bryce & Son, 1884.

MacKenzie, William. *The History of Galloway: From the Earliest Period to the Present Time.* Vol. 2. Kirkcubright: John Nicholson, 1841.

Macpherson, David. *Annals of Commerce, Manufactures, Fishers, and Navigation.* Vol. 3. London: Nichols and Son, 1805.

Martin, Frederick. *Stories of Banks and Bankers.* London: Macmillan and Co., 1865.

Moore, Thomas. "To the Lord Viscount Forbes." In *The Works of Thomas Moore, Comprehending all his Melodies, Ballads, etc.*, vol. 2. Paris: A. and W. Galignani, 1823, 147–157.

M'Ure, John. *The History of Glasgow.* Glasgow: Hutchison & Brookman, 1830.

Mure, William, ed. *Selections from the Mure Family Papers Preserved at Caldwell.* Part 2. 2 vols. Paisley: Alexander Gardner, 1883.

Notes and Queries: A Medium of Inter-Communication for Literary Men, Artists, Antiquaries, Genealogists, Etc. Vol. 8. London: Bell & Daldy, 1859.

Paterson, James. *History of the Counties of Ayr and Wigton.* Vol. 1. Parts 1 and 2. Edinburgh: James Stillie, 1863.

———. *History of the County of Ayr: With a Genealogical Account of the Families of Ayrshire.* 2 vols. Ayr: John Dick, 1847, 1852.

Rae, John. *Life of Adam Smith.* London: Macmillan, 1895.

Robertson, George. *A Genealogical Account of the Principal Families of Ayrshire.* Vol. 1. Irvine, Aryshire: Cunninghame Press, 1823.

Scharf, John. *History of Maryland, 1765–1812.* Baltimore: J. B. Piet, 1879.

Somers, Robert. *The Scotch Banks and System of Issue.* Edinburgh: Adam and Charles Black, 1873.

Stevenson, John Home, ed. *The Scottish Antiquary or Northern Notes & Queries.* Edinburgh: George P. Johnston, 1886.

Story, Alfred Thomas. *The Building of the British Empire: 1689–1895.* London: G. P. Putnam's Sons, 1898.

Tourreff, Gavin, ed. *Antiquarian Gleanings from Aberdeenshire Records.* Aberdeen: George and Robert King, 1859.

Warden, Alex. *The Linen Trade, Ancient and Modern.* London: Longman, Green, Longman, Roberts, & Green, 1867.

Other Printed Materials after 1900

Acheson, Graeme, Charles Hickson, and John Turner. "Organisational Flexibility and Governance in a Civil-Law Regime: Scottish Partnership Banks during the Industrial Revolution." *Business History* 53, no. 4 (July 2011): 505–529.

Acres, Wilfred. *The Bank of England from Within: 1694–1900.* Vol. 1. London: Oxford University Press, 1931.

Allen, Nicholas. *Adderbury: A Thousand Years of History.* Chichester: Phillimore & Co., 1995.

Ashton, Thomas. *Economic Fluctuations in England and Wales, 1750–1800.* Oxford: Oxford University Press, 1959.

Baasch, Ernse. *Holländische Wirtschaftsgeschichte.* Jena: G. Fischer, 1927.

Bonnyman, Brian. "Agricultural Improvement in the Scottish Enlightenment: The Third Duke of Buccleuch, William Keir and the Buccleuch Estates, 1751–1812." Ph.D. diss., University of Edinburgh, 2004.

Bowen, Huw. *East India Company: Trade and Domestic Financial Statistics, 1755–1838* [computer file]. Colchester, Essex: UK Data Archive [distributor], September 2007. SN: 5690, http://dx.doi.org/10.5255/UKDA-SN-5690-1.

Brady, Frank. "So Fast to Ruin." *Ayrshire Collections* 11, no. 2 (1973): 26–44.

Cameron, Rondo. *Banking in the Early Stages of Industrialization.* New York: Oxford University Press, 1967.

Carlson, Mathieu. "Adam Smith's Support for Money and Banking Regulation: A Case of Inconsistency." *History of Economics Review* 29 (Winter 1999): 1–15.

Carr, Jack, and Frank Mathewson. "Unlimited Liability as a Barrier to Entry." *Journal of Political Economy* 96, no. 4 (August 1988): 766–784.

Carr, Jack, Sherry Glied, and Frank Mathewson. "Unlimited Liability and Free Banking in Scotland: A Note." *Journal of Economic History* 49, no. 4 (December 1989): 974–978.

Checkland, Sydney. "Adam Smith and the Bankers." In *Essays on Adam Smith,* edited by Andrew Skinner and Thomas Wilson, 504–523. Oxford: Clarendon, 1975.

———. *Scottish Banking: A History, 1695–1973*. Glasgow: Collins, 1975.
Clapham, John. *The Bank of England: A History*. Vol. 1. Cambridge: Cambridge University Press, 1968.
Clark, Gregory. "The Price History of English Agriculture, 1209–1914." *Research in Economic History* 22 (2004): 41–124.
Cowen, Tyler, and Randall Kroszner. "Scottish Banking before 1845: A Model for Laissez-Faire?" *Journal of Money, Credit and Banking* 21, no. 2 (May 1989): 221–231.
Devine, Thomas. "The Colonial Trades and Industrial Investment in Scotland, c. 1700–1815." *Economic History Review* 29, no. 1 (February 1976): 1–13.
———. "An Eighteenth-Century Business Elite: Glasgow–West India Merchants, c. 1750–1815." *Scottish Historical Review* 57, no. 163 (April 1978): 40–67.
———. "Glasgow Merchants and the Collapse of the Tobacco Trade 1775–1783." *Scottish Historical Review 52,* no. 153 (April 1973): 50–74.
———. "Sources of Capital for the Glasgow Tobacco Trade, c. 1740–1780." *Business History 16* (1974): 113–129.
Diamond, Douglas, and Philip Dybvig. "Bank Runs, Deposit Insurance, and Liquidity." *Journal of Political Economy* 91 (June 1983): 401–419.
Douglas, James. *Scottish Banknotes.* London: Stanley Gibbons, 1975.
Dowd, Kevin. *Laissez-Faire Banking.* New York: Routledge, 1993.
———. "Option Clauses and Bank Suspension." *Cato Journal* (Winter 1991): 761–774.
———. "Option Clauses and the Stability of a Laissez Faire Monetary System." *Journal of Financial Services Research* 1 (December 1988): 319–333.
Friedman, Milton, and Anna Schwartz. *A Monetary History of the United States, 1867–1960.* Princeton, NJ: Princeton University Press, 1963.
Gherity, James. "An Early Publication by Adam Smith." *History of Political Economy* 25, no. 2 (Summer 1993): 241–282.
———. "The Evolution of Adam Smith's Theory of Banking." *History of Political Economy* 26, no. 3 (Fall 1994): 423–441.
———. "The Option Clause in Scottish Banking, 1730–65: A Reappraisal." *Journal of Money, Credit and Banking* 27, no. 3 (August 1995): 713–726.
Gibson, A., and C. Smout. *Wages and Prices in Scotland, c. 1580–1780* [computer file]. Colchester, Essex: UK Data Archive [distributor], June 1995. SN: 3302.
Gipson, Lawrence. "Virginia Planter Debts before the American Revolution." *The Virginia Magazine of History and Biography* 69, no. 3 (July 1961): 259–277.
Goodhart, Charles. *The Evolution of Central Banks.* Cambridge, MA: MIT Press, 1988.
Haldane, Andrew, and Robert May. "Systemic Risk in Banking Ecosystems." *Nature* 469 (January 2011): 351–355.

Hamilton, Henry. "The Failure of the Ayr Bank, 1772." *Economic History Review* 8, no. 3 (1956): 405–417.

———. "Scotland's Balance of Payments Problem in 1762." *Economic History Review* 5, no. 3 (1953): 344–357.

Healer, Edna. *Coutts & Co., 1692–1992: The Portrait of a Private Bank.* Sevenoaks: Hodder & Stoughton, 1992.

Hickson, Charles, and John Turner. "Free Banking and the Stability of Early Joint-Stock Banking." *Cambridge Journal of Economics* 28 (2004): 903–919.

———. "Trading in the Shares of Unlimited Liability Banks in Nineteenth Century Ireland: The Bagehot Hypothesis." *Journal of Economic History* 63, no. 4 (2003): 931–958.

Humphrey, Thomas. "The Real Bills Doctrine." *Federal Reserve Bank of Richmond Economic Review* (September/October 1982): 3–13.

Janeway, William. *Doing Capitalism in the Innovation Economy: Markets, Speculation and the State.* Cambridge: Cambridge University Press, 2012.

Johnson, Simon. "The Quiet Coup." *The Atlantic,* May 2009.

———. *13 Bankers: The Wall Street Takeover and the Next Financial Meltdown.* New York: Random House, 2010.

Kärrlander, Tom. "Douglas Heron and Company, Bankers in Air (Ayr Bank): A Bank Crash in Scotland in 1772." Working Paper 16, Department of Economic History, Stockholm University, Stockholm, 2005.

Kellock, Katharine. "London Merchants and the pre-1776 American Debts." *Guildhall Studies in London History* 1, no. 3 (October 1974): 109–149.

Klein, Benjamin. "The Competitive Supply of Money." *Journal of Money, Credit and Banking* 6, no. 4 (November 1974): 421–453.

Kroszner, Randall. "Free Banking: The Scottish Experience as an Example for Emerging Economies." World Bank Policy Research Working Paper 1536 (November 1995).

Laidler, David. "Adam Smith as a Monetary Economist." *Canadian Journal of Economics* 14, no. 2 (May 1981): 185–200.

Lamoreaux, Naomi. *Insider Lending: Banks, Personal Connections, and Economic Development in Industrial New England.* Cambridge: Cambridge University Press, 1996.

Malcolm, Charles. *The Bank of Scotland, 1695–1945.* Edinburgh: R. & R. Clark, 1948.

———. *The History of the British Linen Bank.* Edinburgh: T. & A. Constable, 1950.

McClure, David. "James McAdam and the Loss of Waterhead." *Ayrshire Notes* 33 (Spring 2007): 7–19.

Meulen, Henry. *Free Banking: An Outline of a Policy of Individualism.* London: Macmillan, 1934.

Munn, Charles. *The Scottish Provincial Banking Companies, 1747–1864*. Edinburgh: John Donald Publishers, 1981.

Munro, Neil. *The History of the Royal Bank of Scotland.* Glasgow: Grimsay Press, 1928.

Norris, John. "The Struggle for Carron: Samuel Garbett and Charles Gascoigne." *Scottish Historical Review* 37, no. 124 (October 1958): 136–145.

Paganelli, Maria Pia. "Vanity and the Daedalian Wings of Paper Money in Adam Smith." In *New Voices on Adam Smith,* edited by Eric Schlieser and Leonidas Montes, 271–289. London: Routledge, 2006.

Paul, James Balfour. *The Scots Peerage: Founded on Wood's Edition of Sir Robert Douglas's Peerage of Scotland; Containing an Historical and Genealogical Account of the Nobility of that Kingdom.* Vol. 1. Edinburgh: David Douglas, 1904.

Pollard, Sidney. "A New Estimate of British Coal Production, 1750–1850." *Economic History Review* 33, no. 2 (May 1980): 212–235.

Price, Jacob. "The Rise of Glasgow in the Chesapeake Tobacco Trade, 1707–1775." *William and Mary Quarterly* 11, no. 2 (1954): 179.

Ragsdale, Bruce. *A Planters' Republic: The Search for Economic Independence in Revolutionary Virginia.* Madison, WI: Madison House Publishers, 1996.

Rait, Robert. *The History of the Union Bank of Scotland.* Glasgow: John Smith & Son, 1930.

Reinhart, Carmen, and Kenneth Rogoff. *This Time Is Different: Eight Centuries of Financial Folly.* Princeton, NJ: Princeton University Press, 2009.

Reinhart, Carmen M., and Belen Sbrancia. "The Liquidation of Government Debt." NBER Working Paper 16893 (March 2011).

Richardson, Ralph. *Coutts & Co., Bankers.* London: Elliot Stock, 1902.

Rockoff, Hugh. "Upon Daedalian Wings of Paper Money: Adam Smith and the Crisis of 1772." NBER Working Paper 15594 (December 2009).

Ross, Ian Simpson. *The Life of Adam Smith.* Oxford: Oxford University Press, 1995.

Rothbard, Murray. "The Myth of Free Banking in Scotland." *Review of Austrian Economics* 2 (1988): 229–245.

Rothschild, Emma. *Economic Sentiments: Adam Smith, Condorcet, and the Enlightenment.* Cambridge, MA: Harvard University Press, 2001.

Rouwenhorst, Geert. "The Origins of Mutual Funds." Yale International Center for Finance Working Paper 04-48 (December 12, 2004).

Royal Bank of Scotland. *The Royal Bank of Scotland: A History.* Edinburgh: Royal Bank of Scotland, 1998.

Saville, Richard. *Bank of Scotland: A History, 1695–1995.* Edinburgh: Edinburgh University Press, 1996.

Schnabel, Isabel, and Hyun Song Shin. "Liquidity and Contagion: The Crisis of 1763." *Journal of the European Economic Association* 2, no. 6 (December 2004): 929–968.

Sechrest, Larry. "White's Free-Banking Thesis: A Case of Mistaken Identity." *Review of Austrian Economics* 2, no. 1 (1988): 247–257.

Selgin, George. *Bank Deregulation and Monetary Order.* London: Routledge, 1996.

———. *A Theory of Free Banking.* Totawa, NJ: Rowman and Littlefield, 1988.

Selgin, George, and Lawrence White. "The Option Clause in Scottish Banking." *Journal of Money, Credit and Banking* 29, no. 2 (May 1997): 270–273.

Sen, Amartya. Introduction to *Adam Smith, The Theory of Moral Sentiments,* edited by Ryan Patrick Hanley. London: Penguin, 2010.

Shah, Parth. "The Option Clause in Free-Banking Theory and History: A Reappraisal." *Review of Austrian Economics* 10, no. 2 (1997): 1–25.

Sheridan, Richard. "The British Credit Crisis of 1772 and the American Colonies." *Journal of Economic History* 10, no. 2 (June 1960): 161–186.

Sloan, Herbert. *Principle and Interest: Thomas Jefferson and the Problem of Debt.* New York: Oxford University Press, 1995.

Soltow, J. H. "Scottish Traders in Virginia, 1750–1775." *Economic History Review* 12, no. 1 (1959): 83–98.

Steuart, James. *Principles of Political Economy.* Vol. 2. London: A. Millar and T. Cadell, 1767.

Stigler, George. "The Theory of Economic Regulation." *Bell Journal of Economics* 2, no. 1 (Spring 1971): 3–21.

Stiglitz, Joseph, and Andrew Weiss. "Credit Rationing in Markets with Imperfect Information." *American Economic Review* 71, no. 3 (June 1981): 393–410.

Stock prices from John Castaing's *Course of Exchange* [computer file], European State Finance Database.

Taleb, Nassim Nicholas. *Antifragile: Things That Gain from Disorder.* New York: Random House, 2012.

Tillson, Albert. *Accommodating Revolutions: Virginia's Northern Neck in an Era of Transformations, 1760–1810.* Charlottesville: University of Virginia Press, 2010.

Turnock, David. *The Historical Geography of Scotland since 1707: Geographical Aspects of Modernisation.* Cambridge: Cambridge University Press, 2005.

Ward, John. "Ayrshire Landed Estates in the Nineteenth Century." *Ayrshire Archaeological and Natural History Collections* 8 (1969): 93–145.

West, Edwin. "Adam Smith's Support for Money and Banking Regulation: A Case of Inconsistency," *Journal of Money, Credit and Banking* 29, no. 1 (February 1997): 127–134.

White, Lawrence. "Antifragile Banking and Monetary Systems." Paper presented at the Cato Institute 30th Annual Monetary Conference, Washington, DC, November 15, 2012.

———. *Free Banking in Britain: Theory, Experience and Debates, 1800–1845.* Cambridge: Cambridge University Press, 1984.

———. "Free Banking in Scotland before 1844." In *The Experience of Free Banking,* edited by Kevin Dowd, 157–186. London: Routledge, 1992.

Wilson, Charles. "The Economic Decline of the Netherlands." *Economic History Review* 9, no. 2 (May 1939): 111–127.

Acknowledgments

The various debts owed for this work far exceed my ability to adequately repay them in thanks here. First and foremost I thank my advisors—Niall Ferguson, Benjamin Friedman, Richard Hornbeck, and Emma Rothschild—for their invaluable guidance, patience, and counsel throughout this project. I also owe immense thanks to George Selgin, Charles Maier, John Turner, Christine Desan, Mauricio Drelichman, Robert Shapiro, Sean Barrett, and James Medoff for innumerable comments, criticisms, and suggestions that no doubt improved and refined the project at each stage of its development. Seminar participants at the Harvard-Cambridge Center for History and Economics and Harvard Law School Institute for Global Law and Policy provided much-appreciated early-stage feedback. Sian Yates at the Lloyds Banking Group Archive was an instrumental navigational guide as I traversed Scottish banking archives.

Financially, this project would not have been possible without funding support from the Harvard Center for European Studies and the Krupp Foundation, the Harvard Weatherhead Center for International Affairs, the Harvard Institute for Quantitative Social Science, and a Clive Fellowship grant.

I further salute the team at Harvard University Press, especially Michael Aronson, Kathleen Drummy, and Stephanie Vyce, whose professionalism, thoroughness, efficiency, and, above all, good humor made them truly an honor and privilege to work with. Mike, in particular, I thank for his invaluable input from start to finish.

Finally, it must be noted that the longest-term debts have a tendency to compound over time to quite considerable sums. Mom, Dad, and Izzy—this work is as much yours as mine. Thank you.

Index

www.ingramcontent.com/pod-product-compliance
Ingram Content Group UK Ltd.
Pitfield, Milton Keynes, MK11 3LW, UK
UKHW041421290926
475585UK00013B/33/J

9 780674 088887